CREATIVITY'S EDGE

CREATIVITY'S EDGE

Unleashing Humanity's Greatest Advantage in the Age of AI

SUSAN M. RILEY

BLOOMSBURY ACADEMIC
NEW YORK • LONDON • OXFORD • NEW DELHI • SYDNEY

BLOOMSBURY ACADEMIC
Bloomsbury Publishing Inc, 1359 Broadway, New York, NY 10018, USA
Bloomsbury Publishing Plc, 50 Bedford Square, London, WC1B 3DP, UK
Bloomsbury Publishing Ireland, 29 Earlsfort Terrace, Dublin 2, D02 AY28, Ireland

BLOOMSBURY, BLOOMSBURY ACADEMIC and the Diana logo are trademarks of
Bloomsbury Publishing Plc

First published in the United States of America 2026

Copyright © Bloomsbury Publishing, 2026

Cover design by Kathi Ha
Cover image © iStock.com/liuzishan

All rights reserved. No part of this publication may be: i) reproduced or transmitted in any form, electronic or mechanical, including photocopying, recording or by means of any information storage or retrieval system without prior permission in writing from the publishers; or ii) used or reproduced in any way for the training, development or operation of artificial intelligence (AI) technologies, including generative AI technologies. The rights holders expressly reserve this publication from the text and data mining exception as per Article 4(3) of the Digital Single Market Directive (EU) 2019/790.

Bloomsbury Publishing Inc does not have any control over, or responsibility for, any third-party websites referred to or in this book. All internet addresses given in this book were correct at the time of going to press. The author and publisher regret any inconvenience caused if addresses have changed or sites have ceased to exist, but can accept no responsibility for any such changes.

A catalog record for this book is available from the Library of Congress.

ISBN: HB: 979-8-8818-0685-9
ePDF: 979-8-8818-6764-5
eBook: 979-8-8818-0686-6

Typeset by Integra Software Services Pvt. Ltd.
Printed and bound in the United States of America

For product safety related questions contact productsafety@bloomsbury.com.

To find out more about our authors and books visit www.bloomsbury.com
and sign up for our newsletters.

CONTENTS

Acknowledgments ix

Introduction: The 212th Degree 1

PART ONE The Preparation 5

1. We Have a Creativity Problem 7
   Chapter Guiding Question: If creativity is the most important skill we can teach in the age of AI, why isn't it a priority for schools? 7
   Education's Focus and Purpose Since the Twentieth Century 10
   The Advent of Artificial Intelligence 12
   Future Career Impact and Societal Implications 14
   Competing Priorities for Future Needs 15
   The Equity Gap 17
   The Measurement Conundrum: Evaluating Creativity 18
   The Expedition Begins 20
   Practice Strategy: Headlines 22

2. The Creative Spectrum: Understanding and Developing Creative Potential 25
   Chapter Guiding Question: What does creativity mean and look like in practice? 25
   The Journey Begins: Defining Creativity 26
   Beyond the "Hard" and "Soft" Skills Divide 29
   The Inner Landscape: Neuroscience of Creativity 31
   The Three Faces of Creativity: Divergent, Convergent, and Lateral Thinking 34
   A Social Symphony: Models for the Process 38
   Levels of Impact: The 4-C Model 41
   Practice Strategy: Magazine Cover 45

PART TWO The Incubation 49

3 Creativity at Work 51
   Chapter Guiding Question: How can we develop our own creative practice? 51
   The Four Branches of Creativity 52
   From Purpose to Practice with Creative Skills 61
   From Practice to Play: Exercises That Spark Creative Thinking 63
   Cultivating Creative Spaces: Where Expression Takes Root 67
   Mindsets for Exploring Creative Application 71
   Practice Strategy: iNotice 75

4 Assessing Creativity 79
   Chapter Guiding Question: Is there a way to measure creativity? Should we measure creativity? 79
   Tracing Creativity's Shifting Value Over Time 81
   Beyond Numbers and Metrics: When Measurement Meets Meaning 82
   The Interplay of Assessment and Evaluation 85
   The Alchemy of Process and Product: Transforming Creative Potential into Reality 85
   Four Models for Assessing Creativity 89
      Measuring the Person: The Guilford Model 90
      Measuring the Work: The Taxonomy of Creative Design 90
      Measuring the Work in Context: The Requirements Model 91
      Measuring the Social Value of the Work: The Systems Model 92
   Bridging the Four Branches and Four Models: The Synergy of Creative Development and Assessment 95
   Using Integrated Creativity Assessment Models 98
   The Case for Subjectivity 100
   Practice Strategy: Theme and Variations 107

PART THREE The Illumination 109

5 The Art and Science of Flow 111
   Chapter Guiding Question: Can humans increase our creativity capacity? 111
   How the Brain Works During Creative Episodes 112

Neuroplasticity: Building the Highway System for Creative Flow 114
Cognitive Persistence and Flexibility 118
Flow State: What It Is, Its Benefits, and How to Get into It 120
How to Use Flow to Increase Your Creativity 124
Practice Strategy: Yes, And… 133

6 Cultivating the Creative Habit 135
Chapter Guiding Question: How can we integrate creativity as a regular practice? 135
Exploring the Connections Between Mind, Body, and Creativity 136
Rituals That Stick: Habits to Nurture Creativity 140
Five Pillars of Creative Practice: Building Your Support System 142
Building Environments to Encourage Creative Implementation: The 20 Percent Rule 148
Personal Margin Design: Creating Your Creative Infrastructure 151
Applying Creative Thinking Practices: The Mosaic Method 154
Reflection Exercises to Expand and Level Up 162
Practice Strategy: Playlist 166

PART FOUR The Offering 169

7 The Creative Edge 171
Chapter Guiding Question: How can we thoughtfully and intentionally fuse all of these ideas about creativity together? 171
Cracking Your Unique Creative Code 172
Developing a Creative and Competitive Edge 177
Sidestepping the Excuses: Time, Overwhelm, and Comparison 184
The Creative Opportunity Cost 190
Your Throughline: Creative Skills, Mindsets, and Applications 194
Practice Strategy: Build-a-Character 198

8 Harnessing the Future 201
Chapter Guiding Question: How can we use our creativity as a guide for the twenty-first century? 201
What Science Tells Us Is Coming: Bridging the Gaps 203
The Hype Cycle: Educational Technology's Rocky History 205
The Double-Edged Sword: AI as Disruptor in Education 208

The Equity Challenge 212
Ethical Crossroads: Navigating AI's Moral Maze 213
The Intersection of Creativity and Technology 216
The Rise of the Creative Machine: Computational Creativity in the Age of AI 223
Tapping into Your Creative Genius 227
Applying the Four Branches to Your Creative Development 230
Where Will You Go Next? 233
Practice Strategy: Stepping In, Stepping Out 235

Appendix A: Arts Integration, STEAM, and Project-Based Learning 238
Appendix B: How I Wrote This Book 254
Bibliography 258
Index 267
About the Author 275

ACKNOWLEDGMENTS

Books, like creativity itself, are never born in isolation. They emerge through a beautiful web of connections, support, and inspiration from others. This book is no exception.

I'm deeply grateful to my agent, Laurie Dennison, and the entire team at Creative Media Agency for shepherding me through the process of my first traditionally published book. From your thoughtful feedback to your unwavering persistence in getting this manuscript into the right hands at Rowan and Littlefield, this has been a wonderfully exciting ride.

To my editor, Nathan Davidson—thank you for believing in the power of the arts in schools and in the potential of this book to transform the education landscape. Your insights and guidance have been invaluable.

The dedicated team at Rowman & Littlefield and Bloomsbury Publishing deserves my heartfelt appreciation for making this book the best it could be and working tirelessly to get it into as many hands as possible.

I'm especially indebted to my friends Sally Baker and Jaime Patterson for their help reading and re-reading drafts, sharing honest feedback, and lifting me out of the dark when I could only faintly see the light at the end of the tunnel. Your friendship has been a lifeline.

To my incredible team members at the Institute for Arts Integration and STEAM—thank you for picking up the slack when I needed to focus for weeks on end to get this manuscript complete. Your dedication to our shared mission made this work possible.

This book draws its heart and soul from the thousands of teachers, leaders, artists, and students I've had the honor to work with in my roles as teacher, administrator, and founder of an institution supporting arts integration and

STEAM. Without you, this work doesn't exist to share with the world. Your creativity, resilience, and passion continue to inspire me every day.

To my family—John, Ginger, Andy, Diana, Art, Vickie, Kim, Dave, and Aileen—your support and belief in not only this project, but in my worth beyond it, are a gift beyond measure. You've always encouraged me to follow my creative instincts, even when the path wasn't clear.

To Emma, Warren, James, Ariah, Connor, and Peyton—you are all the reason I fight to bring a creativity-forward approach to education every day. You deserve a future that exceeds your expectations, and I'm committed to helping create a world where your unique creative gifts are valued and nurtured.

To my husband, Kevin—thank you for being the rock that keeps me steady and the wings that let me fly. Your unwavering support, patience during late-night writing sessions, and belief in my vision mean everything to me.

And finally, to my Lord and Savior—thank you for the peace and security only You can provide. This journey has unfolded through Your grace.

—Susan M. Riley

Introduction: The 212th Degree

Did you know that steam is invisible? When we see pictures of a fog-like substance coming out of a boiling tea kettle, or a mist rising from an engine, we might call it steam. But in reality, it's water vapor that we're seeing, not steam. Steam is an invisible gas.

Water vapor happens when the invisible gas (steam) hits cooler air. In order for us to see this vapor, water needs to transform from a liquid to a gas first. This happens when the water is heated to exactly 212 degrees Fahrenheit. From there, we can no longer see the water, until it collides with something that hasn't yet been transformed. Similarly, our futures are often caused by things we cannot see, and by the time we see them, the transformation has already happened.

What many in education, government, and even general society don't realize is that we've hit the 212th degree with the advent of artificial intelligence (AI). The future for humanity is now irrevocably changed. No longer is it enough to teach subjects individually in our schools. No longer is it enough to spend four to eight years on a college or advanced degree and hope that's enough to be competitive in a future job market. In the world of AI, we must fundamentally question what is the point of learning information for information's sake?

According to the World Economic Forum,[1] the jobs that AI can't replace will be those that fall into two basic branches: creativity and care-based services. Think of skills such as judgment, creativity, physical dexterity, and emotional intelligence. If education is meant to prepare us for the future, and the future now requires skill sets in creativity, critical thinking, and care, then we're missing the mark with our current curricular requirements.

This book is a journey into the transformative power of creativity in education—both in the K–12 environment and in its broadest sense of lifelong learning. At its core, this book is guided by this question: "If creativity is so important to the future of humanity, why isn't it a priority in our schools and our lives—and what can be done to change that?"

I wanted to explore this question through the creative process itself. Generally, there are four stages that most humans go through during any creative endeavor: *preparation, incubation, illumination,* and *verification.* In the preparation stage, we're collecting information and knowledge about a topic of a problem. In the incubation stage, we're ruminating on what we've learned and letting the pieces come together. The illumination stage is where the creative magic happens, and we begin to create our own ideas or fuse together something new, and then we offer it out to the world for verification to see if it's accepted or not.

For this book, I've taken this process and slightly altered it. In part 1—the preparation stage, I'm exploring the central question through research around how our education system has developed thus far and why creativity hasn't been central to its purpose up until now. I've also taken time here to investigate the many layers of meaning around creativity itself—there's a lot here that research helps us to understand specifically surrounding how creativity impacts learning and the brain.

Of course, the more we learn, the more questions we have. So in part 2—the incubation stage—I chased my curiosity around how creativity's impact on the brain changes over time, and whether or not these changes can (and should) be measured.

This led to my favorite part of the creative process: the making and fusing. This happens during part 3—the illumination. This is when all the information we've gathered starts to come together in new and interesting ways. In this section, we'll explore how all the elements of creativity can come together in schools, places of work, and through our lives in ways that address the major pushbacks addressed in chapter 1.

And finally, part 4—which is where I've slightly adjusted the creative model to be the *offering* rather than the verification. In this section, we'll explore how to crack your unique creative code, including how to discern between your creative and competitive edge, and how to deal with the negative feedback loops that will inevitably occur. From there, we'll close out our journey by reflecting on the ways creativity can guide us in harnessing a future that's impossible to predict and that's approaching infinitely faster than ever before. We'll use the strategies, research, and tools from this book to explore the possibilities of what's next for each of us—and how we can begin taking those steps today.

Embedded throughout each chapter are guiding questions, illuminating stories, and insights from others in the field, and practical strategies, models, and examples you can use in your own practice. At the end of each chapter is a new creative strategy that helps you both reflect on the guiding question posed at the beginning and hone your own creative skills.

Just as water becomes something entirely new—steam—with just a slight increase in temperature, so too does the traditional learning framework evolve with the infusion of creativity. This subtle yet significant shift is reshaping how we view and approach education in the twenty-first century.

Creativity often operates like the invisible nature of steam. It's there, all around us, shaping our world in ways we might not immediately see. It's in the way a child learns to solve problems, in the innovative advancements in technology and engineering, and in the rapidly evolving applications of mathematics and science. It's the art in writing, the beauty in the code, the imagination in the equation. This invisibility does not diminish its presence or importance; rather, it challenges us to look closer, to see beyond the obvious.

Artificial intelligence is rapidly changing our landscape, presenting new challenges and opportunities in and out of education. The integration of creativity across the curriculum is not just an enhancement; it's a necessary evolution to equip our learners for a future that's already unfolding.

In the following chapters, we will explore together why prioritizing creativity in schools, our work, and our lives, is not only vital but also natural and inevitable, just like the one-degree change that turns water into steam. This book is a guide for educators, parents, professionals, and all those invested in the future of learning. It's time to harness the 212th degree in education—creativity—and in doing so, unveil the immense potential of our future generations.

Note

[1] World Economic Forum. (2023). "These Are the Jobs That AI Can't Replace." https://www.weforum.org/agenda/2023/05/jobs-ai-cant-replace/

PART ONE

THE PREPARATION

1

We Have a Creativity Problem

> *Chapter Guiding Question: If creativity is the most important skill we can teach in the age of AI, why isn't it a priority for schools?*

The Cove was how most people referred to the impoverished area back at the early turn of the twentieth century. This compact region in south central Pennsylvania is where lesser-known towns like Sylvan, Lemasters, and Cove Gap are triangulated around Mercersburg. It became celebrated for a brief period of time as the birthplace of President James Buchanan, but quickly lost its luster and went back to the sleepy obscurity that deep woods and fertile farmland quietly crave.

This land was rich in hard work and dairy cows but little else. In 1884, the population of Sylvan was just 458. So when Garry Cleveland Myers made his appearance in the heat of the summer on July 15, everyone simply expected another future farmer had joined the Cove's now bursting population of 459 members. But Garry's path would be different from the others. At a time when public education wasn't mandatory or valued much, Garry managed to work his way through a high school diploma in between the morning milkings and afternoon feedings. Through a series of twists and turns, he would come to graduate first from Ursinus College in 1909, attend the University of Pennsylvania for graduate school, and finally receive his PhD from Columbia University in 1913 in child psychology. All of which he would suddenly collide during his work in World War I.

While in college, he met his wife Caroline and the two of them were inseparable, both in work and in life. During World War I, both Garry and Caroline worked in the United States Army, participating in the education of illiterate soldiers. It was during this time that the first standardized tests for intelligence were introduced by Robert Yerkes and six other psychologists, and Garry participated in administering these as well. They were called the Army Alpha tests; it was a group-administered test to evaluate the "intellectual and emotional functioning of soldiers." Scores on these tests were then used to determine whether a soldier was capable of serving, their job classification, and any leadership position. Anyone who was illiterate or non-English speaking would take what was known as the Army Beta test, which was the nonverbal equivalent of the exam. The use of these tests became the model for standardized testing seen today.

Upon returning from the war, Garry and Caroline continued their mission of education. He taught classes at several universities and colleges, and he traveled to classrooms representing *Children's Activities* magazine. But it was in 1946 that he found his true calling. He and Caroline wanted to create a magazine of their own that helped children become curious, creative, caring, and confident individuals. Inside, it would have stories, puzzles, games, and even advice columns, all for young children.

So with a two-room office above a car dealership and a small team, *Highlights for Children* was born. The magazine spread throughout the local community in doctors' and dentists' offices, bringing joy and smiles during a time when children were often otherwise scared or nervous.

Slowly, the magazine began to pick up circulation and subscriptions in more and more towns as parents and their children fell in love with the adventures of beloved characters like Goofus and Gallant and the Timbertoes. Since then, it has become a successful and iconic educational publication, which continues to showcase the philosophy that "children become their 'best selves' by using their creativity and imagination." Garry is proof that despite the circumstances of your birth, the combination of education, persistence, and creativity can yield world-changing results.

We've heard the cry for decades now: creativity in our schools is in crisis. Dan Pink's book *A Whole New Mind* broke the surface in 2005 with the research that creativity was going to be what set us apart in the coming future of robots.[1] Sir Ken Robinson famously asked the question "Do schools kill creativity?" in his 2006 TED Talk that went viral.[2] And yet, here we are—decades and lightyears of technology later—and schools haven't changed. Artificial intelligence has crossed our doorsteps and still schools haven't answered the call. Why?

Ask educators what gets in the way of making creativity a priority in schools and they will overwhelmingly tell you one answer: standardized testing. I know this from twenty years' worth of lunch conversations in teachers' lounges and chats with my colleagues after days of proctoring during the dreaded "testing season" that happens in schools from March to May every year. But to prove it, I also conducted a poll on my organization's Facebook page, which has over forty thousand educators who engage with it on some level. When asked the same question, over 90 percent of respondents said standardized testing was to blame for the lack of creativity in schools today.

And until writing this book, I agreed with them.

But according to research, we would all be wrong. The real killer of creativity in our schools? Poverty. Specifically, the underlying ramifications and effects that poverty brings across all socioeconomic levels.[3] To be sure, standardized testing is wrapped around poverty like a kudzu vine wraps around a white oak tree. One has much deeper roots and a longer history, which must be understood in order for the vine to be cut back or eliminated.

Of course, there's always more than one or even two reasons for a complicated system like education to prioritize certain items over others. Let's explore each of the challenges creativity faces in our current education norms.

Education's Focus and Purpose Since the Twentieth Century

In the sprawling narrative of human civilization, few inventions have had as profound an impact on society as public education. It's a story that intertwines with the fabric of societal evolution, economic shifts, and the unyielding quest for equality and knowledge. Public education, as we understand it today, wasn't born from a single moment of enlightenment, though its seeds were planted there. It evolved as a response to the changing needs of society. As times shifted through the Industrial Revolution to the early days of modern society, so too did the acknowledgment of the need for a basic quality of public education. What began as a way to ensure future factory workers were compliant became a fundamental right that could uplift individuals, and by extension, entire communities.

Initially, education's primary aim was basic literacy and numeracy, tools considered essential for the informed citizenry of a burgeoning democracy. This phase laid the groundwork for a more structured form of public education, which sought to equip citizens with the knowledge needed to participate fully in "good society."

As we crossed the threshold into the twentieth century, the purpose of public education underwent a significant change. The dawn of industrialization saw a shift in educational objectives—from broad-based literacy to the cultivation of specific skills needed in factories and offices. This era marked the beginning of education as a means to an economic end, where schools became factories of human capital, priming students for their roles in the industrial machine.

This shift wasn't merely academic but deeply ingrained in the socioeconomic fabric of the time. Education became a vehicle for social mobility, a ladder for the aspiring masses to climb out of poverty and into the burgeoning middle class. However, this ladder wasn't accessible to everyone. Socioeconomic status played—and continues to play—a pivotal role in the availability and quality of education, creating disparities that echo through generations.

From its inception, public education in the United States has been marred by socioeconomic disparities.[4] In 1965, President Lyndon Johnson set out to do something about this. The son of a tenant farmer, he believed that the key to ending inequality was education. He recognized that schools in affluent areas boasted resources and facilities that schools in poorer districts could only dream of. And so Johnson, along with Congress in 1965, signed the Elementary and Secondary Education Act (ESEA) into law. This was the largest expansion of the role of the federal government in the classroom, an area of public policy that had traditionally been left to state and local governments. Along with this act came funding—lots of it—in the form of federal dollars for things called "Title Programs." These programs, such as Title 1—which provides funding for schools with low-income families—are the topic of much debate each year and are often held hostage in budget seasons. As it turned out, the divide in education wasn't just a matter of funding but a reflection of societal values and priorities. Education policy often went astray, focusing more on the needs of the economy than on the individual learner, exacerbating the divide between the haves and the have-nots. All of this laid the root system for the invader that would come next.

Standardized testing, the most significant educational reform of the twentieth century, promised to level the playing field by offering a uniform measure of student achievement.[5] Its roots can be traced back to the early 1900s during World War I and the Army Alpha tests for soldiers. During Senate hearings to debate the ESEA, Senator Robert Kennedy asked rhetorically, "I wonder if we couldn't have some system of reporting… through some testing system that would be established [by] which the people at the local community would know periodically… what progress had been made," which would end up coming true when the first national assessment of student learning, which would later be known as the National Assessment of Educational Progress or NAEP, was given in 1969 (see note 4). But it was the No Child Left Behind Act of 2001 that cemented testing's place in American education. This act, aimed at closing the achievement gap, instead often widened it.[6] Test scores now became the be-all and end-all of educational success, at the expense of creativity, critical thinking, and the joy of learning.

To be sure, the effects of standardized testing on education have been profound and far reaching. It redefined success in narrow terms, prioritized rote memorization over understanding, and placed undue stress on students and teachers alike. And while the backlash against this myopic focus on testing rages, little has been done to change the situation. Perhaps because there has not been a new revolution to require a change—until now.

The Advent of Artificial Intelligence

Artificial intelligence (AI) isn't just a product of the twenty-first-century imagination; its roots trace back to the mid-twentieth century, a time of great innovation and curiosity about the capabilities of machines. The term "artificial intelligence" was first coined in 1956, during a workshop at Dartmouth College. Here, the brightest minds pondered over machines that could not just calculate at rapid speeds but could also think, learn, and adapt like humans. Since then, AI has evolved from an intriguing concept into a fundamental part of our daily lives, transforming industries, reshaping societal norms, and even altering the fabric of human interaction.

Today, AI's impact on society and individuals is unlike anything we've seen before. From the way we shop, with recommendations tailored to our preferences, to the way we move, with autonomous vehicles navigating the complexities of road travel, AI has made services more efficient and experiences more personalized. In healthcare, AI algorithms analyze data to predict patient outcomes, personalize treatments, and revolutionize diagnostics. In K–12 education, AI isn't just making waves; it's creating a whole new ocean of possibilities. It's reshaping the way students learn, making education a more tailored experience, and easing the administrative burden on teachers. But—and it's a big but—there are a couple of areas where AI can't quite match up to the human touch: creativity and emotional intelligence.

AI can generate music, art, and even write articles, but can it truly be creative? Creativity involves connecting dots in unique ways, having those lightbulb moments, and navigating the messy process of turning an idea into reality. It's about thinking outside the box in ways that AI, with its logical algorithms, can't quite grasp. AI operates within the boundaries of its programming and the data it's fed. It lacks the ability to engage in divergent thinking, to dream, and to imagine in the way humans do.

Similarly, AI's grasp of emotional intelligence is mechanical at best. AI can recognize facial expressions, analyze speech patterns, and even respond to human emotions in a way that simulates empathy. Yet, true emotional intelligence is more than just processing cues; it's about understanding complex human emotions, demonstrating empathy, and building genuine relationships. It involves nuances and subtleties that are deeply human and inherently unquantifiable. AI lacks the capacity for genuine care, compassion, and empathy—the essence of what it means to be human.

However, as AI becomes increasingly integrated into the fabric of daily life, ethical implications bubble to the surface. Privacy concerns, data security, and the potential for bias in AI algorithms are significant issues. The question of how to ensure AI benefits all of society, not just a privileged few, looms large. There's also the issue of job displacement, as AI and automation become capable of performing tasks traditionally done by humans. Balancing the efficiency and innovation AI brings against these ethical challenges is a tightrope walk for policymakers, technologists, and society at large.

Future Career Impact and Societal Implications

As AI tech continues to evolve, so does the landscape of careers and society at large. In a world increasingly run by algorithms, our uniquely human trait of creativity isn't just nice to have; it's essential. Here are a few reasons why we all need to double down on creativity.

First off, the job scene is getting a major makeover. Jobs that involve routine tasks? AI can handle those. In fact, McKinsey Global Institute reports that by 2030, 30 percent of our currently worked hours could be automated.[7] But this isn't necessarily bad news. It means we've got a golden opportunity to shift toward roles that demand our human touch—think creativity, critical thinking, and emotional intelligence. Jobs in AI and tech are booming, sure, but so are roles requiring human creativity, like design, storytelling, and innovation.

Now, let's talk about how AI is shaking up society. On the bright side, AI promises to solve some of our toughest challenges, from climate change to healthcare. It's making our lives easier and more efficient, from smart homes that know just how you like your morning coffee to apps that make it a breeze to connect with people across the globe.

But there's a flip side. The rapid pace of AI development raises big questions about privacy, security, and equity. Who controls AI? How do we protect our data? And how do we make sure the benefits of AI don't just go to a select few? These are tough questions, and finding the right answers won't be easy.

That's where creativity comes in. Navigating the future with AI at our side isn't just about understanding technology; it's about imagining the kind of world we want to live in and then creating it. It's about thinking outside the box to solve ethical dilemmas and ensuring that AI serves the greater good.

In the workplace, the emphasis on creativity is already taking hold. Companies aren't just looking for technical know-how; they're on the hunt for people who can innovate, adapt, and think differently. As AI takes on more of the mundane tasks, the value of creative work is skyrocketing. Whether you're designing the next big app or crafting marketing campaigns that resonate on a human level, creativity is your ticket to standing out.

But embracing creativity isn't just about securing a job; it's about shaping a society that values human connection, ethical thinking, and innovative solutions to global problems. It's about creating art, music, and literature that reflect our times and inspire future generations. In a world where AI can crunch numbers and analyze data, our ability to dream, empathize, and create is what makes us irreplaceable.

Competing Priorities for Future Needs

In the wake of all this, it's clear that our schools are at a crossroads, juggling a bunch of competing priorities as they prepare for the future. It's like they're trying to bake the perfect educational cake, but everyone's arguing about the ingredients. On one side, we've got the tech enthusiasts, pushing for coding, AI, and all things digital. On the other, there's a call for a back-to-basics approach with reading, writing, and 'rithmetic. And across it all, there's creativity, empathy, and teamwork.

Schools are under pressure to teach the skills that'll be in demand, like coding, data analysis, and how to work with AI. This isn't just about preparing kids for jobs; it's about understanding the world they live in. But here's the rub: tech skills alone won't cut it. The digital world is vast and ever-changing, and learning one programming language today might be outdated tomorrow.

Then there's the traditional trio: reading, writing, and arithmetic. Some folks argue we're getting so caught up in the shiny new tech that we're neglecting the basics. And they've got a point. No matter how advanced AI gets, being able to read critically, write clearly, and understand math is foundational. These aren't just academic skills; they're life skills. Think about it—every time you read the news, budget your expenses, or write an email, you're using these core skills.

And in the middle of this crossroads are creativity and empathy. Creativity isn't just an elective; it's the central axis around which all other subjects revolve. Imagine schools where creativity isn't sidelined for the sake of more "practical" subjects but is the heartbeat of the curriculum, integrating seamlessly with every lesson, from tech to the three Rs. This isn't about choosing art over algebra or drama over data science; it's about recognizing that creativity is the key to unlocking potential across all disciplines.[8]

The emphasis on creativity nurtures a mindset that's about more than just generating ideas; it's about critical thinking, problem-solving, and innovation. These are the skills that will matter in a world where AI can take care of the routine tasks. By weaving creativity into the fabric of education, schools can prepare students not just to navigate the future but to shape it.[9]

Tech skills are crucial, no doubt. But when paired with creativity, they're supercharged, leading to breakthroughs in how we interact with technology and use it to solve complex problems. The basics—reading, writing, and arithmetic—become more vibrant when approached creatively, transforming them from mere subjects to be mastered into tools for creative expression and exploration.

Soft skills, too, flourish in a creativity-centric education system. Teamwork, empathy, communication—all are naturally cultivated in an environment that values creative thinking and collaborative problem-solving. It's about preparing students not just for the jobs of the future but for a life of meaningful innovation and connection.

But here's the thing: prioritizing creativity in education isn't just an academic shift; it's a societal one. It opens up a world of possibilities for all students, regardless of background, giving them the tools to think differently, innovate, and lead. However, this vision faces a stark challenge: the widening gap between the haves and have-nots.

The Equity Gap

In the end, advocating for creativity in education isn't just about preparing students for a rapidly changing world; it's about striving for equity. In some schools, students have access to everything: 3D printers, robotics clubs, art studios brimming with supplies, and courses in everything from coding to creative writing. These students are encouraged to think outside the box, make mistakes, and learn from them. Their creative muscles get a serious workout every day.

Then, there are schools struggling with underfunding and overcrowding, where the focus is on getting through the standard curriculum, often through rote learning. Here, creativity isn't just undervalued; it's often seen as a luxury they can't afford. These students are just as capable of innovation and creativity as their more privileged peers, but they're running a race with weights tied to their feet.

This equity gap in schools doesn't just affect academic outcomes; it stifles the potential for creative thinking among a significant portion of the next generation.[10] But what if we flipped the script and used creativity as a tool to bridge this divide?

Imagine a shift toward project-based learning, where students tackle real-world problems with whatever resources they have. It's not about the flashiest tech but about innovative thinking and doing more with less. This kind of creative problem-solving is invaluable, teaching students resilience, adaptability, and outside-the-box thinking.

There are schools that partner with local businesses and communities to provide creative learning opportunities outside the classroom already—think artist residencies, coding bootcamps, or entrepreneurship workshops. These experiences are leveling the playing field, giving all students a taste of diverse creative endeavors. What if we could equip more schools to join in on efforts like these?

Consider the power of mentorship programs that connect students from under-resourced schools with professionals in creative fields. These relationships can ignite passions, open doors, and show students that their creative dreams are valid and attainable, regardless of their current circumstances.

Turning the tide on the equity gap in schools through creativity isn't just a nice idea; it's a necessity for building a more equitable and innovative society. When all students have the opportunity to develop their creative potential, we all benefit from the fresh ideas, solutions, and innovations they bring to the table.

But let's be real: bridging the equity gap in education through creativity is no small task. It requires investment—of time, resources, and belief in the transformative power of creativity. It calls for a collective effort from educators, policymakers, communities, and students themselves. And it means a shift in the collective mindset—toward learning as a process and away from testing for achievement.

The Measurement Conundrum: Evaluating Creativity

This may be the greatest hurdle for prioritizing creativity in schools: our obsession with measurement. And trying to measure creativity is like trying to measure the wind with a ruler. We know it's there, whipping through the air, but pinning it down to a precise number? That's where the head-scratching begins. So, the question remains: can we evaluate creativity in schools, and more importantly, should we?

First off, let's tackle the "can" part. Sure, we can try to measure creativity. Educators have developed rubrics and assessments aiming to quantify students' creative abilities, looking at originality, problem-solving skills, and the ability to connect seemingly unrelated concepts. But here's the thing: creativity is as diverse as the human race itself. What looks like a groundbreaking idea in one context might be everyday thinking in another. Can a standardized rubric truly capture the nuance of every student's creative process? It's a bit like trying to capture a butterfly with a net. You might get a closer look, but you risk damaging its wings in the process.

Now, onto the "should" part. The intention behind evaluating creativity is often well-meaning. We want to encourage innovative thinking, right? Reward those lightbulb moments and nurture our future artists, inventors, and problem solvers. But when we start putting numbers on creativity, things get murky. Creativity thrives in environments where taking risks is encouraged, where there's room to fail and learn from that failure. The moment we start grading it, we risk turning it into just another hoop to jump through. Instead of thinking outside the box, students might start wondering, "What does the teacher want me to say to get a good grade?"

This doesn't mean we throw our hands up and give up on nurturing creativity in schools. Far from it. It means we approach it differently. We encourage it, foster it, and give it space to grow.

Showcase student projects, celebrate innovative ideas, and provide feedback that focuses on the process, not just the end product. Let students know it's the journey of creation that's valued, not just the destination.

But here's the conundrum: in our data-driven world, the pressure to quantify everything is immense. We crave algorithms that can neatly predict and evaluate outcomes, including creativity. Yet, creativity refuses to be boxed in. It's the human spark that ignites new ideas, solutions, and art. It's what makes us stare at a problem until we see a solution no one else thought of, what drives us to doodle, to invent, to imagine worlds beyond our own.

Perhaps creativity must stand alone, without the constraints of an algorithm. Creativity is the essence of being human. It's our innate ability to see connections where none existed before, to dream and to make those dreams a reality. In a world increasingly run by code, our creative capacities distinguish us, making us irreplaceable not just in the workforce, but in the fabric of society.

Evaluating creativity in schools, then, is not just about assigning a grade.[11] It's about acknowledging and nurturing this uniquely human trait, ensuring it flourishes in the next generation. We need creativity now more than ever—to solve the complex problems facing our world, to innovate, to inspire. So, let's give creativity the space it deserves to grow, unencumbered by the need to measure it. Instead, acknowledge that creativity is imperative simply because it's the wellspring of our humanity and our future—one that no algorithm can replicate.

The Expedition Begins

Let's recap and get real about a big issue in our schools: the creativity crunch. It's not that schools don't value creativity; it's that there's a whole tangle of reasons why it's getting squished out of the picture.

First up, a history lesson. Our education system was designed in an era where assembly lines were the future. It was about churning out workers who could fit neatly into predefined roles.

Creativity? Not so high on the agenda. Fast forward to today, and we're still shaking off that old-school dust, trying to make room for creative thinking in a system that was built for a different time.

Enter AI, stage right. It's changing the game, automating tasks left and right, and showing us that what we really need to be teaching is what makes us uniquely human: creativity. But here's the kicker: the future careers our kids will step into? They're not just about being creative; they're about using creativity to navigate a world where humans and machines work side by side. That's a tall order when we're still figuring out the creativity equation in schools.

Now, schools are juggling like never before. Tech skills here, traditional subjects there, and a chorus of voices saying, "Don't forget about creativity!" It's like trying to keep all the plates spinning without letting any crash to the floor. And amid this juggling act, a chasm is forming—an equity gap where not all students get the same shot at flexing their creative muscles. This isn't just unfair; it's a waste of potential that we can't afford.

Even if we all agree that creativity is as essential as breathing, how do we measure it? Slap a grade on an idea? Count the number of lightbulb moments? It's like trying to measure the ocean with a teacup. This conundrum has left us scratching our heads, wondering how to encourage creativity when we can't even agree on what it looks like.

Where does this leave us? Staring down a bunch of challenges that might seem as daunting as climbing Everest in flip-flops. But here's the good news: the next pages are all about the climb. We're going to dive deep into how to untangle this creativity crunch. We're talking processes that work, models that inspire, and examples from schools that have cracked the code.

So buckle up. It's going to be an adventure—a journey to rediscover what makes us human and how to nurture it in the heart of our education system. Creativity isn't just another subject; it's the key to unlocking a future where every student can thrive, innovate, and dream big. Let's get started.

Key Takeaways

1. Research suggests that poverty—not standardized testing—is the primary obstacle to creativity in schools, though testing practices are deeply intertwined with socioeconomic factors.

2. The purpose of public education has evolved from creating compliant factory workers to developing specific job skills, but it has consistently struggled to prioritize creativity despite mounting evidence of its importance.

3. As AI increasingly automates routine tasks, creativity and emotional intelligence emerge as distinctly human capabilities that will be essential for future careers and cannot be replicated by machines.

4. Schools face competing priorities—technical skills, traditional academics, and creative development—creating a tension between preparing students for immediate job markets versus developing adaptable, innovative thinking.

5. The equity gap in education means that creative learning opportunities are often treated as luxuries available primarily to affluent schools, perpetuating disparities in how creativity is valued and developed across different communities.

PRACTICE STRATEGY: HEADLINES

Consider everything you learned from this chapter. If you had to sum up what you read into a single headline for your local newspaper or to share on your social media feed, what would it say? Make it compelling and ensure it grabs the reader's attention right away—write this down.

Notes

1 Pink, D. H. (2006). *A Whole New Mind: Why Right-Brainers Will Rule the Future.* Riverhead Books.

2 Robinson, K. (2006, February). *Do Schools Kill Creativity?* [Video]. TED Conferences. https://www.ted.com/talks/sir_ken_robinson_do_schools_kill_creativity

3   Zelizer, J. E. (2015, April). "How Education Policy Went Astray." *The Atlantic*. https://www.theatlantic.com/education/archive/2015/04/how-education-policy-went-astray/390210/

4   Allegretto, S., García, E., & Weiss, E. (2022). "Public Education Funding in the US Needs an Overhaul." Economic Policy Institute. https://www.epi.org/publication/public-education-funding-in-the-us-needs-an-overhaul/

5   Hinton, J. (2020, December 8). "How Did We Get Here: A Brief History of American Standardized Testing." https://www.jeffreyahinton.com/post/how-did-we-get-here-a-brief-history-of-american-standardized-testing

6   Holmes, S. E. (2010). "No Child Left Behind: A Failing Attempt at Reform." *Inquiries Journal*, 2.

7   Ellingrund, K., et al. (2023, July 26). "Generative AI and the Future of Work in America." McKinsey Global Institute. https://www.mckinsey.com/mgi/our-research/generative-ai-and-the-future-of-work-in-america

8   Catterall, J. S. (2009). *Doing Well and Doing Good by Doing Art: The Effects of Education in the Visual and Performing Arts on the Achievements and Values of Young Adults*. Imagination Group/I-Group Books.

9   Wagner, T. (2012). *Creating Innovators: The Making of Young People Who Will Change the World*. Scribner.

10 Florida, R. (2002). *The Rise of the Creative Class*. Basic Books.

11 Said-Metwaly, S., Van den Noortgate, W., & Kyndt, E. (2017). "Approaches to Measuring Creativity: A Systematic Literature Review." *Creativity: Theories-Research-Applications*, 4(2), 238–75. https://intapi.sciendo.com/pdf/10.1515/ctra-2017-0013

2

The Creative Spectrum: Understanding and Developing Creative Potential

> *Chapter Guiding Question: What does creativity mean and look like in practice?*

Here's the truth: We've been getting creativity wrong for decades.

For the longest time, we've thought of creativity as something that belongs to artists in their studios or designers in their workshops. But some of the most creative breakthroughs happen in the most unexpected places—like in 1982, when NASA engineer Lonnie Johnson was tinkering with a new heat pump design in his bathroom. He had connected a nozzle to the sink and was testing how his invention handled pressurized water, when suddenly … whoosh! A powerful stream of water shot clear across the room. Most engineers would have seen this as a failed experiment. But Johnson saw something else entirely: the potential for pure joy. That accidental discovery eventually became the Super Soaker, transforming summer afternoons for millions of kids and revolutionizing an entire industry of outdoor toys.

I love this story because it shatters that persistent myth about creativity belonging exclusively to "creative professionals." Johnson wasn't trying to invent a toy or even trying to be creative. He was simply doing what engineers do: solving problems, staying curious, and keeping his mind open to unexpected possibilities. His breakthrough came from the uniquely human ability to connect seemingly unrelated dots: a heat pump experiment, a wayward water stream, and the universal appeal of an epic water fight.

We're living in an age where artificial intelligence can write poetry, generate art, and even compose music. Every day, AI gets better at handling routine tasks and recognizing patterns. But Johnson's story hints at something AI hasn't mastered: the human capacity to find meaning in accidents, pivot in response to surprise, and transform technical knowledge into experiences that delight and inspire. As technology advances, understanding creativity—its workings, its transformative power, and its application—becomes increasingly valuable.

The Journey Begins: Defining Creativity

Ask ten different people to define creativity. I guarantee you'll get ten different answers, and they'll all be right in their own way. Some folks will tell you it's a gift you're born with, like being tall or having perfect pitch. Others will break it down into a process, complete with steps and methods. And then there are the people who'll tell you (and I tend to agree with them) that it's way more complicated than a single simplified definition.

Psychologist Mihaly Csikszentmihalyi's work on flow, creative processes, and audience reception led him to an interesting conclusion. Creativity exists beyond what happens in your head. It functions as a conversation between your expertise, what society thinks is valuable, and whether the culture is ready for your ideas.[1]

For years, the world has been trying to nail down exactly what creativity is and give it a nice, neat definition. Many use this one from researchers Robert Sternberg and Todd Lubart:

The production of ideas, insights, or products that are novel, original, and useful in a given context.[2]

I like this attempt because it captures something really important: creativity isn't just about coming up with wild, random ideas. It's about coming up with new ideas that actually matter, that solve problems or touch hearts.

But creativity is more than a product—it's also a process. Harvard researcher Teresa Amabile breaks creativity down into three parts[3] that I think make a lot of sense:

1. **Domain Knowledge**—This is your toolkit, everything you know about your field. Think of it as having the right ingredients before you start cooking.

2. **Cognitive Flexibility**—This is how you use those ingredients in new ways. It's like a chef who knows the rules well enough to creatively break them.

3. **Intrinsic Motivation**—This is your engine, what gets you excited to create. It's that spark of curiosity or passion that makes you want to dive in.

Here's how this expanded definition plays out in the real world:

Imagine an urban planner looking at a run-down neighborhood. They're using their knowledge of city design (domain knowledge), thinking about unconventional ways to use the space (cognitive flexibility), driven by a passion to create better communities (intrinsic motivation).

Or picture a basketball coach watching game footage at 2 a.m., not because they have to, but because they're excited about crafting the perfect play. They're combining their deep understanding of the game with fresh thinking about strategy, all fueled by their love of the sport.

This definition of creativity is less about "thinking outside the box" and more about knowing when to use the box as a stepping stone, when to turn it into a boat, or when to build something entirely new.

Creativity as a Social Phenomenon

Of course, we can't stop there. That would be too easy! Amabile throws in a fourth piece that changes everything: the social element. These are all the things we can't control—the world around us, other people, timing—that shape how our creativity plays out.

This is where Amabile's definition lines up perfectly with what Csikszentmihalyi discovered when studying artists, musicians, and athletes. Creativity is like a three-way dance between the following:

1. **You**—coming up with the ideas
2. **Experts**—the people who can recognize a good idea when they see it
3. **Culture**—the world that either embraces or ignores those ideas

The Wright brothers are a perfect example of these three elements working in tandem for creative innovation to hit it big. Sure, they invented the first successful airplane with their 1903 Wright Flyer, but their story isn't just about two genius brothers tinkering in a bicycle shop creating a new way for humans to travel. Here's what they needed:

- Other aviation pioneers who could test and validate their ideas
- A society that was ready to accept humans flying
- The right moment in history when the technology made it possible

This parallels creativity in the world of artificial intelligence, doesn't it? AI can generate endless variations of poems, paintings, and patterns. But here's what it can't do: give those creations real meaning or emotional depth. That's still our territory. As we prepare our students for careers of the future, we need to shift our focus from knowing for knowing's sake to building the skills and capacities that make us uniquely *us*.

Beyond the "Hard" and "Soft" Skills Divide

How do we identify which skills matter most for preparing children for an uncertain future? Traditionally, we've looked to professional industries for guidance on the skills they need, and then trying to stuff those skills into one of two boxes: hard skills or soft skills. Hard skills are classified as the technical stuff you can put on your resume, like coding or speaking French. Soft skills are the people-focused abilities that help you navigate office life, like communication and teamwork.[4] In schools, we've been busy teaching students the hard skills and hoping that students pick up the soft skills along the way.

The problem with this is that with the advent of artificial intelligence, the hard skills can now be done in a fraction of the time by a bot that's been programmed with the same information students find in their textbooks. So where does that leave our students—and our schools—for the future? While students still need fundamental competencies in reading, writing, and mathematics, future success will increasingly belong to those who can create with those skills rather than merely apply them.

Creativity doesn't fit into a singular box like a hard or soft skill. It's like trying to categorize water—sometimes it's a solid, sometimes it's a liquid, sometimes it's a gas. And that's exactly what makes it so powerful.

For years, employers have listed creativity as the number one skill set they are looking for in candidates.[5] So when they list this as a must-have skill, which column do they place it in? Most people would automatically file it under soft skills, right alongside emotional intelligence and leadership. But that misses something huge about how creativity actually works in today's world.

Consider a detective working a complex case. Effective investigators need hard skills in forensic evidence analysis, legal procedure knowledge, and database proficiency. But they also require that intuitive spark that reveals patterns others miss, the ability to connect seemingly unrelated evidence, and the creativity to think beyond standard procedures when a case takes an unusual turn.

Or think about a trauma surgeon. They've got all the technical skills down cold—they could probably recite surgical procedures in their sleep. But what happens when they encounter a case that doesn't fit the textbook? That's when creativity kicks in, helping them improvise solutions in split-second decisions that could save someone's life.

The old question "Is creativity a hard or soft skill?" completely misses the point. It's both, and it's neither. It's a lens that magnifies both technical expertise and interpersonal abilities into something more powerful. Rather than being another professional tool, creativity becomes a force that helps you use all your tools in new and better ways.[6]

But this brings up an interesting question: are we stuck with whatever creative ability we were born with, or can we develop it?

In 2015, researchers studied this question by following sets of identical twins who had been separated at birth and raised in different households, allowing them to isolate the impact of environment versus genetics on creative ability.[7]

Turns out, twins who grew up in environments rich in diverse experiences, including artistic exposure, complex problem-solving opportunities, and interdisciplinary learning, consistently developed stronger creative skills than their counterparts raised in more rigid, structured settings. The research underscored that creativity is not simply an inherited trait but one that flourishes in the right conditions.

The study ultimately concluded that while some cognitive traits that support creativity are influenced by genetics, the capacity for creative thinking itself is primarily shaped by experience, environment, and mindset. This means that creativity is not an innate gift reserved for a select few, but a skill that can be actively cultivated through deliberate exposure to new ideas, challenges, and cross-disciplinary interactions.

This has huge implications for how we think about education and professional development. Instead of treating creativity as just another soft skill to develop alongside time management and teamwork, we need to recognize it as something more fundamental—a way of seeing and engaging with the world that enhances everything else we do.

The old model of separating technical training from creative development? That's becoming about as useful as a flip phone at a smartphone convention. The most effective learning environments now integrate both, encouraging people to apply creative thinking across everything they do, whether they're crunching numbers or crafting communications.

Creativity is more than a skill you learn or a trait you're born with. It's a mindset you cultivate, a problem-solving approach you develop, and increasingly, it's becoming our secret weapon in a world where AI is mastering routine tasks faster than we can teach them. We need to understand how creativity works in the mind—through internal systems, thought pathways, and within a social context—to develop it for our advantage.

The Inner Landscape: Neuroscience of Creativity

If creativity is a skill, a mindset, and a process we need to nurture, then figuring out how to tap into it is key. While creativity touches the heart, it begins in the mind. The human brain remains nature's most sophisticated creative engine, but contrary to popular belief, there's no single "creativity center" lurking within its folds. Instead, creativity emerges from an intricate dance between different neural networks, each playing a critical role in the creative process.

There are three key players that dominate this neural choreography.[8] First is the **Default Mode Network (DMN)**. The DMN is your brain's daydreaming system. It's what kicks in when you're taking a shower, going for a walk, or staring out the window. This network specializes in spontaneous thinking and free association, often leading to those "Aha!" moments that seem to come from nowhere.

But raw ideas alone don't make for creativity. That's where the **Executive Control Network** (ECN) steps in as an organizer and decision-maker. This network is the part that takes those spontaneous insights and shapes them into something useful. It's the difference between having a random thought about combining a bicycle with a coffee shop and actually figuring out how to create a successful mobile café business.

The **Salience Network** (SN) acts as a switchboard between the DMN and ECN, determining which ideas from the mind-wandering state should be passed to the executive control system for refinement and which should stay in the background.

Of course, creativity doesn't exist in a vacuum. External factors, like stress and mood, have a powerful influence on how these networks function. When stress activates the brain's fear centers, it suppresses the DMN—the very system responsible for generating new ideas. On the flip side, positive moods can enhance our ability to think flexibly and make unexpected connections.

Yet, despite what science tells us about how our brain actually works, certain myths about creativity persist; none more enduring than the idea of the "tortured artist." The image is everywhere: the isolated poet tormented by inner demons, the brooding painter lost in a haze of melancholy, the musician channeling pain into brilliance. It's a romanticized notion that has shaped our cultural narrative, but modern research paints a more nuanced picture.

The fact is you don't need to suffer to be creative. While some mental health conditions might amplify certain aspects of creativity, the relationship isn't one way, nor is struggle a prerequisite for innovation. In fact, creativity itself can be a powerful tool for mental well-being. When we engage in creative acts, we give our brains an outlet to process emotions, relieve stress, and foster joy.[9] In a world where anxiety is as common as a cold, creativity isn't just an artistic pursuit; it's a mental health superpower.

Basically, your brain is a creativity gym. Every time you engage in creative thinking, you're building new neural connections, like forging new paths through a forest. Scientists call this "plasticity"; essentially, it's your brain's ability to stay flexible and nimble. It's why we can keep learning and growing throughout our lives, building our creative muscles along the way.

This is also why some of the best learning approaches mix things up between focused work and free exploration. It's not just because it keeps things interesting (though it does). It's because that's how our brains naturally work when we're being creative. Sometimes we need to zoom in and focus, and sometimes we need to let our minds wander and see what connections pop up.

Your brain doesn't care whether you're being creative about art or science or business. The same neural networks light up whether you're painting a masterpiece, solving a complex equation, or figuring out a new marketing strategy. Your brain is just like, "Cool, we're creating something new here!" and gets to work, regardless of the field.

Think about what this means for a moment. All those times we've put creativity in the "artsy" box? That's like saying you can only use your legs for dancing, not for walking or running or climbing. Your creative brain is more versatile than that and deserves a lot more credit.

This understanding is empowering, especially as we're moving into an age where AI is becoming more prevalent. Yes, AI can mix and match existing patterns to create something new—but it can't match the incredible complexity of the human brain, with its ability to smoothly shift between wild imagination and practical problem-solving, between "what if?" and "how to."

The Three Faces of Creativity: Divergent, Convergent, and Lateral Thinking

Have you ever watched a kid tackle a jigsaw puzzle? They usually start by dumping all the pieces on the table, looking at each one from different angles. Then they might sort them by color or edge pieces. Finally, they start challenging their assumptions about what goes where, discovering surprising connections along the way.

That simple puzzle process is a perfect window into how creative thinking works in our brains. As we travel deeper into understanding creativity, we discover three distinct thinking styles that work together like a well-oiled machine: divergent, convergent, and lateral thinking.[10] Each connects with one of our three neural networks and acts as different gears in our creative engines. They all serve a unique purpose and knowing when to shift between them helps to navigate any creative challenge.

Divergent Thinking: The Explorer

Let's start with divergent thinking—the wild child of the creative family. This type of thinking is strongly associated with the default mode network (DMN). It's your brain in exploration mode, throwing out ideas without judgment, like a kid in a candy store pointing at everything that catches their eye. It's that brainstorming session where no idea is too crazy or that artist's sketchbook filled with half-finished concepts. But divergent thinking isn't just for artists and innovators. Engineers use it to envision multiple solutions to technical problems, teachers use it to find new ways to explain tough concepts, and entrepreneurs use it to spot opportunities everyone else missed.

Here's what makes divergent thinking special:

- It's like your brain on a creative treasure hunt, following every shiny possibility.
- It loves hanging out in the land of "what if?"

- It's comfortable with messy, unfinished ideas.
- It says "yes, and…" instead of "yes, but…"

But divergent thinking alone can lead to chaos—a sea of ideas without direction. That's where convergent thinking steps in.

Convergent Thinking: The Refiner

Meet convergent thinking—the practical problem-solver of the creative process. If divergent thinking is the one tossing out wild ideas left and right, convergent thinking is the one stepping in with a clipboard, saying, *All right, let's sort through this and find what actually works.* This is where the executive control network (ECN) shines, acting like a mental filter that sifts through all the possibilities and zeros in on the best, most logical solution. Think of it as the brain's built-in editor. It helps you refine ideas, cut the fluff, and figure out what's worth pursuing.

This is the thinking style that helps:

- Engineers pick the most efficient design from their options.
- Writers choose the perfect word from a dozen possibilities.
- Business leaders zero in on the most viable strategy.
- Chefs perfect a recipe after trying various ingredients.

It's when you learn to move between divergent and convergent thinking that things become interesting.

Lateral Thinking: The Revolutionary

Lateral thinking is like the rebellious genius of the creative process. It doesn't just think outside the box; it questions whether we even need a box in the first place. Popularized by Edward de Bono,[11] this kind of thinking is all about breaking free from traditional patterns and sparking those *aha!* moments that change everything. It's probably my favorite type of thinking because it has a way of flipping conventional wisdom on its head.

Take a look at some of the biggest game-changers in recent history. Ride-sharing apps didn't just improve taxis; they asked, *why own a car at all?* Streaming services didn't try to build a better video store; they completely reimagined how we consume entertainment. And food delivery apps didn't just make restaurant takeout more efficient; they turned every kitchen into a potential business.

While the salience network (SN) isn't directly responsible for lateral thinking, it plays a key supporting role. The SN helps pinpoint the most important details in any given situation, which in turn fuels the ability to make unexpected connections and see alternative perspectives—both essential to lateral thinking.

At its core, lateral thinking is about challenging the assumptions we take for granted, spotting connections no one else sees, and approaching problems from entirely new angles. It's also about embracing that uncomfortable, squirmy feeling that comes when an idea initially seems too strange to work—because often, those are the ideas that change everything.

Better Together

The real magic happens when these three thinking styles start working together. A product development team might start with divergent thinking to generate tons of product ideas, use lateral thinking to challenge basic assumptions about what customers really need, and then apply convergent thinking to refine and implement the most promising concepts.

This mix of thinking styles becomes super important when we're facing complex challenges. Climate change, public health crises, technological

# 6 Lateral Thinking Prompts

1 A jewelry store was robbed in the middle of the night. The alarm system was fully functional, but the police were never alerted. There were no power outages, technical glitches, or tampering with the system. Yet, the thieves got away clean. How?

Answer: The robbers broke into the store after it had closed but before the alarm was set. The alarm only arms automatically at a scheduled time, and they struck just before that.

2 A woman enters a dark, windowless room with no light. She only has a candle, a match, and a fireplace. The candle is unlit. Yet somehow, she manages to light the fireplace without lighting the candle first. How?

Answer: She lights the match and then lights the fireplace directly. The candle was never needed to light the fireplace.

3 A farmer owns a perfectly square field. He needs to create four separate, equal-sized, enclosed sections using only three straight fences. There are no hills, trees, or other natural dividers. How can he do it?

Answer: The farmer can arrange the three fences in the shape of a capital "Y" within the square field. This will divide the area into four equal triangular sections.

4 A man walks into a room with one chair, sits on it, and after he leaves, there are two chairs. No one entered the room while he was there, and nothing was hidden. How did this happen?

*Answer: The man was sitting on a **folding** chair or a **stackable** chair. When he unfolded or unstacked it, it became two separate chairs.*

5 Two trains are on the same track heading towards each other at full speed. Miraculously, they pass by safely without switching tracks or stopping. How is this possible?

Answer: They are toy trains on parallel tracks, not real trains on the same track. They pass by safely without needing to switch or stop.

FIGURE 2.1

disruption—none of these are problems you can solve with just one type of thinking. You need to be able to

- generate multiple possible solutions (divergent thinking);
- question fundamental assumptions (lateral thinking); and
- figure out practical next steps (convergent thinking).

While artificial intelligence is getting pretty good at convergent thinking like analyzing data and finding optimal solutions, it still struggles with the kind of cognitive flexibility that lets humans smoothly switch between these different thinking modes. Our ability to combine wild exploration, assumption-challenging insights, and practical problem-solving in uniquely human ways is our secret sauce.

So the trick is to develop the thinking skills and learn to orchestrate them as one collective ensemble. Knowing when to let your mind run wild, when to question everything you know, and when to buckle down and make things happen. It's this pivot between different types of thinking that drives real innovation and creative problem-solving in our modern world.

A Social Symphony: Models for the Process

Of course, we don't do all this thinking and creating alone. That old image of the lone genius, working in isolation until—eureka!—they emerge with some world-changing breakthrough? It makes for great movies, but real creativity doesn't quite work that way. Modern research tells us something far more interesting: creativity works like an ecosystem—your individual ideas are just one part of a larger network where everything influences everything else. Scientists call this the dual pathway model,[12] and it helps explain why some environments seem to spark creative breakthroughs, while others make you feel like your ideas are stuck in quicksand.

Creativity is like a garden. Your individual talent and brainpower are the seeds, but the social environment? That's your soil, water, and sunlight. You can have the best seeds in the world, but without the right growing conditions, they're not going to flourish. Let's explore how this plays out through three key elements: social context, group dynamics, and individual differences.

Social context is fascinating because it works as both nurture and nature in the creative process. When people bump into different perspectives and ideas, their own creative thinking expands. It's like cross-pollination in action. You've probably seen this happen countless times:

- A software developer starts working alongside designers and suddenly sees new ways to make their code more user-friendly.
- A teacher collaborates with local artists and discovers fresh ways to explain complex math concepts.
- A chef talks with food scientists and uses traditional recipes as inspiration for something new.

The part that can trip us up is social pressure. This acts like frost on tender shoots. The same environments that could nurture creativity might accidentally squash it. Think about the following:

- corporate cultures that love predictability more than experimentation
- schools that reward following rules or earning higher standardized testing scores over breaking new ground
- social groups where standing out is seen as showing off

Then there's the impact of group dynamics. When groups click, they can reach creative heights that no individual could touch alone. Look at any major breakthrough—smartphones, electric vehicles, renewable energy solutions—

none of these came from a single person working in isolation. They were designed by teams that combined different kinds of expertise and perspectives.

But group creativity isn't necessarily a smooth ride. Teams can easily fall into traps that shut down innovation before it even has a chance to take off. *Groupthink* happens when everyone gets so comfortable that they stop challenging each other. *Status hierarchies* mean the intern with the brilliant idea might never speak up. And then there's the classic *loudest voice wins* scenario, where the quiet genius in the room goes unheard.[13]

Rather than ditching groupwork altogether, it's better to structure it in a way that actually works. With the right setup, collaboration becomes a powerhouse for creativity. The smartest teams put guardrails in place to keep ideas flowing. Anonymous idea submissions help prevent status bias, so the best ideas rise to the top no matter who they come from. Structured turn-taking ensures that everyone gets a voice, not just the most outspoken. Small group breakouts give quiet thinkers space to shine, and mixing up teams brings fresh perspectives into the conversation.

Even with great collaboration, creativity isn't a simple formula. We have to acknowledge our individual differences. Some people are idea fountains, constantly bubbling with new possibilities. Others are more like master sculptors, taking time to deeply refine fewer ideas.

Some folks love radical innovation, while others excel at making small but crucial improvements.

These differences aren't flaws—they're strengths. The best creative environments don't force everyone into the same mold; they embrace these variations and build systems that support them. That means flexible work processes that adapt to different thinking styles, multiple ways for people to contribute ideas, and recognition systems that value both big, game-changing breakthroughs and subtle, incremental refinements. When individuals have the freedom to approach creative challenges in a way that works for them, the results speak for themselves.[14]

Breakthroughs happen when these three elements line up just right. Think about innovation hubs like Silicon Valley or creative powerhouses like Pixar. They're not just throwing smart people together in a room. They're carefully crafting environments where individual talent can flourish, team collaboration clicks, and social barriers to creativity get knocked down.

Intentionally cultivating these three elements also sets humans apart in an AI-powered world. While AI can process massive amounts of information and generate novel combinations, it can't replicate the complex social dynamics that drive human creativity. Our ability to read social cues, build on others' ideas, and navigate group dynamics remains a distinctive advantage for humans.

Levels of Impact: The 4-C Model

We've explored how creativity flows between people—but what about the scope and scale of creative work itself? Researchers James C. Kaufman and Ronald A. Beghetto found that there are different levels or types of creative work, and each exists on a spectrum, like colors blending into one another, each distinct but connected. They called this the 4-C model.[15]

Think about this like a spectrum of light, where each type of creative impact has its own purpose while simultaneously blending with others when needed. Some creative work glows intimately, visible mainly to ourselves, while other work radiates widely, illuminating entire fields of human progress. Here's what each part of the spectrum looks like in practice:

Mini-c: Personal Illumination

This is creativity at its most intimate—like the warm glow of a reading light that illuminates personal discoveries. It's those "aha!" moments that might seem small to others but light up your own understanding in new ways. It's a student suddenly getting why fractions work, or a hobby cook discovering a new flavor combination that brightens their own culinary world.

Little-c: Everyday Brightness

Moving along our spectrum, we find little-c creativity. This is like the practical light of day that helps everyone see better. This is where personal insights start illuminating solutions for others too. For example, a parent could invent a game that makes cleanup time fun, or an office worker could develop a better way to handle email. These innovations might not dazzle the world, but they make daily life brighter for those around us.

Pro-c: Professional Brilliance

Further along, we find Pro-c. Here, creativity shines with consistent professional power. These are the working artists, scientists, engineers, and other professionals who generate steady beams of innovation in their fields. They've learned to focus their creative light precisely where it's needed, often collaborating with others to create even brighter solutions.

Big-C: Transformative Radiance

At the far end of our spectrum, we find Big-C creativity. These are the breakthrough innovations that light up entire fields or societies. Think Einstein's theory of relativity or the invention of the internet. These achievements often combine multiple creative wavelengths, creating something that illuminates the world in entirely new ways.

Keep in mind, this 4-C model isn't a simple progression from dim to bright. Creative impact radiates in all directions across this spectrum. Big-C breakthroughs often spark thousands of mini-c moments for others. Pro-c practitioners frequently shift between personal insights and broader innovations. Each type of creativity reflects and amplifies the others, creating a richer spectrum of human innovation.

Instead of pushing everyone toward Big-C creativity (as we're often tempted to do), we need to appreciate the full spectrum of creativity. It's not just about the game-changing ideas; it's about the everyday sparks that make life and work more innovative.

That means celebrating those personal moments of inspiration, whether it's a clever fix for a daily problem or a fresh approach to an old routine. It also means encouraging small, everyday ideas that might not shake the world but still make a difference. It's about supporting people as they grow their creative skills, whether in their careers, hobbies, or personal projects. And of course, it's about learning from the transformative breakthroughs that redefine industries and reshape our thinking.

When we recognize and nurture creativity in all its forms, we uplift individuals while building a world that's more dynamic, innovative, and full of possibility.

The Path Ahead: Creativity in the Twenty-First Century

Creativity isn't just any way of operating—it's a way of seeing, thinking, and engaging with others, and grows more vital as our world grows more complex. The creative spectrum we've explored serves as a map for navigating an increasingly automated future where human creativity becomes our distinctive strength.

Here's what really excites me about the future: we're entering an era where understanding creativity means reimagining what humans can achieve when we combine our unique creative capabilities with powerful new tools. Consider what this means for different fields:

- In education, we're shifting from teaching creativity as a separate subject to integrating creative development across all learning experiences.

- In business, companies are redesigning work environments to nurture the full spectrum of creative capabilities.
- In technology, we're creating tools that amplify rather than replace human creative potential.[16]
- In science and research, we're seeing how creative thinking leads to breakthrough insights that pure computation might miss.

The rise of AI isn't making creativity less important—it's revealing just how extraordinary human creativity really is. Every advance in artificial intelligence helps us better understand what makes human creativity unique: our ability to find meaning, to care deeply about outcomes, to connect seemingly unrelated ideas, and to discover truly novel possibilities.[17]

After all, we're more than passive consumers of culture or cogs in an economic machine. We're natural-born creators, equipped with cognitive tools that have evolved over millions of years to help us shape better futures.

As we move deeper into the twenty-first century, our challenge isn't just to be more creative—it's to be more intentional about developing and expressing our creative capabilities. Whether you're an artist, entrepreneur, educator, or engineer, understanding how creativity works helps you engage with it more fully and purposefully.

Because here's the reality: In an age of artificial intelligence and automation, creativity is our superpower. It's the thing that sets us apart and pushes us forward. And the better we understand it, the better we can nurture and develop it, both now and in the future.

The path ahead is uncharted, but that's exactly why we need creativity more than ever. Each advance in technology expands the canvas for human imagination. Our creative capabilities—refined across millennia of evolution, strengthened through practice, and amplified by new tools remain our most powerful means of shaping what comes next.

Key Takeaways

1. Creativity exists on a spectrum, from personal insights to world-changing innovations.
2. Creativity expands connections between multiple areas in our brain simultaneously.
3. Creative development is a process that includes interconnected components that contribute to overall creative potential.
4. The dynamic interplay and integration of different creative elements are more crucial than any single component in isolation.

While AI is transforming the creative landscape, it doesn't diminish the significance of human creativity; instead, it fosters new avenues for creative expression and collaboration.

PRACTICE STRATEGY: MAGAZINE COVER

Imagine you're writing a cover story for a national magazine about the creative spectrum. What would you include in each of the following sections:

- The headline (give the big idea)
- The sidebar (interesting facts about the story)
- Quotes (either from the chapter or from people you would interview)
- Images (what images would you include to capture the essence from this chapter?)

List these out or doodle them onto a single page in the format of a magazine cover.

Notes

1. Csikszentmihalyi, M. (1990). *Flow: The Psychology of Optimal Experience*. Harper & Row.

2. Feist, G. J. (2019). "The Function of Personality in Creativity: Updates on the Creative Personality." In J. C. Kaufman & R. J. Sternberg (Eds.), *The Cambridge Handbook of Creativity* (pp. 353–373). Cambridge University Press. https://doi.org/10.1017/9781316979839.019

3. Amabile, T. M. (1996). *Creativity in Context: Update to The Social Psychology of Creativity*. Westview Press.

4. Vedhar, R. (n.d.). "What's the Difference Between Hard and Soft Skills?" Walden University. https://lifelonglearning.waldenu.edu/resource/what-is-the-difference-between-hard-skills-and-soft-skills.html

5. Riley, S. (2021). "Creativity Is Not a Soft Skill. It Is a Must-Have Mindset for the 21st Century." The 74 Million. https://www.the74million.org/article/riley-creativity-is-not-a-soft-skill-it-is-a-must-have-mindset-for-the-21st-century-how-teachers-can-nurture-it-in-their-students/

6. Guilford, J. P. (1967). *The Nature of Human Intelligence*. McGraw-Hill.

7. Velázquez, J. A., Segal, N. L., & Horwitz, B. N. (2015). "Genetic and Environmental Influences on Applied Creativity: A Reared-Apart Twin Study." *Personality and Individual Differences*, 75, 141–46. https://doi.org/10.1016/j.paid.2014.11.014

8. Jung, R. E., & Haier, R. J. (2007). *The Neuroscience of Creativity*. Creativity Research Journal.

9. Feist, G. J. (2019). "The Function of Personality in Creativity: Updates on the Creative Personality." In J. C. Kaufman & R. J. Sternberg (Eds.), *The Cambridge Handbook of Creativity* (pp. 353–373). Cambridge University Press. https://doi.org/10.1017/9781316979839.019

10. Teeter, C. (2022). "The 3 Modes of Thought: Divergent, Convergent Thinking." TeachThought. https://www.teachthought.com/critical-thinking/3-modes-of-thought-divergent-convergent-thinking/

11. De Bono, E. (2016). *Lateral Thinking: A Textbook of Creativity*. Penguin.

12. Sawyer, R. K. (2012). *Explaining Creativity: The Science of Human Innovation*. Oxford University Press.

13. Edmondson, A. C. (1999, June). "Psychological Safety and Learning Behavior in Work Teams". *Administrative Science Quarterly*, 44(2), 350–383.

14 Deci, E. L., & Ryan, R. M. (1985). *Intrinsic Motivation and Self-Determination in Human Behavior*. Springer Science & Business Media.

15 Kaufman, J. C., & Beghetto, R. A. (2013). "Beyond the Big and the Little: The Four-C Model of Creativity." *Review of General Psychology*, 13(1), 1–12. https://www.normanjackson.co.uk/uploads/1/0/8/4/10842717/four_c_model_of_creativity.pdf

16 Neff, G. (2021). "Can Robots Be Creative?" BBC Science Focus. https://www.sciencefocus.com/future-technology/can-robots-be-creative

17 Aguilera, A. M. (2022). "Theories of Creativity Explained." Ana Maria Aguilera. https://anamariaaguilera.com/creativity-theories/

PART TWO

THE INCUBATION

3

Creativity at Work

> *Chapter Guiding Question: How can we develop our own creative practice?*

In 1967, a petite, soft-spoken nun in horn-rimmed glasses walked away from her religious order and plunged headfirst into creating radical political art during the Vietnam War era. Sister Corita Kent defied every stereotype of a revolutionary. Yet her vibrant screen prints—serigraphs that blended advertising slogans, biblical verses, and bold social commentary—became iconic symbols of the 1960s peace movement.

Kent's most enduring legacy, though, wasn't hanging on gallery walls. It was taped to the door of a small art department classroom at Immaculate Heart College in Los Angeles.

"RULE 7: The only rule is work. If you work, it will lead to something. It's the people who do all of the work all the time who eventually catch on to things."

This was just one of Kent's famous "rules" guiding her art students. Unlike the tired stereotype of the solitary creative genius waiting for divine inspiration, Kent knew creativity was a practice. Her classroom days began with ten minutes of focused observation. Students might examine a single leaf, study reflections in a puddle, or trace shadow patterns on a wall. This seemingly simple ritual trained their brains to notice details others overlooked.

Kent filled notebooks with these observations, which later transformed into her acclaimed artwork tackling pressing social issues. She didn't wait for the muse to visit. She worked steadily and deliberately, turning the creative process into a daily practice rather than a mystical event.

What made Kent's approach compelling was both her art (though her works now hang in the Metropolitan Museum of Art, the Museum of Modern Art, and the National Gallery) and her insistence that creativity isn't some mysterious gift bestowed on a lucky few. It's a practice we cultivate through deliberate habits, thoughtful engagement, and consistent effort—a message that matters now more than ever for today's educators.

The Four Branches of Creativity

Here's the real question: How do we move beyond just talking about creativity to actually building it? Theory is great, but without application, it's just fuel for a lively dinner conversation. Most of us have sat through those passionate discussions about "schools today" that somehow never make it past the appetizers. What does teaching creativity actually look like? How do we help our students (and ourselves) develop creative skills, deepen creative thinking, and apply creativity[1] in meaningful ways?

Years ago, my husband Kevin and I celebrated our anniversary with a trip to Charleston, South Carolina. While there, we visited the Angel Oak tree just outside the city. Considered the largest live oak east of the Mississippi, this towering giant is estimated to be over four hundred years old. Its trunk spans an astonishing twenty-five feet in circumference, with sprawling, gnarled branches stretching wide enough to cast over seventeen thousand square feet of shade.

Standing beneath those massive limbs, I felt more than just awe at its size and beauty—I was struck by its sheer endurance. This tree has weathered centuries of storms, stood firm through both the Civil and Revolutionary Wars, and silently witnessed the rise and fall of entire civilizations. It has survived hurricanes, earthquakes, and relentless human expansion, yet it continues to grow. If trees kept journals, this one would make our history books look like CliffsNotes.

The Angel Oak's strength comes partly from its ability to adapt, but even more so from the way its roots and branches work together. Deep roots anchor it, providing stability and nourishment, while its sprawling branches stretch outward, each playing a vital role in the tree's survival.

Creativity works exactly the same way. Think of this oak not just as a tree, but as a model for creativity itself—four primary branches reaching in different directions, yet all connected to the same powerful core. Together, they form something far greater than any single branch could achieve alone.

Branch 1: Creative Skills

The first branch—creative skills—is like the strongest limb of our tree, the one you'd trust to hold a treehouse. These are concrete, learnable abilities you can actually measure and improve.[2] While most people immediately think of artistic skills like painting or playing music, that's barely scratching the surface. Creative skills show up everywhere in daily life:

- a business analyst who masters data visualization to tell compelling stories with numbers
- a teacher developing new methods to explain complex concepts when "just read the textbook" clearly isn't working
- an engineer learning to rapidly prototype solutions
- a marketing professional crafting engaging social media campaigns that transform "buy our stuff" into content people actually want to see

In schools, this branch is most visible in dedicated arts classes. While creative skills aren't limited to the arts, they certainly thrive there. This is where students build foundational techniques in music, theater, dance, visual art, and media arts. I firmly believe every student should have access to these classes, taught by trained arts educators. Not just because it's ideal, but because research consistently shows it's what works best for developing creative skills in these disciplines.[3]

I refer to creative skills as an "assessable" branch. That means we can measure progress in concrete ways. Take music, for example—when a student plays a musical scale, you can immediately measure whether they've mastered it based on accuracy, fluidity, and tempo. The same applies in visual art when a student demonstrates perspective drawing, or in theater when they refine vocal projection. These are tangible skills with clear indicators of growth.

And let's be honest—schools love anything they can measure. Testing, data, accountability—it's baked into the system. Sometimes I wonder if something that can't be turned into a spreadsheet even exists in education. That's why creative skills often get prioritized over other, less quantifiable aspects of creativity. But here's the problem: creativity isn't two-dimensional. There are branches of creativity that standardized assessments simply can't capture.

Branch 2: Creative Thinking

The second branch—creative thinking—is where innovation truly develops. This is your brain's creative engine room, where different thinking patterns (divergent, convergent, and lateral) merge to spark new ideas.[4] But it's not just about generating random thoughts—it's about developing the mental agility to

- see problems from multiple angles;
- make unexpected connections that nobody else notices;
- challenge assumptions everyone else takes for granted; and

- navigate fluidly between thinking styles, switching from detail-oriented analysis to big-picture vision as needed.

This branch is less like a checklist and more like a fire—you can't measure creativity with exact numbers, but you can fuel it with the right conditions. With enough curiosity, experimentation, and an open mind, that initial spark can grow into something powerful.

I consider this branch "explorable" rather than assessable. Creative thinking can be assessed in some ways but pinning it down gets tricky. And even if we could measure it, should we? It's like trying to catch a shadow—you can see its movement and sense its presence, but the moment you try to grab it, it shifts and changes.

As we saw in the previous chapter, we must cultivate creative thinking if we want our students to become true innovators and problem-solvers in tomorrow's workforce. Yet we don't need a separate class for that in school. Creative thinking is something we foster across disciplines as part of our teaching approach,[5] rather than something separate from everything else.

Branch 3: Creative Expression

The third branch—creative expression—is where your unique perspective enters the picture. Creative expression is a way of representing yourself as you interpret the world around you—your experiences, emotions, and insights.[6] This is where the idea of providing "arts for arts sake" comes in. And I'm not just talking about writing poems or singing songs in class. Creative expression shows up in everyday life through:

- **Journaling or Personal Writing**—Whether jotting thoughts in a journal, writing poetry, or crafting a social media post, creative expression helps you process emotions, reflect on experiences, and make sense of your inner world.

- **Curating Playlists or Making Music**—From creating the perfect mood-matching playlist to playing an instrument or singing along to your favorite song, music offers one of the most accessible ways to express yourself.

- **Personal Style and Fashion**—How you dress, accessorize, or style your home reflects your personality, mood, and cultural influences. Even small choices, like wearing a bold color on a tough day, communicate something about how you feel.

- **Photography and Capturing Moments**—Whether taking candid snapshots, framing a beautiful sunset, or experimenting with angles and filters, photography is a way you express how you see the world and which moments matter most to you.

- **Movement and Physical Expression**—From dancing around the kitchen to the way you gesture while talking, movement powerfully expresses your inner state. Activities like yoga, improvisational dance, or even the way you walk with confidence or slump when you're sad communicate your inner experiences without words.

This branch plays a crucial role in developing belonging, emotional intelligence, and self-awareness—skills increasingly valuable in both personal and professional contexts. While creative expression can be deeply individual, it also connects us with others when we share collective work in community. When choirs sing, artwork goes on display, or a play gets performed, something special happens. These shared expressive moments transcend both skills and thought.

Like creative thinking, this branch is more exploratory than assessable. The value of creative expression isn't in its measurable outcomes but in its ability to facilitate authentic communication and personal growth.[7] Can we assess the play and grade the choir? Sure. But that only evaluates the product's execution, not the process itself.

Creative expression also offers a powerful way to process personal experiences. Think about students who use drawing or music-making during traumatic events like school shootings or natural disasters to make sense of overwhelming emotions or loss. The value doesn't always lie in sharing their creative work (though sometimes it does). The real magic happens in the act of creating itself.

Branch 4: Creative Application

The fourth branch—creative application—is where everything comes together. This is where theory meets reality, ideas transform into solutions, and creativity "proves its worth" in our results-driven world. It's that moment when

- a product designer turns user feedback into a revolutionary new feature,
- a community organizer transforms a neighborhood challenge into an opportunity,
- a healthcare worker develops a better way to track patient care, or
- a teacher adapts a traditional lesson for remote learning.

In schools, creative application comes alive through approaches like arts integration, STEAM (science, technology, engineering, arts, and math), and project-based learning (PBL). These methods move beyond rote memorization and passive learning, inviting students to actively engage with concepts in meaningful, hands-on ways. Rather than simply learning about topics in isolation, students apply knowledge across multiple disciplines, making connections that spark new ideas and possibilities.

For example, in an arts-integrated lesson, a history class studying the Civil Rights Movement might create spoken word performances or murals that convey the emotional impact and messages of the era. In a STEAM project, students could design and prototype eco-friendly housing using principles of engineering, math, and environmental science while incorporating artistic elements into the design process. Meanwhile, project-based learning tasks students with exploring real-world challenges and developing innovative solutions—whether designing a community garden to address food insecurity or building a multimedia campaign to raise awareness about climate change.

These hands-on, minds-on experiences do more than reinforce academic concepts. They develop critical thinking, problem-solving, collaboration, and adaptability[8]—skills essential for navigating an unpredictable future. More importantly, they help students see the relevance of what they're learning, fostering curiosity and engagement that extends far beyond classroom walls.

This branch falls firmly in the "assessable" category because it produces tangible results. Unlike more abstract forms of creativity, creative application gives us measurable outcomes we can evaluate for effectiveness, impact, and success. In a classroom setting, we can assess a student's STEAM project based on how well it integrates scientific principles, artistic creativity, and problem-solving skills. In business, we can measure an innovative marketing campaign by customer engagement, brand awareness, or sales growth.

We can analyze creative solutions by asking the following: Does it actually work? Is it practical? Does it introduce something new? Similarly, we can evaluate the impact of creative initiatives by examining real-world outcomes, such as how a community art project fosters engagement or how a redesigned user interface improves accessibility.

While creativity itself resists easy quantification, creative application thrives on iteration and refinement. Prototypes, feedback loops, and performance metrics allow for adjustments and improvements, making creativity a dynamic process rather than a one-time event. What sets this category apart is its ability to be tested, improved, and measured, ensuring creative ideas don't just remain concepts but evolve into impactful, real-world innovations.

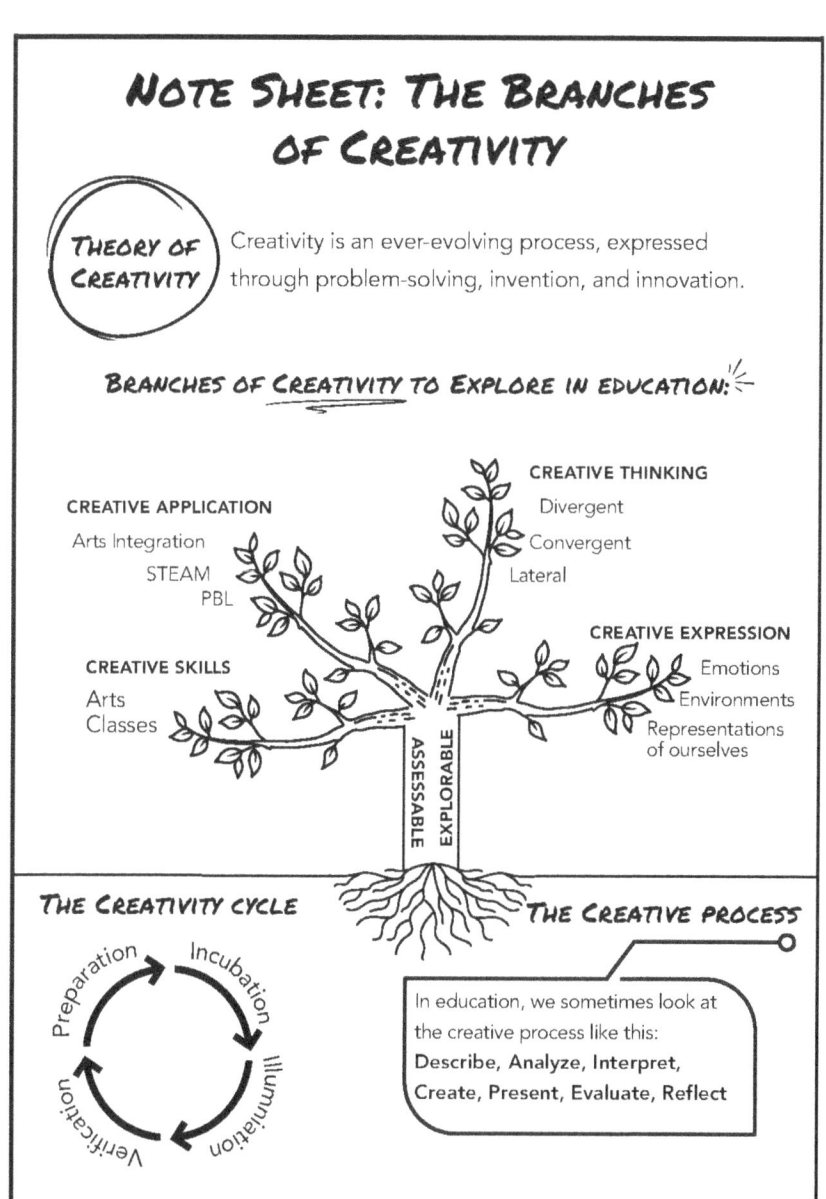

FIGURE 3.1

The Interplay of Branches: More Than the Sum of Their Parts

These four branches don't exist in isolation. They form an ecosystem, where each element nourishes and strengthens the others.[9] Think about a software developer who might use technical skills to write elegant code, creative thinking to solve complex problems, personal expression to design intuitive interfaces, and practical application to implement solutions that actually improve users' lives.

I've noticed arts teachers sometimes worry that arts integration or STEAM will dilute their content or even replace their classes. Classroom teachers often worry they lack the skills to teach in and through the arts. But when we recognize that each creative branch serves a purpose and can work separately or together, these fears become unnecessary.

The Angel Oak tree hasn't survived for centuries just because its branches are strong and its roots run deep. Its ability to thrive depends on an intricate ecosystem of freshwater wetlands and maritime forests. Surrounding trees shield it from harsh winds and intense sunlight, while the wetlands maintain the perfect water balance.

Just as the Angel Oak thrives through its connections to the broader ecosystem, your creative abilities flourish when they interact and support each other. Like that ancient tree, the strength of your creativity doesn't come from any single element, but from the rich network of connections between them.

And before you dismiss teaching creativity because it "can't be measured" with a traditional standardized test, ask yourself if testing is the only reason we teach anything. As we've seen, some aspects of creativity absolutely *can* be measured—like how well someone has mastered a specific technical skill or whether a solution effectively solved a problem. Other elements—like the spark of inspiration or the authenticity of expression—resist easy assessment.

This isn't a weakness; it's simply how creativity works in practice. The measurable and the mysterious work together, each making the other more powerful.

Creativity isn't some lofty, abstract concept—it's woven into our daily lives in countless ways we often overlook. Whether we're tackling workplace challenges, finding new ways to express ourselves, or improving the world around us, creativity is always at play. To see it in action, let's dive into real-world examples from each branch and explore how they show up in both personal and professional spaces. From problem-solving breakthroughs to artistic expressions that bring people together, these branches highlight the many ways creativity shapes our experiences.

From Purpose to Practice with Creative Skills

Many of us find ourselves staring at blank canvases—both literally and metaphorically. The pressure to inject creativity into classrooms while juggling standards, benchmarks, and the daily reality of teaching thirty to forty young humans can feel overwhelming. We know creativity matters, but how do we actually develop it in ourselves and our teaching practice?

Harvard education researcher Shari Tishman tackled this question head-on in her work with Project Zero, documenting how teachers develop creative practices over time. In her book "Slow Looking: The Art and Practice of Learning Through Observation," Tishman chronicles how educators transform their teaching through deliberate attention to observation and creative engagement.[10]

Jennifer Roberts, a professor at Harvard who collaborated with Project Zero, exemplifies this approach. Roberts developed a methodology requiring students to observe a single artwork or object for three hours.

Initially, this approach seemed counterintuitive in our fast-paced educational environment. Roberts asked students "to spend a painfully long time looking at a single work of art." This practice of extended observation wasn't a skill she was born with but one she cultivated deliberately over time.

Her method evolved gradually. She began implementing structured observation assignments where students document what they see over extended periods, noticing details that reveal deeper meanings and connections that would be missed in cursory viewings.[11] This approach transforms not just how students look at artwork, but how they approach all kinds of complex material.

I often tell my teenage daughter that she "looks but doesn't see." This typically gets thrown around when I've asked her to find a spice from the pantry or some other simple household item, and she comes back with the phrase all parents dread: "It's not there." How many of us go through life this way? By employing these close observational skills, we begin to notice more deeply and make stronger connections to the world around us.

Roberts emphasizes that this sustained attention creates cognitive shifts that would otherwise be inaccessible. According to her research, the first thirty minutes of looking are just the beginning, with the most thought-provoking insights often emerging in the second or third hour of observation.

The results from her approach? Roberts documented how students in her classes demonstrated improved analytical abilities, more sophisticated written responses, and greater willingness to revisit initial assumptions—all crucial components of creative thinking.

Roberts's journey illustrates the first fundamental principle of creativity development: it grows through deliberate practice rather than sudden inspiration. She developed her approach through structured experimentation, reflection, and application—building habits that transformed her teaching and her students' learning experiences.

A 2016 study by Teresa Amabile and Michael Pratt reinforces this idea of incremental skill growth. Their research indicates that people who engage in regular creative activities develop what they call "progress loops"—cycles of creative work that build on themselves and generate increasing creative capacity over time.[12]

Their model suggests that creativity develops through a self-reinforcing process. Small creative experiences and successes help build both technical skills and intrinsic motivation, which in turn leads to more creative engagement. These regular creative practices help people reinterpret challenges, find joy in the process, and envision new possibilities.

This research points to the second principle of creativity development: it flourishes through incremental growth and skill practice rather than dramatic transformation. By cultivating small creative habits consistently, you build resources that help you find deeper meaning in your work, even during challenging days (and let's be honest, teaching has plenty of those).

Developing creativity isn't about generating flashy lesson ideas or Pinterest-worthy bulletin boards. It's about building what researchers call "creative self-efficacy"—your belief in your ability to solve problems creatively. Each time you try a new approach, whether it succeeds brilliantly or fails spectacularly, you strengthen both your skills and your confidence in using them.

This gives us a pathway to deeper meaning and purpose in teaching and in life. Every creative engagement, whether designing curriculum or crafting learning experiences, strengthens not just your creative ability but also your neural foundations for resilience, problem-solving, and professional growth.

From Practice to Play: Exercises That Spark Creative Thinking

A few years ago, I learned an unexpected lesson about creativity in the most painful way possible—by wiping out on a slick cobblestone path in Puerto Rico. One bad step, a sharp twist, and suddenly, my right knee was out of commission with a torn meniscus. The road to recovery wasn't quick or easy.

For six grueling weeks, I showed up to physical therapy, where my therapist had me perform what seemed like ridiculously simple exercises. Tiny movements, subtle shifts—nothing flashy. But each one had a purpose: to restore flexibility and build strength.

At first, I was impatient. I wanted big, dramatic progress. Instead, I faced slow, steady work—stretching a little further each time, holding my balance a few seconds longer. Eventually, I realized that flexibility and strength weren't just goals; they formed the foundation of my recovery. Neither could succeed without the other. Strength gave my knee stability. Flexibility allowed it to move freely again.

The same is true for creativity. Strong creative habits give us the discipline to show up and do the work. Flexibility in thinking lets us stretch, adapt, and explore new possibilities. Without both, we either stay stuck in rigid patterns or lack the endurance to follow through.

So how do we develop this balance in our creative lives? Just like physical therapy, we need targeted exercises. Here are three powerful ways to stretch and strengthen your creative capacity:

Exercise 1: The Power of Constraints

Most people assume creative breakthroughs come from total freedom—an open canvas, a blank page, unlimited resources. But here's a counterintuitive truth: some of the most innovative solutions emerge from constraints.[13]

The game designers at Nintendo faced a serious technical limitation when creating Mario for early gaming systems. They couldn't render detailed facial features at such low resolution. Their solution? Give Mario a mustache and a cap. These constraints led to one of the most iconic character designs in gaming history.

Or, take Dr. Seuss's most famous work, *Green Eggs and Ham*. His publisher bet him he couldn't write an engaging children's book using only fifty different words. The result? A beloved classic that's sold millions of copies. The constraint didn't limit his creativity—it enhanced it.

The key lies in embracing constraints rather than fighting them. Try these approaches:

- Give yourself a time limit: Set a timer for thirty minutes and solve a problem before it runs out.
- Limit your tools: Write a lesson plan using only materials students already have at home.
- Create artificial boundaries: Solve a classroom management issue without speaking or design a learning experience using only materials you already have.
- Challenge your assumptions: What if you had to teach this concept without technology? Without using words? Without following the standard approach?

When forced to work within limits, our brains become remarkably creative at finding solutions. It's like packing for a weekend with only a small carry-on bag—suddenly you become impressively innovative about what you really need and how to fit it all in.

Exercise 2: Make Unexpected Connections

Innovation often lives at the intersection of different ideas, fields, or perspectives.[14] This isn't about waiting for inspiration to strike—it's about actively creating conditions where new ideas can emerge.

James Dyson revolutionized vacuum cleaners by observing how sawmills remove dust using industrial cyclones. He asked himself, "What if household vacuums worked the same way?" The result was a billion-dollar innovation born from connecting two seemingly unrelated fields.

Here's how to practice making connections:

- Read outside your field: If you teach science, grab a book on architecture. If you teach English, read about business innovation.
- Play "what if": Take a solution from one field and apply it to another. What if classrooms operated like restaurants? What if report cards worked like video game achievements?
- Create weird combinations: Pick two random objects and find ways to connect them to your teaching.
- Cross-pollinate your interests: How might your hobby inform your teaching strategies?

Exercise 3: The Space for Structured Reflection

In our always-on world, this third practice might seem impossible: creating intentional space for your mind to wander productively. This isn't passive daydreaming. It's fostering what psychologists call "constructive internal reflection."[15] Albert Einstein famously credited his daily violin practice with helping him solve complex physics problems. When he felt stuck, he would step away from his calculations and lose himself in music. Not only did this give him a break, it also shifted his thinking about other projects. The rhythm, patterns, and fluidity of playing the violin allowed his mind to make unexpected connections, ultimately leading to some of his greatest breakthroughs in theoretical physics.

Try these approaches to structured reflection:

- Schedule "thinking walks" where you focus on a specific teaching problem while moving.
- Practice "brain dumping"—set aside fifteen minutes to write down every idea that comes to mind about an upcoming unit, without judgment.

- Create "white space" in your calendar—blocks of time specifically for reflection and ideation.
- Use "productive procrastination"—grade papers or organize materials while letting your mind work on a problem in the background.

These strategies are ingredients for flexible thinking, not rigid recipes. Mix them up. Experiment. Combine structured reflection with unexpected constraints. Try solving a classroom management issue during a walk, but give yourself only the walk's duration to find solutions. Or intentionally connect ideas from different domains while working within specific limitations.

Creativity's biggest impact doesn't come from generating wild, fantastical ideas—it comes from finding practical solutions that work within real-world constraints while bringing something fresh to the table. It's about playing seriously and working playfully.

Cultivating Creative Spaces: Where Expression Takes Root

You can teach someone every creative practice under the sun, but if they're trying to implement them in a toxic environment, it's like planting seeds in barren soil. Nothing grows. The spaces we inhabit—whether physical, emotional, or cultural—seriously shape how our creative expression emerges and evolves.

And despite what that teacher down the hall with the color-coordinated supply caddy and hand-lettered inspirational quotes might suggest, fancy supplies don't significantly develop creativity. Environments that support creativity provide the right conditions for ideas to flourish. Gardening teaches us this—you need the right combination of light, water, and nutrients, but you also must protect young shoots from harsh conditions that might kill them before they have a chance to grow.

Creative Workplaces and Learning Environments

Walk into any preschool classroom and you'll see creativity in its purest form. Young children naturally experiment, play, and create without fear of judgment. But something often happens as we move up through the education system—that natural creativity gets squeezed out by rigid structures and fear of failure. It's like watching a beautiful butterfly slowly transform back into a caterpillar—nature in reverse.

Psychological safety—the belief that you won't be punished or humiliated for speaking up with ideas, questions, or mistakes—is absolutely crucial for creativity to thrive.[16] In fact, when Google studied what made their most effective teams successful, psychological safety topped the list.

But what does this look like in practice?

Pixar's headquarters features central gathering spaces that deliberately encourage unplanned encounters between employees from different departments. The theory? Some of the best ideas emerge when an animator bumps into a storyteller on the way to get coffee. But it goes deeper than random encounters. Their workspace includes the following:

- studios where artists can retreat for focused technical work,
- common areas filled with toys and games that spark playful thinking,
- walls covered with work-in-progress art that invites feedback,
- prototype labs where ideas can be tested and refined, and
- informal meeting spots where people feel comfortable sharing unfinished thoughts.

Then there's design firm IDEO's workspace: portable whiteboards and movable furniture allow teams to reconfigure their space based on project needs. They maintain a "tech box"—a collection of interesting materials and mechanical objects anyone can rummage through for inspiration. Instead of focusing on fancy tools, they craft an environment that sparks connections.

The most innovative classrooms today are taking cues from artists' studios. At High Tech High in San Diego, classroom walls are transparent and covered with student work in progress. The message? Creative work isn't something to hide until it's perfect—it's something to share and develop openly. These spaces are designed to

- make tools and materials easily accessible to remove barriers to creation;
- display work at all stages of development to normalize the creative process;
- create different zones for different types of work (quiet focus, messy experimentation, collaborative creation); and
- enable multiple forms of expression through diverse materials and media.

McDonogh School in Owings Mills, Maryland, uses learning spaces almost as a third teacher: flexible seating arrangements, areas for quiet reflection alongside spaces for collaborative work, and materials organized to encourage independent exploration. They even have a "collaboratory" with spaces deliberately designed to provoke questions and investigation.

The most effective learning environments, whether in schools or professional development settings, share some key characteristics.[17]

- They encourage experimentation and validate multiple approaches to problems.
- They treat mistakes as learning opportunities rather than failures.
- They balance structure with freedom.
- They foster collaboration while respecting individual work styles.
- They make space for both focused work and playful exploration.

Leaders play a crucial role here, not by trying to control creativity, but by removing the obstacles that kill it. The best leaders and administrators aren't the ones with all the answers—they're the ones who ask the right questions and create spaces where educators, students, and staff can innovate freely.

The Home Studio

As education and work evolve, so does where our learning and work take place. Our homes host our most personal—and sometimes professional—creative work. And size in this instance, truly doesn't matter. Author Stephen King wrote his first novel at a makeshift desk wedged between a washer and dryer. Author Austin Kleon transformed a corner of his basement into what he calls his "bliss station"—a simple desk with basic tools, surrounded by inspiring quotes and artifacts. Visual artist Lisa Congdon started her career working at her kitchen table after her day job, gradually claiming more space as her practice grew.

Here are some key elements of an effective home creative space:

- a designated area, however small, that signals "creative work happens here"
- easy access to frequently used tools and materials
- protection from daily life interruptions
- room for movement and different working positions
- elements that inspire without overwhelming
- clear boundaries between creative space and other areas of life
- flexibility to adapt as your practice evolves

The Digital Environment

We can't ignore the impact of digital spaces on creativity. Virtual environments can either enhance or hinder creative work. The key is being intentional about how we use them:

- Create different user profiles for creative work versus other activities.
- Use website blockers during dedicated creative time.

- Design your digital desktop as thoughtfully as your physical one.
- Maintain digital archives that inspire without overwhelming.
- Set clear boundaries between online connection and creative solitude.

Some of history's most innovative work has emerged from basement offices, kitchen tables, and borrowed spaces. The creative process doesn't demand perfection—it thirsts for possibility.

Whether you're working from a corner desk or a coffee shop, a classroom or a corporate office, what matters is cultivating a space that nurtures rather than neglects your creative spirit.

Mindsets for Exploring Creative Application

Most people first encounter the concept of mindset in school. On the surface, it seems straightforward: a fixed mindset means believing abilities are set in stone—either you're good at math or you're not, creative or not, musical or not. A growth mindset, on the other hand, is the belief that skills can be developed with effort, smart strategies, and feedback. Psychologist Carol Dweck's research on this completely changed the way we think about learning and success.[18] Suddenly, teachers began shifting focus, praising effort over raw talent. Parents swapped out "You're so smart" for "You worked so hard," reinforcing that ability isn't just something you have—it's something you build.

But when applying creativity in real situations, mindset becomes far more complex and dynamic. It develops our mental agility to shift between different creative modes as the work demands.

Think about jazz musicians. During practice, they need a growth mindset—methodically working on scales, studying theory, mastering their instrument. But during improvisation, they need what psychologists call a "flow mindset"—

letting go of conscious effort and trusting their creative instincts—same musician, different mindsets for different creative demands.

This shape-shifting nature of creative mindsets shows up everywhere if you know where to look. An elementary teacher developing a new lesson plan oscillates between analytical and intuitive thinking. A scientist needs methodical skepticism while designing experiments but wild speculation while theorizing new possibilities.

Sometimes too much expertise actually hinders creative application. When people become highly skilled in one area, they often develop what researchers call "creative overconfidence"—they stop questioning their assumptions, stop seeing new possibilities.[19] Meanwhile, beginners in a field often make breakthrough innovations precisely because they don't know what's "impossible."

This paradox plays out in schools, too. Put a group of veteran teachers together, and you might get less creativity than a mixed group of veterans and newcomers. The newcomers ask those "naive" questions that spark fresh thinking. That's why some of the most innovative schools deliberately mix teams across grade levels and experience levels.

But perhaps the most powerful aspect of creative mindset is its transferability. Someone who has experienced the creative process in one domain—say, music—can apply that creative confidence to completely different areas. They viscerally understand that creative work involves false starts, dead ends, and unexpected breakthroughs. They've developed what we might call "creative resilience."

Creativity rarely follows a straight path. More often, it moves in a spiral—you keep circling back to familiar challenges, but each time, you bring new skills, insights, and experiences to the table. To effectively apply creative skills, thinking, and expression, you need a mindset that stays fluid, transitioning between different ways of seeing and solving problems.

Sometimes, you need the beginner's mind, the one that asks, *"Why not?"* and sees possibilities without limitations. Other times, the expert's mind takes over, drawing on past knowledge to recognize what usually works. Then there's the experimenter's mind, willing to test, tweak, and push boundaries, followed by the editor's mind, which refines and polishes ideas into something stronger. And finally, the observer's mind steps back, gaining perspective and clarity on the bigger picture.

Creativity expands our mental agility, helping us know when to shift gears. It relies on intuition, trusting that gut feeling when an idea just *clicks*. When it's time to bring ideas to life, a systematic mindset helps implement solutions in a structured way. But just as important is reflection—learning from both success and failure to fuel the next creative cycle.

This transforms how we approach creative development. Instead of just practicing skills, we can practice mindset shifts. Instead of just setting up physical spaces for creativity, we can establish mental spaces that support different kinds of creative thinking. Instead of just collaborating with others, we can learn from how they see and think about creative work.

The most sophisticated creative practitioners don't just use different tools—they think in different ways at different times. They've learned to navigate the full spectrum of creative mindsets, choosing the right mental stance for each phase of their work.

Through the Looking Glass: Bringing It All Together

Everything we've explored—from establishing purpose to cultivating mindsets—serves a larger goal: developing a rich, sustainable creative practice that transforms your teaching and learning. Like a skilled rock climber who combines technical knowledge, physical training, strategic planning, and intuitive response to the changing rock face, effective creative development requires bringing all these elements together to navigate the future landscape.

Our creative purpose guides which skills we develop and how we apply them. Our habits build the foundation for both technical mastery and innovative thinking. Our practices sharpen our ability to generate and refine ideas. Our environments support both structured work and spontaneous discovery. And our mindsets allow us to move fluidly between different creative modes as our work demands.[20]

Developing our creative practice isn't about reaching some final destination. It's about engaging in an ongoing dialogue between structure and spontaneity, between mastery and experimentation, between individual expression and collaborative innovation. Every new project, every creative challenge, every breakthrough or setback becomes part of this larger conversation.

Chemistry teacher Ramsey Musallam exemplifies this integrated approach. After experiencing a life-threatening health crisis, he completely reimagined his teaching practice. He established a clear purpose: sparking student curiosity through creative exploration. His habits include recording teaching ideas the moment they strike. His practices incorporate unexpected connections between chemistry and everyday life. His classroom environment supports both messy experimentation and structured reflection. And his mindset shifts between scientific precision and playful exploration as lessons demand.

The most effective educators understand this dynamic nature of creative development. They know when to focus on building teaching skills and when to trust their intuition. They recognize when to stick with proven lesson approaches and when to experiment with new ones. They create classroom environments that support both focused study and playful exploration. And they cultivate the mental agility to shift between different creative teaching modes as their students' needs change.

This is how creativity truly evolves—through the thoughtful integration of all these elements.[21] It's a journey requiring both patience and persistence, both structure and flexibility, both individual effort and a supportive community.

Your creative teaching practice will be uniquely your own. But by understanding how these different elements work together, you can cultivate it more intentionally and effectively. The question isn't whether you're creative or not—it's how you'll develop and apply your creativity in ways that matter most.

Key Takeaways

1. Creative practice starts with understanding your purpose—recognizing how creativity shows up across all areas of your life and how different aspects of creativity work together to help you accomplish what matters.

2. Building consistent habits and rituals creates the foundation for creative work, while specific practices like embracing constraints and making unexpected connections help develop creative muscles.

3. The environments we create—physical, emotional, and digital—shape how creativity emerges and evolves, making it crucial to design spaces that support both structured work and spontaneous discovery.

4. Creative mindsets need to be fluid and dynamic, shifting between different modes of thinking as your work demands.

5. Developing a creative practice isn't about reaching some final destination but about engaging in an ongoing conversation between different creative approaches and finding what works best for your unique situation.

PRACTICE STRATEGY: iNotice[3]

It's time for some deep observation and reflection on how creativity currently shows up in your own life.

1. Think about a time when you made or performed something you were proud of (even if you didn't share it).

2. Write down everything you can remember about what you created, how you felt before, during, and after creating it, and what your process looked like as you were developing your work. Capture as many details as possible.

3. Read it all back to yourself and circle three things that stand out to you.

4. For each of those items, answer these three questions:
   - Why did this stand out to me?
   - What does this tell me about myself?
   - How can I use this in the future?

Notes

1 Kotler, S. (2021). "3 Science-Based Strategies to Increase Your Creativity." Ideas.TED.com. https://ideas.ted.com/3-science-based-strategies-to-increase-your-creativity/

2 American Psychological Association. (2009). "The Science of Creativity. GradPSYCH, 7(1), 14. https://www.apa.org/gradpsych/2009/01/creativity

3 Drexel University School of Education. (n.d.). "How to Inspire Creativity in the Classroom." https://drexel.edu/soe/resources/teacher-resources/inspire-creativity-in-the-classroom/

4 Kupers, E., & van Dijk, M. (2020). "Creativity in Interaction: The Dynamics of Teacher-Student Interactions During a Musical Composition Task." *Thinking Skills and Creativity*, 36. https://doi.org/10.1016/j.tsc.2020.100648

5 Gnezda, N. M. (2011). "Cognition and Emotions in the Creative Process." *Art Education*, 64(1), 47–52. https://doi.org/10.1080/00043125.2011.11519111

6 Bielec, S. (2022, January). "A Growth Mindset in the Arts." Learn Quebec. https://blogs.learnquebec.ca/2022/01/a-growth-mindset-in-the-arts/

7 Giles, R. M. (2024). "10 Ways to Promote Artistic Expression." Exchange Press. https://hub.exchangepress.com/articles-on-demand/27403/

8 Runco, M. A., & Albert, R. S. (2010). "Creativity Research: A Historical View." In J. C. Kaufman & R. J. Sternberg (Eds.), *The Cambridge Handbook of Creativity* (pp. 3–19). Cambridge University Press. https://doi.org/10.1017/CBO9780511763205.003

9 Samara, T. (2023). "The Psychology of Creativity: Exploring the Mindset Connection." Medium. https://medium.com/@drthediasamara/the-psychology-of-creativity-exploring-the-mindset-connection-46e0f1bbc443

10. Tishman, S. (2017). *Slow Looking: The Art and Practice of Learning Through Observation* (1st Ed.). Routledge. https://doi.org/10.4324/9781315283814

11. Roberts, J. L. (2013, October). "The Power of Patience." *Harvard Magazine*. https://www.harvardmagazine.com/2013/10/the-power-of-patience

12. Amabile, T. M., & Pratt, M. G. (2016). "The Dynamic Componential Model of Creativity and Innovation in Organizations: Making Progress, Making Meaning." *Research in Organizational Behavior*, 36, 157–83. https://doi.org/10.1016/j.riob.2016.10.001

13. Karwowski, M. (2013). "Creative Mindsets: Measurement, Correlates, Consequences." *Psychology of Aesthetics, Creativity, and the Arts*, 8, 62–70. 10.1037/a0034898.

14. Samara, T. (2023). "The Psychology of Creativity: Exploring the Mindset Connection." Medium. https://medium.com/@drthediasamara/the-psychology-of-creativity-exploring-the-mindset-connection-46e0f1bbc443

15. Gaines, J. (2020). "Fostering Creativity: 12 Strategies to Boost Creative Skills." PositivePsychology.com. https://positivepsychology.com/creativity/

16. NeuCollins, T. (2019, March). "Encouraging a Growth Mindset Through Art." National Education Association. https://www.nea.org/professional-excellence/student-engagement/tools-tips/encouraging-growth-mindset-through-art

17. VLS. (n.d.). "Cultivating Creativity and Innovation: Environments and Materials." Virtual Lab School. https://www.virtuallabschool.org/fcc/creative-expression/lesson-3

18. Dweck, C. S. (2006). *Mindset: The New Psychology of Success*. Random House

19. Karwowski, M., Royston, R., & Reiter-Palmon, R. (2019, February). "Exploring Creative Mindsets. Variable and Person-Centered Approaches." *The Psychology of Aesthetics, Creativity, and the Arts*, 13(1), 36–48. https://doi.org/10.1037/aca0000170

20. Lee, J. H., & Lee, S. (2023). "Relationships Between Physical Environments and Creativity: A Scoping Review." *Thinking Skills and Creativity*, 48. https://www.sciencedirect.com/science/article/pii/S1871187123000469

21. Wilson, R. E., Jr. (2013, June). "Surprise! Creativity Is a Skill Not a Gift." *Psychology Today*. https://www.psychologytoday.com/us/blog/the-main-ingredient/201306/surprise-creativity-is-skill-not-gift

4

Assessing Creativity

Chapter Guiding Question: Is there a way to measure creativity? Should we measure creativity?

The question seemed simple enough on paper: What makes some fighter pilots extraordinary while others remain merely competent?

For US Air Force commanders in the 1950s, the answer held life-or-death consequences. Their data revealed something striking: of the 823 enemy aircraft shot down by the Fifth Air Force during the Korean War, over a third had been brought down by just thirty-eight pilots. That meant a mere 5 percent of fighter pilots accounted for more than 30 percent of victories.[1]

What separated these "aces" from everyone else? It wasn't educational background or physical attributes—those were essentially identical across the board. The military's traditional measurements showed nothing useful.

The Air Force's psychologist, E. Paul Torrance, knew he couldn't use standardized measurements to answer these questions from the top brass. But he had been working on a different kind of assessment since his days as a high school teacher in the 1940s.

Back then, Torrance found himself drawn to students who didn't quite fit the mold. These so-called problem students had a tendency to challenge authority, disrupt class with unexpected questions, and approach assignments in unconventional ways. Yet over the years, Torrance noticed many of these same students went on to excel not just in school, but in life. Some became influential figures in politics, business, and science.

Torrance was intrigued. What was it about these students that set them apart? How could educators nurture rather than stifle their unconventional thinking? And could there be a test that assessed creative potential as rigorously as IQ tests measured intelligence?

These questions led him to develop his first creativity test in 1943, refining it over decades. Perhaps this unorthodox assessment could reveal what made those exceptional pilots so effective.

After studying the pilots, Torrance identified three crucial characteristics in the aces: aggressiveness, self-confidence, and a complete devotion to flying. These qualities allowed them to take calculated risks, solve problems on the fly, and see possibilities others missed. In short, the pilots were more creative. Torrance reached this conclusion because his test examined areas traditional assessments typically overlooked: fluency, flexibility, originality, and elaboration.

By 1966, Torrance had formalized his research into the *Torrance Tests of Creative Thinking* (TTCT). Unlike standard tests, the TTCT asked people to complete unfinished drawings, improve products, and create unusual titles for stories. These activities measured someone's ability to generate multiple ideas, think flexibly across categories, produce original solutions, and elaborate on their thinking—all essential components of creativity that classroom teachers instantly recognize in their most innovative students.

Research consistently showed the TTCT predicted creative achievement better than IQ tests. People who scored high on these creativity measures were more likely to pursue creative careers, patent inventions, and excel in innovative fields. The studies confirmed what many had suspected but couldn't prove: creativity, more than IQ, was a strong predictor of future success.[2]

Over the decades, the TTCT has become one of the most widely used creativity assessments in schools worldwide. Yet, like any standardized measure, it has limitations. Can a test truly capture the depth and unpredictability of creativity? Can creative genius be distilled into a score?

These questions echo through schools and classrooms as educators wrestle with a fundamental tension: how do we assess something as elusive as creativity without diminishing it in the process?

To understand this challenge, we need to start at the beginning—with how different cultures and eras have perceived creativity's value. Their struggles to define and measure creative worth still reverberate in our attempts today.

Tracing Creativity's Shifting Value Over Time

Every era has wrestled with how to value and measure creativity.[3] For most of human history, the very idea of measuring creativity would have seemed absurd—not because creativity didn't matter but because it wasn't seen as something human at all.

In ancient Greece, creativity wasn't a skill to be measured but a gift from the Muses. When a sculptor carved a masterpiece or a poet composed an epic, they were seen as vessels for divine inspiration rather than creative agents. Their work was judged not by originality but by how well it channeled these divine forces. The ancient Greeks had detailed systems for measuring everything from architectural proportions to musical harmonies, but creativity itself? That belonged to the gods.

This view persisted well into the Renaissance. Even as figures like Leonardo da Vinci and Michelangelo upended art and engineering, their creativity was often attributed to divine inspiration or extraordinary genius—something to be admired but not measured. The master craftsmen's guilds of the time did assess technical skill with incredible precision, but they saw innovation as emerging from mastery rather than something to evaluate independently.

Everything changed during the Enlightenment. As human reason replaced divine inspiration as the source of innovation, people began viewing creativity as something that could be understood, developed—and potentially measured. Scientists started documenting their creative processes. Artists began writing about their techniques. For the first time, creativity was seen as something human rather than divine.

Our modern obsession with measuring creativity began in earnest during the Space Race, when identifying innovative thinkers became a matter of national urgency. The problem? No one quite agreed on what they were measuring. Suddenly, the inability to quantify creativity wasn't just a philosophical problem—it was an economic and strategic one.[4]

Now, in the age of artificial intelligence and global challenges, creativity is more valuable than ever. Yet, our methods for assessing it still feel woefully inadequate. We've moved from divine inspiration to data analytics, but the fundamental challenge remains: how do we measure something that is, by its nature, about creating something new?

The answer isn't choosing between past wisdom and modern metrics, but in understanding how different ways of valuing creativity can inform how we assess it today.

Beyond Numbers and Metrics: When Measurement Meets Meaning

I once watched an assistant superintendent of a school system toss a thick binder of metrics onto a conference table with a sigh. "We've measured everything possible about our students' academic progress," he said, "but somehow we're still missing what actually matters."

His frustration echoes what those Air Force commanders discovered decades ago. When they tried to identify what made their ace pilots special, traditional measurements revealed nothing useful. They were looking at all the wrong things.

This pattern plays out everywhere. Organizations default to measuring what's easy to count, not what truly counts. But around the world, some places are trying something radically different.

In Finland, schools don't obsess over standardized test scores. Teachers aren't evaluated by student performance metrics. Yet Finnish students consistently outperform most of their global peers.[5] Why? Because Finnish society values education intrinsically, not just for measurable outcomes. Teachers are respected professionals trusted to know what works. Creativity flourishes because it's valued, not because it's measured.

This isn't limited to education. When business schools began integrating ethics and values into their programs, something fascinating happened. Future executives didn't just become "more well-rounded"—they fundamentally changed how they understood success. Beyond profit margins and quarterly returns, they started seeing how values drive innovation and create meaningful impact. Their very definition of value expanded.

Some of the most successful companies have discovered this too. When Southwest Airlines defined "fun" as a core value, it wasn't just a nice sentiment for the break room wall. It transformed how they hired, designed customer experiences, and yes—evaluated creative work. Their success didn't come from ignoring metrics but from measuring what aligned with their values.

The data backs this up. People who align their work with their values take more creative risks and produce more innovative solutions. It's not that values are separate from performance—they actually drive better performance, just not in the ways we traditionally measure.[6]

This creates an uncomfortable reality for many schools and organizations. Most claim to value creativity while simultaneously using assessment systems that kill it. They say they want bold, innovative thinking but reward only safe, predictable outcomes. It's like telling someone to explore uncharted territory but only paying them when they stick to the marked tourist path.

Look at how this plays out in everyday work life. Traditional performance reviews rarely capture creative contributions. In schools, standardized tests tell us that reading and math scores are falling, but they don't explain why or how to fix it. Companies and educational systems that once dominated have faltered because they measured everything except what actually mattered for the future.

What we need is a more balanced approach to assessment that connects what we're assessing with our values and purpose.

In education, this might mean moving beyond traditional grading systems to incorporate more holistic assessments. Portfolios allow students to showcase their creative journey, highlighting not just the final product but their process of exploration and growth. Peer and self-assessments offer valuable insights into how the work resonates with others and how a creator's understanding has evolved. By diversifying assessment methods, educators can create a richer picture of a student's creative development.

In business, integrating creative value might mean supplementing traditional metrics like sales and return on investment (ROI) with more qualitative measures. This could include user feedback that captures the emotional impact of a product, or employee surveys that gauge the level of creative engagement within the company culture. By valuing these "softer" aspects alongside hard data, businesses can make smarter decisions about where to invest their creative resources.[7]

I'm not advocating choosing between hard data and soft feelings. I am suggesting we recognize that the most valuable assessment approaches capture both—measuring what can be measured while honoring what can't be. The key lies in placing assessments within a larger context, making them part of a broader conversation about what we value and why.

The Interplay of Assessment and Evaluation

Picture a dancer in the studio, experimenting with movements, refining their technique. This is assessment—a continuous process of feedback and adjustment, all in service of growth. Now picture that same dancer on stage, performing the finished piece for an audience. The audience watches, critics weigh in, and a final judgment is made. This is evaluation—a summative judgment of the final product.

Both play a role in creativity, but they serve different purposes. Assessment fosters development, guiding students or professionals toward greater creative fluency. Evaluation determines the effectiveness of the final product.[8] The problem is that our current systems overwhelmingly favor evaluation at the expense of assessment. Schools, businesses, and organizations obsess over final outcomes, often failing to nurture the creative process itself.

The result? People become reluctant to take creative risks, to experiment, or to explore new ideas, knowing they'll be judged solely on results. They hide their process, presenting only finished work that seems effortlessly produced. They play it safe, sticking to what they know will meet established criteria. And we end up with a collection of sameness, while the world rapidly evolves and innovates around us.

We need balance—a way to value both the journey and the destination of creativity.

The Alchemy of Process and Product: Transforming Creative Potential into Reality

Creativity lives in a constant flux between process and product. While the end goal matters—a breakthrough idea, a masterpiece, a game-changing innovation—the real magic happens in the messy, nonlinear process of getting there.

Look at the groundbreaking work of choreographer Martha Graham. Her iconic dance pieces didn't spring fully formed onto the stage; they were the product of countless hours in the studio, experimenting with movement, refining techniques, and pushing the boundaries of what the human body could express. For Graham, the process was just as important as the performance. "I am absorbed in the magic of movement and light," she once said. "Movement never lies."

The Intricacies of Process

The creative process is where ideas are born, nurtured, and transformed. It's a space of experimentation and discovery, of breaking down and building up. It's not always pretty or efficient, but it's essential.

I often describe this as "building the plane while flying it." You're constantly making iterations, tweaks, and pivots as your creation takes shape. The first version of an idea rarely resembles the final one; it's through the process of testing, feedback, and refinement that it evolves into something truly innovative.

This iterative approach is at the heart of design thinking, a creative problem-solving method used across industries. The process involves empathizing with users, defining the problem, ideating solutions, prototyping, and testing. The emphasis isn't on getting it perfect the first time but on learning and improving with each cycle.

The process is also where we as creators grow and develop. Through the act of creating, we stretch our skills, confront our doubts, and discover new facets of ourselves. The challenges we encounter—the writer's block, the technical roadblocks, the creative dead-ends—aren't just obstacles to overcome; they're opportunities for growth and self-discovery.

The Power of Product

While process is vital, it's the product that ultimately makes an impact in the world.[9] The final creation is what communicates the creator's vision, elicits emotion, and sparks change.

Like millions of others, I rely on Apple's products daily. My personal and professional lives connect through my MacBook Pro, iPhone, iMac, and iPad. Their sleek design, intuitive interface, and powerful capabilities have streamlined the way I communicate, share ideas, and access information.

But these devices didn't just materialize out of thin air. They were the result of countless iterations, failures, and refinements. The same goes for great works of art, scientific discoveries, and revolutionary social movements. Creativity is an ongoing process of trial, error, and transformation.

The Symbiosis of Process and Product

While we can examine process and product separately, the truth is that they're inextricably linked—just like assessment and evaluation. The process shapes the product, and the vision of the product guides the process. They're two sides of the same creative coin.

On a trip to the central coast of California, I was lucky enough to head out on a whale watching tour. After making it over the choppy waters of the bay, our boat came to an abrupt stop. Our captain explained that two juvenile humpback whales were immediately below the boat, and we couldn't get back underway until they were at least a hundred feet away from the vessel.

Suddenly, a huge creature arose out of the water off the starboard side, causing me to hang onto the railing for dear life as our boat dipped and swayed. Barnacles were scattered across the whale's beautiful face, and I watched in awe as he took another dive below. Just beyond us, I also noticed a few dolphins jumping in the distance. The marine biologist who was on board explained that both the barnacles and the dolphins were in a symbiotic relationship with the young whale. Barnacles attach to whales for shelter, food, and transportation, while dolphins guide humpbacks to schools of fish. In return, humpbacks protect the dolphins and sometimes use barnacles as protective armor—two unlikely partnerships supporting each other.

This symbiosis extends beyond nature. In architecture, you see it in Frank Gehry's iconic structures like the Guggenheim Museum in Bilbao or the Walt Disney Concert Hall in Los Angeles. These striking, sculptural forms emerge directly from Gehry's unique creative process, which involves extensive sketching, model-making, and digital experimentation. The organic, fluid nature of his buildings is a direct result of the way he works.

The relationship between process and product is evident when a screenplay goes through numerous drafts before becoming a film. Or when musicians compose, arrange, rehearse, and record a song before releasing it. Each stage of the process informs and refines the final product.

Even after a product enters the world, the process often continues. User feedback, market responses, and changing contexts can all spur further iterations and improvements. The product isn't a static endpoint but a milestone in an ongoing creative journey.

Balancing Process and Product

Like assessment and evaluation, finding balance between process and product is crucial in creative work. Overemphasizing process can lead to endless tinkering and perfectionism, while fixating on product alone can produce work that feels shallow or soulless.

In the startup world, this balance is often described as the difference between "shipping" and "perfecting." Successful companies recognize that while a product needs to be good enough to meet a need and attract users, the real learning and improvement happens after it's released. The process of iteration and refinement based on real-world feedback is what ultimately leads to a successful product.

In creative fields, balance might mean setting constraints or deadlines to prevent the process from stalling, while still allowing room for experimentation and serendipity. It takes trusting the process while knowing when to step back and let the product stand on its own.

The goal is creating a cycle where process and product feed into and enhance each other. The process is enriched by the clarity of the final vision, while the product is deepened by the insights and discoveries of the creative journey.

Embracing the Dance

Recognizing the interplay between process and product unlocks our full creative potential. By valuing both the journey and the destination, we open ourselves up to more meaningful, impactful, and fulfilling creative experiences.

This means celebrating the messy, iterative nature of the creative process, and recognizing that mistakes and missteps are often necessary on the path to breakthrough. It means giving ourselves permission to experiment, explore, and follow our curiosity down unexpected paths.

At the same time, it means keeping an eye on the final goal and using that vision to guide and focus our efforts. It means pushing through the challenges and doubts, trusting that the process will lead us to a product worth sharing with the world.

Ultimately, embracing this dance honors the full complexity and richness of the creative experience. It recognizes that creativity isn't just about those fleeting moments of inspiration or the glamour of the final result, but about the gritty, challenging, and ultimately transformative work of bringing our ideas to life.

Four Models for Assessing Creativity

To assess creativity more effectively, we can draw on four key models.[10] Each serves different purposes depending on your learning environment.

Measuring the Person: The Guilford Model

J. P. Guilford's model, which heavily influenced Torrance's work, focuses on the cognitive skills that underpin creative thinking. It's especially useful for developing creative thinking capabilities.

The model highlights four key creative thinking skills:

1. **Fluency**—generating many ideas (quantity)
2. **Flexibility**—generating different types of ideas (variety)
3. **Originality**—generating unusual ideas (uniqueness)
4. **Elaboration**—developing ideas with details (depth)

In practice, these skills can be assessed through activities like

- asking people to list all possible uses for a common object (fluency);
- challenging teams to solve a problem in multiple ways (flexibility);
- evaluating the uniqueness of solutions compared to peers (originality); or
- assessing how thoroughly ideas are developed (elaboration).

These assessments might be formal (like Torrance's standardized tests) or informal (like a teacher noting a student's ability to generate multiple solutions to a series of math challenges).

The strength of Guilford's model lies in its focus on specific, teachable thinking skills rather than some mysterious creative quality. Its limitation? These thinking skills are necessary but not sufficient for meaningful creative achievement—they're tools that must be applied purposefully.

Measuring the Work: The Taxonomy of Creative Design

While Guilford's model focuses on thinking skills, the Taxonomy of Creative Design gives us a framework for assessing creative products—solutions, designs, performances, or innovations.

This model evaluates creative work along three dimensions:

1. **Novelty**—How original or surprising is the work?
2. **Resolution**—How well does it solve the problem or accomplish its purpose?
3. **Synthesis**—How well does it integrate different elements into a coherent whole?

In practical settings, this model helps develop evaluation rubrics that balance originality with effectiveness. A product isn't creative just because it's unusual—it must also work. A marketing campaign isn't creative just because it's different—it must also engage target audiences.

The strength of this model is its recognition that creativity is more than just about originality—it's about purposeful originality that works. Its limitation? It focuses on outcomes without necessarily revealing how creators arrived at them.

Measuring the Work in Context: The Requirements Model

Teresa Amabile's Componential Model of Creativity, which I often think of as the Requirements Model, recognizes that creativity always happens within constraints—whether physical limitations, audience needs, or project parameters. This model works particularly well for understanding creativity as purposeful problem-solving rather than unrestrained self-expression.

This approach involves the following:

1. **Defining clear requirements** for a creative task
2. **Giving people freedom** within those boundaries
3. **Assessing** how well solutions meet requirements while demonstrating originality

Here's what this might look like:

- Marketing teams creating campaigns that must reach specific demographics while operating within budget constraints
- Students designing solutions for community problems that must meet technical specifications while offering new benefits
- Healthcare professionals developing treatment plans that must follow medical protocols while addressing unique patient needs

The strength of this model is its real-world authenticity—outside academic settings, creative professionals always work within constraints. Its limitation? Overly rigid requirements can squash innovation, so there must be careful balance between structure and freedom.

Measuring the Social Value of the Work: The Systems Model

We saw this model in chapter 2. Mihaly Csikszentmihalyi's Systems Model recognizes that creativity doesn't exist in isolation—it emerges from the interaction between creators, their fields of knowledge, and the communities that evaluate and adopt new ideas. This model helps us see creativity as inherently social.

In this view, creativity involves the following:

1. **Individuals** with knowledge and creative skills
2. **Domains** with established knowledge, practices, and standards
3. **Fields** composed of people who evaluate and validate creative contributions

Applications might include

- entrepreneurs presenting innovations to investors who evaluate their originality and market potential;

- scientists submitting research to peer-reviewed journals where experts assess contributions; and/or
- artists developing work that art critics and audiences evaluate according to evolving standards.

This model's strength is recognizing creativity's social dimension—ideas become creative when communities recognize them as valuable. Its limitation? Formal validation systems may privilege established approaches and miss genuinely revolutionary ideas that challenge existing paradigms.

Four Models in Action: Assessment Scenarios

The true test of assessment models is how they function in the real world. Here's how these four frameworks can operate:

Educational Setting: Student Project

A high school launches a community problem-solving project. Their assessment strategy includes the following:

- **Guilford-inspired prewriting activities** where students generate and categorize potential community challenges, with assessment focused on their thinking flexibility
- **A Design Taxonomy-based rubric** evaluating solutions on originality of approach, effectiveness of implementation, and integration of community context
- **Requirements Model elements** including feasibility constraints, timeline requirements, and community partnership guidelines
- **Systems Model components** where proposals are reviewed by actual community stakeholders who might implement the most promising student solutions

This layered approach helps teachers assess both individual creative development and the quality of final projects, while maintaining authentic connection to real community needs.

Business Setting: Product Development Team

A technology company is developing next-generation wearable devices. Their assessment approach integrates multiple models:

- Using **Guilford's model**, team leaders document each member's ideational fluency during brainstorming sessions, noting who generates many ideas, diverse ideas, and unique ideas

- Drawing from the **Taxonomy of Creative Design**, their project rubric evaluates prototypes on novelty (unique features), resolution (meeting user needs), and synthesis (technical elegance)

- Following the **Requirements Model**, they establish clear parameters—the device must use existing manufacturing infrastructure, maintain eighteen-hour battery life, and stay within target price points

- Embracing the **Systems Model**, they invite potential users and retail partners to review prototypes and provide authentic feedback

These approaches complement each other. Guilford's model helps assess thinking processes. The Design Taxonomy guides evaluation of prototypes. The Requirements Model ensures practical constraints. The Systems Model connects development to market realities.

Healthcare Setting: Quality Improvement Initiative

A hospital department is tackling patient experience challenges. Their creativity assessment includes the following:

- **Guilford-based assessment** of staff problem analysis, tracking their ability to identify multiple facets of complex issues and generate diverse solution pathways

- **Design Taxonomy** criteria evaluating improvement proposals on originality, practicality, and coherence
- **Requirements Model** elements including regulatory constraints, budget limitations, and staffing realities
- **Systems Model** authenticity through pilots where actual patients evaluate the effectiveness of proposed changes

This approach balances rigorous thinking assessment with real-world impact, helping healthcare professionals understand that creativity isn't just about having unusual ideas—it's about developing viable solutions to genuine problems.

Across these scenarios, different assessment models serve complementary purposes. Process-focused models guide development. Product-focused models evaluate outcomes. Constraint-based models create realistic parameters. Systems-based models connect creativity to authentic contexts.

The most effective creativity assessment doesn't choose between these approaches—it integrates them into a coherent system that both measures and develops creative capabilities.

Bridging the Four Branches and Four Models: The Synergy of Creative Development and Assessment

When we place the Four Branches of Creativity we explored in chapter 3 alongside these Four Models of Assessment, a remarkable relationship emerges. Each assessment model naturally aligns with aspects of our creative branches, creating a powerful framework for developing and evaluating creativity in balanced, meaningful ways.

The **Guilford Model**, with its focus on cognitive processes like fluency and flexibility, provides an ideal approach for assessing **Creative Thinking** (Branch 3). When we use this model, we're examining the mental agility that allows people to see problems from multiple angles and make unexpected connections. This assessment approach helps us develop specific thinking patterns that fuel innovation.

The **Taxonomy of Creative Design** naturally complements **Creative Skills** (Branch 1). Just as creative skills represent concrete, learnable abilities, this assessment model evaluates tangible creative products. The taxonomy's dimensions—novelty, resolution, and synthesis—provide clear criteria for assessing how well technical skills translate into effective creative outcomes.

The **Requirements Model** offers a perfect framework for assessing **Creative Application** (Branch 2), where creativity meets real-world constraints and opportunities. This model recognizes that application always happens within boundaries—whether technological limitations, audience needs, or project parameters. By evaluating how well solutions balance originality with effectiveness within these constraints, we can assess applied creativity in authentic contexts.

The **Systems Model** aligns beautifully with **Creative Expression** (Branch 4), acknowledging the deeply communal aspect of sharing one's unique perspective with others. This assessment approach recognizes that creative expression gains meaning through its reception and impact within communities. Just as Branch 3 emphasizes the importance of expressing oneself authentically, the Systems Model examines how that expression resonates within social contexts.

These sample alignments reveal something important about assessing creativity: different aspects of creativity require different assessment approaches. When we match each branch with a complementary assessment model, we create a more comprehensive framework that captures creativity's multidimensional nature. Look at figure 4.1 to see how this is visually represented:

That's not to say these are the only alignments available for each of the creativity branches. Certainly, there are times when we want to evaluate flexibility and fluency (from the Guilford model) when we're assessing creative

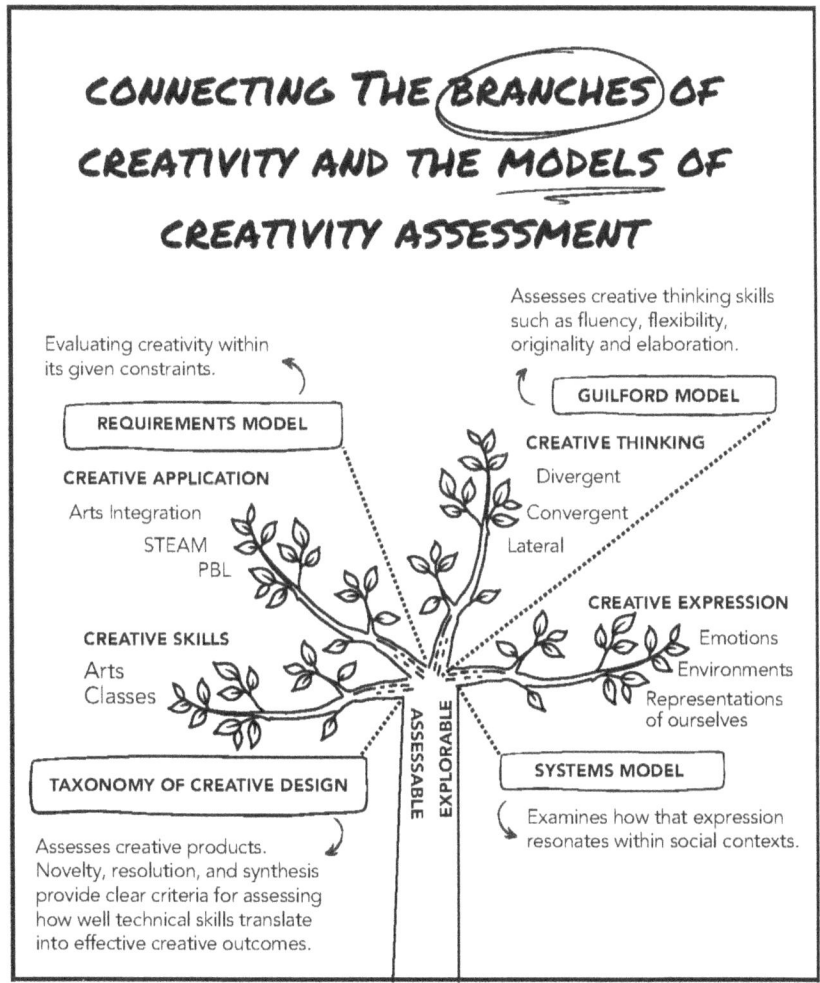

FIGURE 4.1

skill mastery. Or we may want to look at the use of novelty and synthesis during an arts integration project from the creative application branch. All assessment models can be used for each branch, depending upon the intent for which you plan to use them. The point here is to start to notice the natural connections for assessment models to the purposes and methods for engaging in creative action.

While we could use each model distinctively in different classrooms (like using the Taxonomy of Creative Design for an art class skill assessment, or the Requirements Model for an arts integration project in math class), a more authentic approach might be to integrate elements from all models in assessing a project holistically.

For example, imagine a student developing a documentary about local environmental issues:

- We might use Guilford's model to assess their research process, examining how fluidly they generate questions and how flexibly they connect different perspectives (Creative Thinking).

- The Taxonomy of Creative Design could evaluate their technical execution, assessing how well they employ filmmaking techniques to create an effective, cohesive story (Creative Skills).

- The Requirements Model would examine how well their documentary addresses the specific community issues within practical constraints like time limitations and available resources (Creative Application).

- The Systems Model would consider how the documentary resonates with different audiences, from environmental activists to local residents to policymakers (Creative Expression).

Using Integrated Creativity Assessment Models

Table 4.1 provides a sample documentary assessment rubric to focus on local environmental issues:

This integrated approach avoids reducing creativity to a single dimension. Instead of asking, "Is this student creative?," we can examine specific aspects of their creative development across all four branches, using appropriate assessment tools for each.

Table 4.1 Sample Documentary Integrated Assessment Rubric

Criteria	4–Excellent	3–Proficient	2–Developing	1–Needs Work
Creative Thinking (Guilford's Model—Research and Ideation)	Demonstrates exceptional fluency in generating research questions and exploring multiple angles. Effectively integrates diverse perspectives and sources.	Generates a variety of relevant research questions and connects different perspectives. Sources are credible and varied.	Research is somewhat limited in scope, with few connections between perspectives. Some sources lack credibility or depth.	Research is minimal or lacks coherence. Few or no connections between perspectives. Sources are weak or missing.
Creative Skills (Taxonomy of Creative Design—Filmmaking Techniques)	Cinematography, editing, and sound design are skillfully executed, enhancing storytelling. Strong use of visual and narrative elements.	Good use of filmmaking techniques; visuals and editing support the story effectively. Minor issues in execution.	Some basic filmmaking techniques are applied, but execution is inconsistent or lacks impact.	Weak or minimal use of filmmaking techniques. Poor execution affects the overall effectiveness of the documentary.
Creative Application (Requirements Model—Addressing Community Issues and Constraints)	The documentary effectively addresses the environmental issue with depth and relevance. Overcomes constraints creatively (time, budget, access).	Addresses the issue with some depth and shows effort in working within constraints. Some creative problem-solving.	The issue is addressed but lacks depth. Limited adaptation to constraints.	Fails to effectively address the issue or ignores constraints, resulting in an incomplete or weak documentary.
Creative Expression (Systems Model—Audience Engagement and Impact)	Engages multiple audiences (activists, residents, policymakers) with a compelling and balanced narrative. Inspires action or discussion.	Engages at least one key audience effectively. Narrative is clear but may not resonate as strongly across all groups.	Some effort to engage the audience, but the message lacks clarity or depth. Limited appeal beyond a niche group.	Little to no audience engagement. Message is unclear or fails to connect with viewers.

This doesn't mean developing four separate assessments for a project. Rather, it means creating an assessment that incorporates elements from each model—perhaps a rubric, checklist, or portfolio review that includes specific elements from the Guilford, Taxonomy, Requirements, and Systems models.

The relationship works in both directions. The Four Branches provide a roadmap for developing creativity in balanced ways, while the Four Models offer complementary approaches to assessing that development. Together, they create a powerful framework for nurturing and evaluating creativity in education, work, and life.

The Case for Subjectivity

Throughout our exploration of measuring creativity, one truth has become increasingly clear: creativity assessment inevitably involves subjective judgment. Unlike measuring height or weight, there's no purely objective way to assess creative quality. Different observers reasonably disagree about what makes work creative, and these judgments shift across cultural and historical contexts.

This subjectivity makes many people uncomfortable. We're trained to strive for objectivity in assessment—clear criteria, consistent application, reliable results. The inherent subjectivity of creativity assessment seems to contradict everything we've learned about good assessment practice.[11]

But what if this discomfort with subjectivity actually undermines effective creativity assessment? What if, by trying to make creativity assessment perfectly objective, we miss what matters most about creative work?

Vincent van Gogh's story offers a powerful reminder of judgment's limitations. During his lifetime, critics and collectors largely dismissed his work. Only after his death did the world recognize his genius, as new generations found meaning in his expressive paintings. This dramatic shift didn't happen because the paintings changed—they remained exactly the same. What changed was the subjective judgment of those viewing them.

When we pretend we can evaluate creativity with complete objectivity, we risk several problems:

1. We focus on the most easily measurable aspects of creativity while ignoring less quantifiable but equally important dimensions.
2. We present our subjective judgments as objective facts, denying others the opportunity to understand different perspectives on their work.
3. We imply there's one "correct" form of creativity rather than recognizing diverse forms of creative expression.
4. We miss how our own cultural biases and preferences shape our evaluations, potentially putting people from different backgrounds at a disadvantage.

The alternative is embracing more honest approaches that acknowledge subjectivity while still providing valuable guidance. Educators who assess creativity effectively tend to

- use multiple evaluators to provide diverse perspectives on student work;
- make their assessment criteria explicit while acknowledging these represent particular values;
- engage students in evaluating their own and others' creative work;
- recognize that creative judgment is contextual and evolving, not universal and fixed;
- focus assessment on growth over time rather than absolute standards; and
- balance structure with openness, providing clear expectations while allowing for unexpected forms of creativity.

Schools like Central Park East Secondary School in New York demonstrate how this more nuanced approach works in practice. Students there complete graduation portfolios that include creative work across disciplines. Rather than receiving a single grade from one teacher, students present their work to diverse committees including teachers, external experts, parents, and peers. These committees engage in substantive discussions about the work's strengths and limitations, modeling how creative work is actually evaluated in the world beyond school.

This approach prepares students for the reality that creative work always faces diverse, subjective judgments. Success doesn't come from pleasing a single evaluator with one set of criteria, but from understanding different perspectives while developing one's own creative voice and standards.

The most effective creativity assessment makes subjectivity transparent and educational. It shows students that creative evaluation involves genuine human judgment, not just mechanical application of universal criteria. It prepares them for a world where creative success means navigating diverse perspectives while maintaining clear purpose and vision.

This more honest approach doesn't make creativity assessment easier, but it does make it more authentic and valuable. It acknowledges what teachers already know from experience—that assessing creativity requires professional judgment and wisdom that can't be reduced to simple checklists or formulas.

Toward a Balanced Approach: Practical Assessment Strategies

For educators committed to nurturing and assessing creativity, the path forward isn't eliminating evaluation or pretending perfect objectivity is possible. It's developing balanced approaches that both guide creative development and evaluate creative achievement, that provide structure while allowing for surprise.

Here are practical strategies for creating more effective creativity assessment in schools:

1. *Clarify what kind of creativity you're assessing*
   Different learning contexts call for different types of creativity:

   - Sometimes we want **adaptive creativity**—novel solutions within established parameters.
   - Sometimes we want **transformative creativity**—ideas that challenge fundamental assumptions.
   - Sometimes we value **personal creativity**—new-to-the-student insights and expressions.
   - Sometimes we seek **historical creativity**—truly original contributions to a field.

By clarifying what type of creativity matters in a particular context, teachers can create more appropriate assessment approaches.

2. *Balance process and product assessment*
   Effective creativity assessment examines both how students create and what they create:

   - Process assessment tools include creativity journals, thinking portfolios, and documented iterations.
   - Product assessment tools include rubrics evaluating originality, effectiveness, and craftsmanship.
   - Integrated approaches connect process quality to product outcomes, helping students see relationships between their creative approaches and results.

3. *Make assessment criteria transparent but not restrictive*
   Students deserve to understand how their creative work will be evaluated:

   - Share rubrics and examples before students begin work.

- Discuss what makes work creative in your field or context.
- Distinguish between nonnegotiable requirements and areas for creative freedom.
- Allow room for students to surprise you with unexpected forms of creativity.

4. *Use multiple measures and evaluators*

   No single assessment tool or perspective captures creativity completely:

   - Combine quantitative measures (like ideational fluency counts) with qualitative judgments.
   - Include self-assessment, peer feedback, teacher evaluation, and when possible, feedback from field experts.
   - Use different assessment formats—written reflections, presentations, demonstrations, exhibitions.
   - Look for patterns across multiple assessments rather than relying on single measures.

5. *Make assessment developmental, not just evaluative*

   The best creativity assessment helps students grow:

   - Provide specific, actionable feedback on both process and product.
   - Focus on growth over time rather than just current performance.
   - Help students develop metacognitive awareness of their creative approaches.
   - Use assessment to guide instruction, not just document achievement.

6. *Create authentic contexts for creativity assessment*

   Creativity assessment is most meaningful when connected to real purposes:

   - Develop projects addressing genuine problems or needs.
   - Connect students with authentic audiences for their work.

- Create exhibitions where students present work to the broader community.
- Partner with organizations that might actually use students' creative solutions.

These balanced approaches help resolve the tension between structure and freedom in assessing creativity. The most effective assessment isn't completely standardized, but it isn't completely open-ended either.[12] It provides clear guidance while remaining open to surprise. It offers specific feedback while respecting diverse creative paths. It evaluates against standards while acknowledging different forms of creative excellence.

This also serves a deeper educational purpose. It teaches students that creativity isn't magic or mystery—it involves learnable skills, deliberate practice, and critical reflection. But it also teaches that creativity can't be reduced to formulas or algorithms—it requires risk-taking, personal voice, and genuine engagement with meaningful problems.

Thoughtful assessments don't just measure creative development—they actively foster it. They show students that their creative growth matters enough to be taken seriously, guided carefully, and evaluated honestly.

Weighing Sunlight: The Ongoing Quest

Trying to measure creativity often feels like trying to weigh sunlight. We can see its effects, feel its warmth, watch how it transforms everything it touches—but our scales and metrics never quite capture its essence.

This doesn't mean we should abandon the attempt. Each model we've explored opens a window into different aspects of the creative process. Each perspective reveals something true, even if incomplete.

What matters most isn't finding the perfect measurement but recognizing what our current attempts reveal and conceal. In education, in business, in our personal development—understanding creativity's complex nature helps us nurture it more effectively, even when we can't fully define it.

Think back to those Air Force pilots who became aces. They weren't just following procedures better than everyone else. They spotted possibilities others missed, made connections others overlooked, and took calculated risks others avoided. Their creativity wasn't separate from their technical excellence—it was the multiplier that transformed competence into brilliance.

The same principle applies whether you're teaching a classroom of students, leading a team at work, or simply trying to live a more imaginative life. Creativity isn't just one more skill to develop—it's the force that amplifies everything else.

Key Takeaways

1. Creativity can be assessed, but not through traditional standardized measures. Effective creativity assessment requires approaches that capture both measurable skills and less quantifiable qualities like originality and significance.

2. The most powerful creativity assessment examines both process and product—how students create as well as what they create. This dual focus is especially important in an age of AI-generated content.

3. Creativity assessment inevitably involves subjective judgment. Rather than pretending complete objectivity is possible, effective assessment makes evaluation criteria explicit while remaining open to unexpected forms of creative excellence.

4. Different creativity assessment models serve complementary purposes and align with different branches of creativity, creating a comprehensive framework for development and evaluation.

5. Well-designed creativity assessment doesn't just measure creative development—it actively fosters it. By making creative processes visible, providing specific feedback, and connecting creative work to authentic purposes, assessment becomes a powerful tool for developing the creative capabilities students need in a rapidly changing world.

PRACTICE STRATEGY: Theme and Variations

Musicians organize compositions through a main idea (theme) and variations on that theme. You're going to use this same idea to explore assessment:

1. Write down a creative project or process you'd like to assess. It could be something you've already done or something you plan to do in the future.

2. Think about the assessment ideas presented in this chapter. Which of these would you like to apply to your creative project? You can select one method/practice or multiples. This is your theme.

3. Next, write down the answer to this question: "What does DONE look like for this project or process?"

4. Set a timer for five minutes. For each assessment method you've selected, write down three ways you could use that assessment for your creative project. These are your variations. You only have five minutes to come up with these three variations—so think quickly!

Tip: Don't get caught up in outlining all the details for your assessment right now. Focus instead on the purpose of your assessment and what you're hoping to evaluate in your project or process. Use these big ideas to help you in determining whether you met your statement of "This is what done looks like for this project/process."

Notes

1 Time. (1954, May 31). "Science: Portrait of an Ace." *Time.* https://time.com/archive/6884620/science-portrait-of-an-ace/

2 Alabbasi, A. M. A., Paek, S. H., Kim, D., & Cramond, B. (2022). "What Do Educators Need to Know About the Torrance Tests of Creative Thinking: A Comprehensive Review." *Frontiers in Psychology*, 13, 1000385. https://doi.org/10.3389/fpsyg.2022.1000385

3 Perri, V. (2019). "The History of Creativity." Sari Studio. https://www.sari.studio/blog-1/the-history-of-creativity

4 Franklin, S. W. (2023, September). "The Surprising Origins of Our Obsession with Creativity." Behavioral Scientist. https://behavioralscientist.org/the-surprising-origins-of-our-obsession-with-creativity/

5 Ripley, A. (2013). *The Smartest Kids in the World: And How They Got That Way*. Simon & Schuster. "Amanda Ripley Compares US Education System to Best Education System in the World" (February 13, 2014). Aspen Institute. https://www.aspeninstitute.org/blog-posts/amanda-ripley-smartest-kids-in-the-world-aspen-institute/

6 Mind Tools. (n.d.). "What Are Your Values?" https://www.mindtools.com/a5eygum/what-are-your-values

7 Park, N. K., Chun, M. Y., & Lee, J. (2016). "Revisiting Individual Creativity Assessment: Triangulation in Subjective and Objective Assessment Methods." *Creativity Research Journal*, 28(1), 1–10. https://doi.org/10.1080/10400419.2016.1125259

8 Georgia Department of Education. (n.d.). "Assessment and Evaluation: What's the Difference?" https://www.gadoe.org/Curriculum-Instruction-and-Assessment/Special-Education-Services/Documents/Co-Teaching%20Modules/Module%202/10%20Assessment_and_Evaluation_Whats_the_Difference.pdf

9 Beloglovsky, M. (n.d.). "Navigating the Dichotomy of a Creative Process vs. Creative Product." Miriam Beloglovsky. https://miriambeloglovsky.com/navigating-the-dichotomy-of-a-creative-process-vs-final-product

10 Said-Metwaly, S., Van den Noortgate, W., & Kyndt, E. (2017). "Approaches to Measuring Creativity: A Systematic Literature Review." *Creativity: Theories-Research-Applications*, 4(2), 238–75. https://intapi.sciendo.com/pdf/10.1515/ctra-2017-0013

11 Wieschermann, D. (2024, February). "Four Principles of Navigating Subjectivity in Creative Work." LinkedIn. https://www.linkedin.com/pulse/four-principles-navigating-subjectivity-creative-work-wieschermann-ed6xe/

12 Yang, H. C., & Cheng, H. Y. (2010). "Creativity of Student Information System Projects: From the Perspective of Network Embeddedness." *Computers & Education*, 54(1), 209–21. https://doi.org/10.1016/j.compedu.2009.08.004

PART THREE

THE ILLUMINATION

5

The Art and Science of Flow

> *Chapter Guiding Question: Can humans increase our creativity capacity?*

In December 1973, Philippe Petit walked into a Manhattan bookstore and spotted a magazine article about the World Trade Center's construction. Time stopped. The world around him vanished. A single vision consumed him—one that would dominate the next three years of his life: walking between those Twin Towers of the World Trade Center on a high wire.

What followed was a daring masterclass in how flow and creativity intertwine. For forty-five minutes on August 7, 1974, Petit made eight crossings on that high wire in what he describes as "a state of perfect concentration." He didn't just walk—he performed. He danced, lay down, and even saluted to the crowds 1,350 feet below. At the same time, he solved countless unexpected problems mid-wire, from changing winds to cable movement, all while in a state of complete immersion.[1]

"I was not conscious of any fear," Petit later wrote. "Time had disappeared. I was in a world where normal rules had no reality." This wasn't just bravado talking. He'd experienced one of the most dramatic documented examples of what psychologists now call "flow state."[2] A seemingly magical condition where challenge and skill meet perfectly, where self-consciousness slips away, and where creative solutions bubble up with surprising ease.

This extraordinary state isn't reserved for daredevils or artistic geniuses; it's available to us mere mortals as well. In an age where artificial intelligence can calculate risks and probabilities faster than any human brain, this uniquely human ability to enter profound states of creative problem-solving has never been more valuable.

This chapter explores how we can tap into this flow state and use it to access otherwise dormant solutions hiding in our own minds. Drawing on cutting-edge neuroscience and decades of psychological research, we'll uncover practical steps anyone can take to enhance their creative potential. Because flow performs the most stunning feat of all: it unlocks the full power of the distinctly human mind.

How the Brain Works During Creative Episodes

In our hustle-obsessed world, it's tempting to believe that becoming more creative means thinking harder, pushing more, and forcing our brains to innovate by sheer willpower. But neuroscience reveals the exact opposite truth. Just like Petit discovered on his high wire, our most creative moments typically arrive when we allow our usual mental chatter to quiet down.

In chapter 2, we explored the fundamentals of creativity and how various neural networks interact during creative thinking. Now, we'll dive deeper into how these networks function during states of peak creative performance—what happens in our brains when we're not just being creative, but when we're experiencing that magical state of flow.

Think of your brain as a bustling city at night. Certain neighborhoods pulse with activity while others grow quiet. During creative episodes, this pattern shifts in fascinating ways. The default mode network (DMN) and executive control network (ECN) stop their usual pattern of taking turns—instead, they begin to work in concert. It's like a neural jazz improvisation where networks that normally clash suddenly find perfect harmony. Advanced fMRI research confirms that during creative tasks, these networks don't just activate sequentially—they synchronize.[3]

In flow, the transition between these networks becomes remarkably fluid. The salience network orchestrates their interaction with unusual efficiency, allowing ideas to flow seamlessly from generation (DMN) to evaluation and implementation (ECN) without the usual friction or self-doubt that typically interrupts creative thinking.

When you're engaged in creative work, your brain waves shift, too. Creative tasks trigger increases in both alpha waves (8–12 Hz) and theta waves (4–8 Hz). Alpha waves, associated with relaxed alertness, create what neuroscientists call a "neural inhibition" state—essentially quieting the parts of your brain that might interfere with creative thinking. Meanwhile, theta waves, linked to deep meditation and memory integration, help forge new connections between previously unrelated ideas.[4]

Most creative solutions actually emerge through a specific chemical sequence. Your brain releases what we can cheekily call "the creative cocktail":

- first comes a dopamine surge, enhancing pattern recognition and cranking up your motivation;
- next, norepinephrine levels rise steadily, sharpening your focus and attention;
- then endorphins flood in, creating that sense of well-being that keeps you engaged and helps cement those fresh neural connections; and
- finally, anandamide (the "bliss molecule") appears, producing feelings of joy that reward your creative efforts.

Additionally, the left and right hemispheres of your brain collaborate more effectively during creative episodes.[5] The outdated notion of being "left-brained" (logical) or "right-brained" (creative) has been thoroughly debunked. Creativity emerges from dynamic collaboration between hemispheres.

This hemispheric teamwork shifts based on the type of creative task. During the early stages of creativity—when you're generating new ideas—the right hemisphere shows more activity, particularly in areas linked to novel connections and holistic thinking. As you refine those ideas, the left hemisphere kicks into higher gear, helping structure and articulate your creative insights. But it's the fluid communication between these hemispheres that ultimately allows creativity to flourish. Most creative breakthroughs happen when both hemispheres actively exchange information.[6]

If our brain is like a city at night, think of the brain's two hemispheres as opposite sides of town. Most of the time, traffic between them follows predictable patterns—main highways, scheduled transit, designated crossing points. But during creative states, the traffic authority takes a coffee break and unusual patterns emerge. Temporary bridges connect neighborhoods that rarely interact. Side streets and alleyways that normally see little activity become bustling thoroughfares of exchange.

This is what neuroscientists call "transient hypofrontality"—a temporary quieting of your brain's executive control centers that allows spontaneous and novel connections to emerge. This isn't your brain malfunctioning; it's your brain operating in a special mode perfectly suited for creativity.

Neuroplasticity: Building the Highway System for Creative Flow

Your brain's remarkable ability to rewire itself, called neuroplasticity, forms the foundation for flow-based creativity.[7] Like constructing new highways that become smoother and faster with use, our brains physically change with each creative experience, making subsequent creative states more accessible.

These neural modifications can occur even when logic tells us they shouldn't be possible.

João Carlos Martins, once celebrated as one of the world's greatest Bach interpreters, saw his career as a pianist devastated in 1995. A mugger in Bulgaria struck him on the head with a metal pipe, causing severe neurological damage. After multiple surgeries and eventually developing focal dystonia (a neurological condition causing involuntary muscle contractions), Martins lost the use of his fingers. Doctors delivered a devastating verdict: he would never play again.[8]

Martins refused to accept this fate. He began experimenting with ways to rewire his brain's musical pathways. He took up conducting, which maintained his neural connections to music while finding different physical expressions. Eventually, through innovative bionic gloves developed by industrial designer Ubiratã Bizarro Costa, Martins returned to the piano at age eighty.

The gloves helped position his fingers correctly, but it was his brain's plasticity, and its ability to create new neural pathways around the damaged areas, that allowed him to reinterpret how to make music.

Then there's Auguste Rodin. Unable to see details clearly due to severe nearsightedness, he developed an extraordinary ability to understand form through touch. This adaptation not only compensated for his visual limitation but essentially shaped his sculptural style. What seemed like a barrier became a catalyst for artistic innovation as his brain built new neural pathways for understanding and creating three-dimensional art.

The ability of our brains to rewire themselves lies at the heart of creativity. Every time we engage in creative activities, we're not just producing something new—we're physically reshaping our neural pathways and deepening our capacity for creative thinking. Scientists have documented this plasticity in action:

- When jazz musicians improvise, their brains create new neural pathways connecting memory, emotion, and motor control in unique ways. These pathways strengthen with practice, making future improvisation more fluid and natural. What begins as conscious effort gradually becomes intuitive expression.

- Writers who practice daily show increased connectivity between language centers and creative regions of the brain. The more they write, the stronger these connections become, making it easier to access creative flow in future sessions.
- Visual artists develop enhanced connections between visual processing areas and motor control regions, enabling them to translate what they imagine into what they create with greater precision.

When we engage in creative activities, three big things happen in our brains: First, we strengthen connections between our default mode network (our imagination center) and our executive control network (our focusing system). It's like building better bridges between the brain regions that generate ideas and those that help us execute them. Even more exciting, this ability to rewire our brains doesn't diminish with age as dramatically as we once thought.

While your brain may not be as malleable as a child's, it maintains significant plasticity throughout your life. A 2019 study of artists over sixty showed they maintained robust connections between their default mode and executive control networks, both key neural players in creativity.[9] Second, our brains release BDNF (brain-derived neurotrophic factor), often dubbed "Miracle-Gro for the brain." This protein helps neurons form new connections and strengthens existing ones. The more we engage in creative activities, the more BDNF we produce.

Third, we develop "cognitive reserve"—essentially backup pathways in our brains. This is exactly what allowed Martins to find new ways to express music when his primary neural pathways were damaged. His brain had built enough alternative routes through years of practice that it could forge new paths when the original ones were blocked.

Here's the catch: this plasticity works in both directions. Just as Martins's brain adapted and found new ways to create music, our neural pathways can weaken if we don't use them. As neuroscientists often say, "neurons that fire together, wire together"—but the opposite holds true as well. When we fall into rigid routines or avoid creative challenges, these pathways begin to fade.

For students, this means creativity is a capacity that grows with practice; it is not just a fixed trait. A student who initially struggles with creative problem-solving isn't "uncreative"—they simply haven't yet built the neural pathways that facilitate creative flow. With appropriate guidance and regular practice, these pathways develop and strengthen.

It isn't just that our brains can change—it's that we can actively direct this change through deliberate practice. Every creative act, every moment of flow, every new challenge we embrace helps rewire our brains for greater creative capacity.

This is especially evident in arts education, where consistent practice yields nonlinear improvements. A student practicing drawing might experience months of steady progress followed by a sudden leap in ability when neural connections reach a critical threshold. These jumps often coincide with their first experiences of flow.

Creative capacity develops through consistent engagement with appropriate challenges, not through occasional bursts of inspiration. This understanding should fundamentally change how we approach creativity development in education. Classroom environments that incorporate regular creative practice—whether in mathematics, science, literature, or dedicated arts programs—literally change students' brains, building the architecture needed for innovative thinking.

This plastic nature of our brains—their ability to forge new pathways and strengthen existing ones—leads to a serious question: What mental qualities should we cultivate to maximize this adaptability?

Think about João Carlos Martins again. His recovery required both dogged persistence (practicing repeatedly despite setbacks) and remarkable flexibility (a willingness to completely reimagine how he made music). This combination of persistence and flexibility is essential for all creative endeavors—including our own healing.

Cognitive Persistence and Flexibility

As we move from understanding creativity to actively applying it, one critical skill emerges: balancing persistence and flexibility. Creativity demands two seemingly contradictory qualities—the persistence to stick with challenging problems and the flexibility to approach them from multiple angles. This paradox mirrors the neural dance between focused attention and open awareness that characterizes flow states.[10]

In educational settings, students typically struggle in one of two ways: either abandoning challenging tasks too quickly when obstacles arise (lacking persistence) or becoming rigidly attached to unproductive approaches (lacking flexibility). Students who learn how to persist through challenges, while remaining willing to pivot their approach, demonstrate higher creative achievement and problem-solving success.[11]

Neuroscience helps explain this dynamic. Persistence engages the brain's executive control network, maintaining focus despite difficulties. Flexibility, meanwhile, involves temporarily relaxing this control to allow the default mode network to generate alternative approaches. Flow states are characterized by the ability to shift fluidly between these modes as needed—staying focused without becoming rigid, remaining open without becoming scattered.[12]

You can intentionally develop these capacities through structured practices.

Building Persistence:

- Break complex projects into manageable milestones with clear feedback loops.
- Celebrate effort and process, not just outcomes.
- Share stories of "productive struggle" where difficulty preceded breakthrough.
- Teach explicit strategies for pushing through challenging moments.

Cultivating Flexibility:

- Practice divergent thinking through regular brainstorming exercises.
- Challenge yourself to generate multiple solutions to problems.
- Incorporate perspective-shifting exercises ("How would a biologist approach this history question?").
- Create safe spaces for experimental thinking where the risk of being "wrong" is minimized.

The key lies in learning to toggle between these modes effectively. Think of it as interval training for your brain—alternating between focused persistence and open, flexible thinking. Here are some specific practices that help develop this ability:

1. **The "Yes, And" Exercise:** When problem-solving, first persist with one approach for a set time, then force yourself to generate three evolutions of that solution by saying "Yes, and" to your original approach three times. For example, if my first approach to a classroom management problem is providing more brain breaks, I might say, "Yes, and the breaks should include thirty seconds of movement." Then: "Yes, and the movement should include both individual and partner opportunities."

Finally: "Yes, and the movement can be guided for transitions between activities."

2. **The Perspective Shift:** When stuck, deliberately view your challenge through different lenses—as a child would see it, as someone from a different field would approach it, as nature might solve it.

3. **The Documentation Practice:** Keep a journal of both your persistent efforts and your moments of insight. Looking for patterns helps you learn when to push through and when to pivot.

The goal with all of this is developing the wisdom to know when persistence or flexibility serves you best. This balance allows our neuroplastic brains to both strengthen existing pathways and forge creative new ones.

Flow State: What It Is, Its Benefits, and How to Get into It

In the summer of 1944, geneticist Barbara McClintock made a discovery that would eventually win her the Nobel Prize. But it wasn't just *what* she discovered that was astonishing, it was *how*. Working alone in her Cold Spring Harbor laboratory with rows of maize plants, McClintock experienced something scientists rarely admit to: a dramatic shift in consciousness.

"Suddenly I was seeing things about genes that no one else had seen," she told her biographer. "I found myself literally inside the kernels of corn." For hours, she forgot about herself, her surroundings, even time itself. This wasn't just intense concentration. She described how "everything was going like lightning" and how the corn plants seemed to be revealing their genetic secrets directly to her.[13]

This state led McClintock to insights about genetic transposition—how genes can move along and between chromosomes—that were so far ahead of their time, the scientific community took decades to catch up. When colleagues doubted her findings because they seemed impossible, she simply replied, "I just knew I was right."

McClintock had entered her flow state. Her ability to access this state repeatedly throughout her career enabled her to see patterns others missed, eventually revolutionizing our understanding of genetics.

Here's what makes McClintock's story particularly fascinating: she didn't just stumble into this state once. She learned to recognize its onset and create conditions that made it more likely to occur. She worked in the early mornings when her mind was freshest. She alternated between intense observation and periods of reflection. She eliminated distractions, often working alone with her corn plants for hours at a time. This optimal flow state is a natural capacity we all possess; one that can be developed and enhanced through understanding and practice.

Flow is that elusive but powerful state where time seems to warp, self-consciousness falls away, and you become fully immersed in the task at hand. Athletes call it "being in the zone." Artists describe it as losing themselves in their work. Researchers recognize it as a unique state of consciousness where we do our most creative and fulfilling work.

Flow isn't just a pleasant state of mind. Research confirms it creates distinct changes in brain activity. Remember those neural networks we discussed earlier—the default mode network and executive control network? In flow, they stop competing and start collaborating. It's like your brain's jazz musicians finally finding their groove.

The benefits of flow extend far beyond just feeling good:

- **Enhanced creativity:** Studies show we make more novel connections in flow.
- **Improved learning:** We absorb and retain information more effectively.
- **Increased motivation:** Flow experiences make us want to return to challenging tasks.

- **Greater satisfaction:** People report their highest levels of fulfillment during flow states.

This carries huge implications for educators. When you notice a student completely absorbed in learning—time forgotten, self-consciousness vanished, fully engaged with a challenging problem—you're witnessing this neural networking in action.

These aren't just "good learning moments"; they represent optimal brain states where learning isn't just faster but fundamentally different—more integrative, more meaningful, and more likely to spark creative connections. Understanding how to create conditions for these moments can transform your educational practice.

So how do you access this optimal state more reliably? The science points to several key conditions:

1. **The Challenge-Skill Balance**

    The project or challenge you select matters tremendously. You need something that stretches your abilities without overwhelming them. Too easy leads to boredom. Too hard triggers anxiety. The sweet spot is what researchers call "the flow channel"—where the challenge matches your skills.

2. **Clear Goals and Immediate Feedback**

    Your brain needs to know what it's aiming for and how it's doing. Think of a basketball player who immediately knows if their shot went in, or a writer who can sense when a sentence lands just right.

3. **Deep Focus**

    Our modern world is wired to destroy flow with constant interruptions. Creating the right environment is crucial:

    - Find hours when your energy and focus naturally peak.
    - Create a dedicated space for deep work.

- Turn off notifications and eliminate potential distractions.
- Let others know you need uninterrupted time.

4. **The Goldilocks Zone of Pressure**

    Once you're working on the project or challenge, you have to be mindful of the pressure you place on yourself to find creative solutions. A little pressure actually helps you enter flow. Too much stress activates your brain's fear centers, while too little urgency leads to procrastination. Find what scientists call "optimal anxiety"—just enough pressure to sharpen your focus without overwhelming you.

5. **Prime Your Brain**

    Getting your brain ready for flow can help you enter it more easily. These specific activities can make flow more likely to find:

    - brief meditation or mindfulness practice beforehand
    - light physical exercise to increase blood flow
    - a consistent pre-work ritual that signals "it's time to focus"
    - review of clear objectives before starting

Researcher Jo Boaler's work on mathematical mindset incorporates these flow conditions in classroom settings. Her approach involves structuring tasks as clear, sequential challenges matching students' abilities, creating focused work periods, emphasizing student choice, and normalizing mistakes as valuable learning opportunities.

The results prove transformative: students previously disengaged from mathematics begin experiencing flow states during problem-solving, developing deeper understanding and genuine enthusiasm for challenges they would have previously avoided.[14]

The most powerful insight from flow research might be this: while you can't force flow, you can create conditions that make it more likely to occur.

But here's what most people miss: it's not just about external conditions. It's also about developing what researchers call "flow proneness"—your personal capacity to enter this state. Like any skill, this can be strengthened through practice.

How to Build Flow Proneness:

- Start with shorter periods of focused work and gradually extend them.
- Practice moving between different levels of challenge to find your sweet spot.
- Learn to recognize early signs of flow so you can protect and extend these states.
- Keep a flow diary to identify your personal triggers and blockers.

For educators, these principles provide a framework for our own creative practice. Planning lessons, designing assessments, or developing curriculum can all become flow experiences when approached with the right conditions.

A word of caution: Don't turn flow-seeking into another source of pressure. Sometimes the harder we try to enter flow, the more elusive it becomes. Instead, focus on setting up the conditions and then, paradoxically, letting go of the need to control the experience. This creates a virtuous cycle where our personal flow states inspire flow experiences for our students.

How to Use Flow to Increase Your Creativity

Remember McClintock's moment of insight among her corn plants? She didn't just stumble into a one-time flow state. She learned to access this state reliably, using it to make breakthrough after breakthrough in genetics. Her experience reveals a crucial truth: flow isn't just about feeling good—it's a powerful tool for enhancing creativity.

Here's how to systematically use flow states to boost your creative capacity (and that of your students):

1. **Identify Your Flow Triggers**

   Each person has specific conditions that make flow more likely. These personal "triggers" might include the following:

   - **Environmental factors**: specific locations, ambient sounds, lighting conditions
   - **Temporal patterns**: times of day when focus comes more naturally
   - **Entry rituals**: activities that signal to your brain it's time to enter a focused state
   - **Challenge levels**: the types of problems that hit your personal sweet spot

   Through simple self-observation, you can identify your personal flow triggers. Keep a "flow journal" for two weeks, noting when you experience even brief moments of complete engagement. Look for patterns in when, where, and how these states occur.

   Teachers can facilitate this self-awareness in students by periodically asking reflective questions: "When did you feel most engaged today?" "What helped you stay focused during that activity?" This metacognitive practice helps students recognize and eventually recreate their optimal learning conditions.

2. **Structure for Flow**

   Once identified, flow triggers can be deliberately incorporated into your work routine:

   - **Create flow-friendly spaces**: Designate physical environments with minimal distractions that signal "deep work happens here."
   - **Schedule around energy peaks**: Align your most challenging creative work with your personal periods of peak cognitive energy.

- **Design entry sequences**: Develop consistent pre-work routines that prepare your mind for focused states.
- **Set clear session intentions**: Define specific, achievable goals for each creative session.

In educational settings, this might mean establishing special "creation stations" in classrooms where focused work is expected, scheduling creative activities during students' natural energy peaks, or developing class rituals that signal transitions into deep learning modes.

3. **Train Your Attention Muscle**

    Flow requires sustained attention, a capacity you can systematically strengthen through the following:

    - **Progressive duration practice**: Begin with shorter periods of focused work (fifteen to twenty-five minutes) and gradually extend as your capacity increases.
    - **Meditation and mindfulness**: Regular practice of present-moment awareness strengthens the neural circuits, supporting sustained attention.
    - **Single-tasking discipline**: Deliberately resist the multitasking impulse to train your brain for deeper focus.
    - **Distraction prevention protocols**: Develop systems to minimize both external interruptions and internal distractions.

Teachers can incorporate these principles through structured focus periods that gradually increase in duration, simple mindfulness practices at the beginning of class, and explicit instruction in attention management strategies.

4. **Build Flow Cycles, Not Marathons**

    Rather than attempting to maintain flow indefinitely (which is neurologically impossible), aim for strategic cycles of deep engagement followed by genuine recovery:

- **Work in focused blocks**: Sixty-to-ninety-minute periods of concentrated effort align with your brain's natural ultradian rhythms.
- **Take genuine breaks**: Complete disconnection between sessions allows neural networks to reset.
- **Incorporate movement**: Physical activity between deep work sessions enhances cognitive flexibility.
- **Practice strategic reflection**: Brief periods of intentional review between sessions help consolidate insights.

This cyclical approach can transform classroom scheduling. Instead of trying to maintain attention for long, undifferentiated periods, design learning experiences around focused engagement blocks separated by strategic breaks—creating conditions where flow becomes neurologically more likely.

5. **Develop a Growth Relationship with Challenge**

    Your relationship with difficulty profoundly affects your ability to enter flow. Approaching challenges with what psychologist Carol Dweck calls a "growth mindset" makes flow more accessible:

    - **Reframe obstacles as growth opportunities**: View difficulties as fascinating puzzles rather than frustrating roadblocks.
    - **Celebrate productive struggle**: Recognize that the feeling of stretching your capabilities marks the pathway to growth.
    - **Practice deliberate skill-building**: Identify and focus on developing specific capabilities that enhance your creative work.
    - **Seek calibrated challenges**: Continuously adjust the difficulty of your work to maintain that optimal challenge-skill balance.

Remember, flow states compound over time. Each time you enter flow while working creatively, you're not just producing better work—you're strengthening your ability to enter flow in the future and expanding your creative capacity.

Think of flow states as powerful moments of creative acceleration. But just as an athlete can't perform at peak levels constantly, we can't—and shouldn't—try to stay in flow 24/7. What matters more is building sustainable creative practices that make flow states more accessible when we need them.

This brings us to perhaps the most important question in creative development: How do we turn these optimal states from rare occurrences into regular features of our creative lives?

The answer lies in understanding that creativity isn't just about peak moments. It's about the daily practices, routines, and habits that support them. Flow states might be where we do our best work, but it's our regular creative habits that create the foundation for these experiences.

The Classroom as a Flow Environment: Special Considerations

While flow principles apply across contexts, educational settings present unique opportunities and challenges for cultivating creative flow states.

Social Dimensions of Flow

Unlike many professional creatives who work in solitude, students typically learn in social environments. Research on "group flow" reveals that collective creative states have their own distinct characteristics:

- **Shared goals**: when a group aligns around clear, compelling objectives
- **Close listening**: deep attention to others' contributions
- **Yes-and thinking**: building upon rather than blocking others' ideas
- **Equal participation**: balanced input without domination by single voices
- **Familiarity with teammates**: sufficient trust to take creative risks

Educators can design for group flow through carefully structured collaborative activities that incorporate these elements—from scientific investigations to artistic productions to problem-based learning projects.

Assessment Considerations

Traditional assessment approaches can undermine flow by focusing attention on extrinsic rewards rather than intrinsic engagement. However, thoughtfully designed evaluation can actually enhance flow:

- **Process portfolios**: documenting the creative journey, not just final products
- **Real-time feedback**: Providing information for improvement during the creative process
- **Self-assessment**: developing students' ability to evaluate their own work
- **Authentic audiences**: creating for real purposes beyond teacher evaluation

When students understand that assessment serves their growth rather than just measuring compliance, the evaluative dimension becomes part of the creative challenge rather than a flow-disrupting threat.

Developmental Variations

Flow experiences manifest differently across developmental stages. Young children naturally enter flow-like states during play, while adolescents may experience their first profound flow states through athletics, gaming, or artistic pursuits. Understanding these variations helps educators design age-appropriate flow opportunities:

- **Early childhood**: open-ended exploratory play with appropriate challenges embedded

- **Elementary years**: structured challenges with clear rules but multiple solution paths
- **Adolescence**: meaningful challenges connected to emerging identity and values
- **Young adulthood**: complex problems with real-world impact and relevance

By matching flow opportunities to developmental stages, educators can build a progressive sequence of experiences that develop students' capacity for creative engagement.

Systemic Supports for Creative Flow

Individual techniques matter, but environmental and organizational factors are equally important in enabling creative flow. Schools and educational systems can either nurture or inhibit flow-based creativity through their structures and cultures.

- **Time structures**: block scheduling and flexible time allocations allow for deep engagement that traditional forty-five-minute periods make difficult
- **Physical environments**: spaces designed for different modes of work—from collaborative creation to focused individual effort
- **Technological integration**: tools that enhance creative capabilities without introducing constant distraction
- **Community values**: shared understanding of creative process that normalizes both the struggle and the breakthrough moments
- **Leadership modeling**: administrators who demonstrate creative engagement in their own work and decision-making

When teachers themselves experience flow regularly in their professional practice, they naturally become more attuned to creating these conditions for their students. As a good friend of mine says, "You can't teach what you don't live." Professional development that incorporates flow principles doesn't just enhance teacher creativity—it creates a cascade effect throughout the educational ecosystem.

The Future of Flow: Creativity in an AI-Enhanced World

As artificial intelligence reshapes how we work and learn, our capacity for innovative flow states becomes increasingly valuable. While AI excels at certain types of problem-solving, it lacks the embodied, emotional, and intuitive dimensions that characterize human creative flow.

Future-focused educational approaches will explicitly develop the uniquely human capacities that complement rather than compete with artificial intelligence:

- **Divergent possibilities**: generating multiple unconventional approaches to problems
- **Meaningful synthesis**: integrating information across seemingly unrelated domains
- **Aesthetic judgment**: evaluating quality based on subtle qualitative factors
- **Purpose-driven creation**: making things that express values and meaning, not just utility

These capabilities flourish in flow states and represent distinctly human creative contributions even as AI systems evolve. By understanding and cultivating flow, educators aren't just enhancing current learning; they're preparing students for a future where creative human consciousness remains irreplaceable.

In the next chapter, we'll build upon these principles. You'll learn specific strategies for developing sustainable creative practices, from morning routines that prime your brain for creativity to evening rituals that help integrate the day's insights. And we'll look at how successful creators structure their environments, manage their energy, and maintain their creative momentum over the long term. Because ultimately, building a creative life offers learning experiences where flow states become natural expressions of well-established habits.

Key Takeaways

1. Flow states represent optimal conditions for creativity and learning that you can actively cultivate. Apply this by identifying your personal flow triggers and deliberately structuring environments to activate them in your work or classroom.

2. Through neuroplasticity, every creative experience physically reshapes your brain. Put this into practice by establishing consistent creative rituals, knowing that each session builds capacity regardless of immediate outcomes.

3. The balance between persistence and flexibility forms the foundation of creative capability. Apply this by teaching explicit strategies for both pushing through obstacles and recognizing when approaches need to change.

4. You can systematically cultivate flow states through practical techniques like progressive challenge calibration, distraction management, and strategic work cycles that align with your cognitive rhythms.

5. Learning environments can be redesigned around flow principles by implementing specific changes: restructured time blocks, reconfigured physical spaces, and assessment approaches that enhance rather than interrupt creative engagement.

PRACTICE STRATEGY: Yes, And...

In theater and improv, you try to accept the premise suggested by your fellow actors and run with it. You're going to use this strategy to "go with the flow" as you consider new ways of approaching old problems or lessons.

1. Write down one problem that has you stuck or one lesson that you'd like to revamp.
2. What's one thing about this problem or lesson you wish would change? Write this down.
3. Without much thought, write down a possible solution or change you'd make.
4. Immediately below your solution or change, write the word *Yes... and...*
5. Add onto your solution or change. For example, if I wanted to change the beginning of my lesson to include more movement, I could write: "Yes... and... the movement should be in response to directions."
6. Repeat step 5 for as many times as you'd like.
7. When finished, look back at the ideas your mind came up with! Some of these may be useful and others may not. The point is to allow yourself to see what possibilities emerge.

Notes

1. Newsham, G. (2024, July 27). "Twin Towers Tightrope Walker Philippe Petit Recalls Daring Feat 50 Years Later: 'Artistic Crime of the Century.'" *New York Post.* https://nypost.com/2024/07/27/us-news/twin-towers-tightrope-walker-philippe-petit-recalls-daring-feat-50-years-later-artistic-crime-of-the-century/

2. Villines, Z. (2022). "What Is a Flow State and How to Achieve It." Medical News Today. https://www.medicalnewstoday.com/articles/flow-state#flow-vs-hyperfocus

3. Technology Networks. Neuroscience News and Research. (2024, July). "Study Pinpoints Origins of Creativity in the Brain." Technology Networks Neuroscience News and Research. https://www.technologynetworks.com/neuroscience/news/study-pinpoints-origins-of-creativity-in-the-brain-388735

4   Magsamen, S., & Ross, I. (2023). *Your Brain on Art: How the Arts Transform Us.* Random House.

5   Creative Live. (n.d.). "Science of Creativity." https://www.creativelive.com/blog/science-of-creativity/

6   Topolinski, S., & Reber, R. (2010). "Gaining Insight into the "Aha" Experience." *Current Directions in Psychological Science*, 19(6), 402–5. https://doi.org/10.1177/0963721410388803

7   FlowLab. (n.d.). "Neuroplasticity and Flow." https://flowlab.com/en/mental-fitness-blog/neuroplasticity-and-flow-training/

8   Ceria, M. (Host). (2024, June 20). "João Carlos Martins: The Maestro Finds New Hope." (No. 16). [Audio podcast episode]. In *The Loss Encounters*. https://www.thelossencounters.com/episodes/2024-06-20-joao-carlos-martins

9   Chacur, K., Serrat, R., Villar, F., et al. (2024). "'You Must Learn to Age': Reflections on and Adaptations to Age-Related Changes Among Older Artists and Craftspeople." *Population Ageing*, 18(2), 391–414. https://doi.org/10.1007/s12062-024-09466-5

10 Wu, Y., & Koutstaal, W. (2022). "Creative Flexibility and Persistence." *Consciousness and Cognition*, 105, 103410. https://www.sciencedirect.com/science/article/abs/pii/S1053810022001490

11 Almulla, M. A. (2023). "Constructivism Learning Theory: A Paradigm for Students' Critical Thinking, Creativity, and Problem Solving to Affect Academic Performance in Higher Education." *Cogent Education*, 10(1). https://doi.org/10.1080/2331186X.2023.2172929

12 Peterson, T. W. (2020). "The Positive Psychology of Persistence and Flexibility." Dr. Paul Wong. http://www.drpaulwong.com/the-positive-psychology-of-persistence-and-flexibility/

13 Keller, E. F. (1984). *A Feeling for the Organism: The Life and Work of Barbara McClintock.* Henry Holt.

14 Boaler, J. (2016). *Mathematical Mindsets: Unleashing Students' Potential Through Creative Math, Inspiring Messages, and Innovative Teaching.* Jossey-Bass.

6

Cultivating the Creative Habit

> *Chapter Guiding Question: How can we integrate creativity as a regular practice?*

When the Vietnam Veterans Memorial competition launched in 1981, nobody expected a twenty-one-year-old undergraduate to create one of the most powerful commemorative spaces in American history. Yet there was Maya Lin, sitting in her Yale architecture class, surrounded by research about the Vietnam War and the fallen soldiers she hoped to honor for an upcoming class project. Once finished, she submitted her project to the largest design competition in American history. Her black granite design—two walls meeting at a gentle angle, inscribed with the names of more than fifty-eight thousand service members—beat out 1,420 other submissions and forever changed how we experience public memorials.[1]

What visitors to the memorial don't see is the years of daily creative practice that made her design possible. Since childhood, Lin had developed what architect Juhani Pallasmaa calls a "thinking hand"—translating complex emotions into physical form through consistent practice. Growing up in

Athens, Ohio, she spent countless hours in her father's ceramic studio, running her fingers along pottery forms, absorbing how material could express feeling. At home, she built miniature cities from paper and cardboard, creating, destroying, and recreating environments day after day.

What looked like overnight success to the outside world was actually the culmination of a lifetime of deliberate creative practice.

In this chapter, we'll dig into how to make creativity a daily practice rather than an occasional visitor. We'll look at the connection between the mind and body in creative work, uncover behaviors and systems that support creative growth, and learn how to build environments that encourage creative implementation.

Exploring the Connections Between Mind, Body, and Creativity

We've all experienced that moment when the solution appears only after we've stepped away from the problem. You've been staring at your computer for hours, wrestling with a lesson plan that isn't clicking, a presentation that feels flat, or a difficult email you can't seem to write.

Finally, you stand up, stretch, and take a walk. And somehow, in the simple act of moving your body, the solution appears. Almost as if it had been waiting for you to get out of your own way.

This isn't coincidence. It's one of creativity's most overlooked secrets: the profound connection between our physical and mental states.[2] While we often think of creative work as happening solely in our minds, research tells a different story. Creativity lives in our bodies.

Our minds and bodies are connected through an intricate network of nerves, bones, muscles, and blood. And creativity manifests itself across the thoroughfare of these connections. Take walking, for example. Whenever

I'm stuck on a creative project, I will typically leave my desk, put my dog in her harness, and go for a twenty-minute walk around our neighborhood. More often than not, when I come back to the project, I've figured out a way around the creative block. The data tells us this happens a lot. One Stanford University study found that walking increases creative output by up to 60 percent. People who walk, whether on a treadmill or outdoors, generate significantly more creative ideas than those who remain seated.[3] I guess that walking treadmill and standing desk I purchased were good investments after all.

Other studies have shown that people who engage in regular mindful movement practices demonstrate higher levels of creative thinking and develop greater confidence in their creative abilities.[4] Perhaps a weekly yoga class is something you've always wanted to try but have never started because of lack of time or money. Instead, think of that yoga class as an investment in your creative future.

And it's not just big movements that count. Small, purposeful movement can be just as effective for creative and critical thinking. My husband Kevin is neurodivergent and has both dyslexia and attention deficit hyperactivity disorder (ADHD). One of the many ways he works with these learning differences is to keep his hands busy while listening to others speak. This movement allows him to focus and activates his creative thought processes.

Your body and mind move together like dance partners. When one leads, the other follows. Sometimes we need to let our bodies lead the creative process. This might mean

- taking a walk when you're stuck on a lesson plan or curriculum design;
- using your hands to physically manipulate materials while you think through a problem; or
- changing your physical position when you need a new perspective on a challenge.

While small, purposeful movement can jumpstart our creativity, there are instances when we need more than just general movement to really turn on the creative faucet. In her research at Alanus University, Dr. Sabine Koch discovered that specific types of movement directly influence how we think. She found that when people engaged in fluid, expansive movements like those found in dance, they showed increased creative thinking compared to when they made rigid, constrained motions.[5]

The art form of dance is more than simply choreographed movement. Since time began, humans have instinctively used dance as a conduit to both explore and express our feelings, and to shape how we think and create. And when combined with other arts areas like music, visual art, and theater, we begin to lift our humanity into its full power and purpose.

Bringing all areas of the arts holistically into our lives can have a powerful impact not only on our creative potential, but also on our health, well-being, and our capacity to learn new things. When we are actively using our minds and bodies through creative mediums like art, music, theater, or dance, we tend to feel better and do better at both life and work.

I've often been curious about why the arts have this kind of impact, especially in education. We have hundreds of studies that show us the arts make a tangible difference in both student and teacher achievement and well-being.[6] Schools that use arts integration regularly see students' attendance increase and fewer classroom disruptions. Why do the arts make such a difference compared to other approaches?

To understand this, we need to look beyond our brains to our hearts—and I don't mean this metaphorically. I'm talking about your actual heart organ. In education, we hyperfocus on the brain, forgetting that the body is more than just one organ and that the whole body impacts how we learn and process information.

According to researchers at the HeartMath Institute, the connection between our head and our heart isn't a one-way street with the brain simply telling the heart what to do. Instead, it's a two-way dialogue where each organ is communicating with the other. The heart contains its own intrinsic nervous system with both short- and long-term memory functions. What impacts your heart affects memory transfer to your brain.[7] Why is this important?

Think about an intense memory you'll never forget. You probably remember more than just the sequence of events in that memory. You can probably remember how the moment felt, smelled, maybe even tasted.

That's because your heart also remembers that event and has communicated the memory to your brain through nerve impulses, hormones, a pulse wave, or an electromagnetic field. Our most intense experiences imprint themselves onto the heart, which communicates the experience with our mind. This explains why trauma takes such care and time to heal.

This heart-brain connection also explains why the arts so effectively boost learning outcomes. The arts tap directly into our emotions, and an emotion is essentially an arousal of the nervous system. When you listen to music or look at a photograph that moves you, neurotransmitters carry hormonal responses throughout your body, including your brain and heart.[8]

When we learn through the arts, our hearts and minds transfer that knowledge as a whole-body experience.

This impacts both how we approach our own creative work and how we structure learning environments. Educators who have implemented programs that incorporate the arts into their lessons see increased student creativity, improved problem-solving skills, and higher academic achievement. Students engaged in arts-based learning often demonstrate a deeper understanding of the material and greater excitement for learning.

Our creative capacity is not confined to our minds—it lives in every cell of our bodies. By embracing movement as an essential part of creative practice, we not only enhance our own abilities but also model an engaging approach to learning for our students. This happens by moving creative practice from an optional outlet to a daily habit.

Rituals That Stick: Habits to Nurture Creativity

To consistently access and nurture creativity, it must become a reliable habit—a deliberate, integrated practice woven into the fabric of daily life. A habit is more than a repeated action; it's a neural pathway that converts sporadic inspiration into a sustainable approach.[9] Developing a creative habit means intentionally embedding creativity into your routines in ways that engage your entire cognitive and emotional landscape.

For educators, this isn't just about personal growth (though that's valuable). It's a strategic approach to reimagining learning environments. When you cultivate creativity as a habit, you naturally design more engaging, flexible learning experiences. When students are exposed to creativity as a systematic practice, they develop critical skills of resilience, adaptability, and innovative thinking—precisely the capabilities most valued in our rapidly evolving workforce.[10]

Each branch of creativity we explored in chapter 3 requires its own set of habits

- to build technical skills, establish a daily practice routine—like a musician working through scales or a teacher testing different questioning techniques.
- to nurture creative thinking, develop habits of curiosity—reading outside your field or engaging in regular brainstorming sessions.
- for creative expression, maintain a reflection journal or set aside time for experimental work.
- and to strengthen creative application, create habits around project completion and real-world implementation.

Effective habits don't just build skills—they create the conditions for all aspects of creativity to flourish. Let's look at some examples in action.

When Haruki Murakami is writing a novel, he wakes at 4 a.m. and writes for five to six hours straight. He then spends his afternoons running or swimming, activities he uses to maintain the physical stamina needed for creative work. "The repetition itself becomes the important thing," he explains in his memoir, *What I Talk About When I Talk About Running*. "I've written books and stories this way for thirty years. I've run every day for more than twenty years."[11]

Maya Angelou took a different approach but was no less rigorous with her habitual process. She would rent a local hotel room and arrive there at 6:30 a.m., armed with a Bible, a thesaurus, and a bottle of sherry. She'd write until 2 p.m., then go home to edit her work. The hotel room, stripped of distractions, became her creative sanctuary.

"I have kept a hotel room in every town I've ever lived in," she told the *Paris Review* in 1990. "I never allow the hotel people to change the bed.... I only allow them to come in and empty wastebaskets. I insist that all things are taken off the walls. I don't want anything in there. I go into the room and I feel as if all my beliefs are suspended. Nothing holds me to anything (Paris Review, 1990)."

Georgia O'Keeffe started each morning with a walk at sunrise, carefully scanning for rattlesnakes on her New Mexico property. By 7 a.m., she was back for breakfast, and soon after, she'd immerse herself in her studio, painting until noon.

What these diverse approaches share is intentionality and consistency. These creators didn't wait for inspiration to strike—they showed up regularly and created conditions where inspiration was more likely to find them.

One of the most powerful habits you can develop is "mistake mapping." Think of it as turning your creative stumbles into stepping stones. Simply keep a journal or digital note where you document three things about each creative attempt that didn't quite work out:

- What was the original intention?
- What actually happened?
- What insight did this give you?

This practice shifts failure from an emotional setback into a strategic learning opportunity. By documenting intention, outcome, and insight, you move from an emotional reaction to an analytical process. This neutralizes the negative charge of a "failed" attempt and transforms it into valuable data for your next creative endeavor.

The beauty of creative habits is that they can be as unique as you are. Some people find inspiration in early morning solitude, others come alive in the buzz of collaboration. Some need physical movement to spark ideas, and others find clarity in stillness. The key isn't which specific habits you choose—it's finding rituals that resonate with you and practicing them consistently.

Start small. Pick one habit, try it for a week. Keep what works, adjust what doesn't, and gradually build your own collection of creative rituals. Creativity isn't about waiting for lightning to strike—it's about showing up day after day, creating conditions where lightning is more likely to find you.

Five Pillars of Creative Practice: Building Your Support System

When Duncan Wardle stepped into his role as head of innovation and creativity at Disney, he noticed something interesting about consistently creative people. They weren't necessarily the most naturally talented—they were the ones who had developed specific, intentional behaviors that nurtured their creative thinking.[12]

Wardle discovered that habits alone aren't enough—they need to be supported by robust systems and routines. Here are five key pillars that support sustainable creative practice:

1 Daily Rituals: The Power of Small Practices
Research shows that consistent creative rituals don't just help us produce more work—they fundamentally change how your brain approaches creative tasks.

When we engage in specific pre-work rituals, we demonstrate higher levels of cognitive flexibility and original thinking compared to simply diving into work without preparation.[13]

In a high school English classroom, this might look like a teacher playing the same piece of instrumental music while reviewing student writing, creating a mental cue that it's time for creative feedback. An elementary art teacher might rearrange materials in a particular way before developing new project ideas, signaling to her brain that it's creation time. A middle school science teacher uses a brief meditation practice between classes to reset his mental focus.

For our students, this might look like practicing the same morning routine when they enter the classroom during the first week of school. This helps them transition from home to school so they're more ready to learn. It could also look like playing a chime each time a transition happens from one activity to another or moving from one space to another in the room, indicating to the students' brains that it's time to move on to something new.

James Clear, author of *Atomic Habits*, has documented how small rituals create what neuroscientists call "context-dependent memory." His research into habit formation shows that the specific ritual matters less than its consistency. As Clear explains, "The more you ritualize the beginning of a process, the more likely it becomes that you can slip into the state of deep focus that is required to do great things." The consistency creates a psychological container for creative work, signaling to your brain that it's time to shift into a focused state.

The most effective rituals share three key characteristics:

1. They're personalized to your natural rhythms and preferences.
2. They create clear boundaries between "normal" time and creative time.
3. They're simple enough to maintain even under stress.

2 Environmental Design: Crafting Your Creative Space

Surprisingly, the physical environment plays a more significant role in creative productivity than many people realize. Research shows that the design of our workspaces directly impacts our creative output. A 2015 global study of 7,600 office workers found that employees working in environments with natural elements—such as plants, natural light, and views of nature—reported being 15% more creative overall compared to those in environments lacking these features. The research also revealed that layout and interior design emerged as key predictors of workplace creativity, with visual stimulation and collaborative social spaces constituting the most significant physical aspects supporting creative output.[14]

Importantly, the effectiveness of your environment isn't about luxury or Instagram-worthy aesthetics—it's about intentional design that supports your creative habits. Before you start thinking you need to build a Hogwarts-inspired classroom complete with a drawbridge and house cup, think again. Your classroom could have a very minimalistic approach and still provide an environment that is conducive to highly creative habits and learning.

In classroom settings, this might mean designating specific areas for different types of thinking: one space for hands-on exploration and another for reflective thought. For curriculum developers, it could mean creating visual systems for tracking different projects, using color-coding or spatial arrangement to help shift mental gears between tasks.

Research consistently shows that people who implement clear systems for organizing their tools and ideas outperform those who work in chaotic environments. Tidiness itself doesn't spark creativity—but an intentionally designed environment reduces cognitive load and frees up mental energy for creative work.

3 Feedback Loops: Capturing Creative Insights

The most successful innovators aren't distinguished by how many ideas they generate, but by their systematic approach to capturing and reviewing those ideas. People who maintain consistent feedback loops experience breakthrough moments that often lead to new innovations.[15]

That "mistake book" we looked at previously can offer a terrific way to prompt feedback loops and embrace failure as a transporter to success. Paula Scher, one of the most influential graphic designers of our time, shares this: "You have to see where the failure takes you."[16] Sometimes what looks like a mistake in one season becomes the solution to a problem in another.

You can create similar feedback systems in your own work. A fourth-grade teacher might take quick voice memos after trying a new instructional approach to capture immediate reflections before they fade. A high school drama teacher could photograph different stage arrangements during rehearsals to create a visual record for future productions.

Three critical components make feedback loops effective:

1. **Immediate Capture:** the ability to record ideas and observations in the moment they occur

2. **Regular Review:** scheduled time to revisit and reflect on collected insights

3. **Pattern Recognition:** systems for identifying connections between seemingly unrelated ideas

Implementing these components doesn't require complex systems. In fact, simpler systems are more likely to be maintained long-term. Simply having a record to refer back to provides valuable feedback and unexpected inspiration. It also allows you to begin seeing connections between disparate areas that you may have missed earlier.

4 Connection Points: The Power of Cross-Pollination
Here's something that might surprise you: professionals who regularly engage with fields outside their expertise are more likely to make breakthrough innovations in their own work.[17] The most creative solutions often come from

what researchers call "distant analogies"—applying principles from one field to solve problems in another.

I've watched this play out in schools across the country. Elementary music teachers who spend time with the math department discover new ways to think about patterns and rhythm. High school history teachers who explore theater techniques find fresh approaches to historical storytelling. Principals who establish regular cross-disciplinary meetings create environments where teachers share challenges and brainstorm solutions from different perspectives.

One of my favorite examples comes from the unexpected collaboration between musician Brian Eno and painter Peter Schmidt in 1975. Their chance meeting led to the creation of "Oblique Strategies," a deck of cards containing random prompts that transformed creative problem-solving across industries. What began as a personal tool for breaking through creative blocks has influenced everyone from David Bowie to the world's top tech innovators.

The path to creative success isn't becoming a jack-of-all-trades; it's becoming a master of connection—someone who can see patterns and possibilities where others see only boundaries. Create your own connection points by

- joining a monthly book club that reads outside your field;
- taking a class in something completely different from your primary work;
- setting up coffee dates with people from diverse professional backgrounds;
- creating an inspiration wall where you collect images, quotes, and ideas from various sources; or
- regularly observing practices in different subject areas or domains.

You can build these connections into classroom practice through simple creative thinking routines. These are a set of questions, or a brief sequence of steps, used to scaffold and support student thinking. Harvard's *Project Zero* provides a series of thinking routines across ten categories that can be used as entry points into learning, deepen discussion, or close a unit by reflecting on key concepts.[18]

5 Recovery Periods: The Art of Strategic Rest

The most innovative minds aren't those who work the longest hours, but those who understand the value of deliberate rest. In our productivity-obsessed culture, rest has become almost a radical act. But for those who value creativity, strategic downtime isn't laziness—it's a sophisticated cognitive tool.

Creative insights often arise during periods of mental rest—not through forceful concentration, but through strategic disengagement. When we allow our minds to wander, we create the neural space for breakthrough thinking.[19]

I've seen this in schools where administrators build short breaks between meetings and find the pauses lead to better decision-making. Or teachers who step away from lesson planning to take a brief walk and return with fresh approaches to instructional challenges. These aren't lucky coincidences—they're evidence of our brain's strategic recovery processes at work.

Strategic rest is about creating structured, intentional periods of cognitive recovery with ideas like these:

Cognitive Detachment Techniques

- Scheduling deliberate "unfocus" time in your day
- Practicing mindfulness meditation
- Engaging in physical activities that require minimal cognitive load

Creative Incubation Strategies

- Keeping a notebook for capturing post-rest insights
- Creating transition rituals between work and rest periods
- Experimenting with different rest modalities: walking, napping, creative hobbies

Environment Design for Recovery

- Creating dedicated spaces that signal mental reset

- Minimizing digital distractions during rest periods
- Using natural environments to support cognitive recovery

Rest is a necessary part of productivity and creativity. By using strategic recovery, we transition rest from a passive state into an active creative practice. Your brain is constantly working, even (maybe especially) when you think it's not. The most powerful creative insights often occur not through grinding effort, but through graceful surrender.

Building Environments to Encourage Creative Implementation: The 20 Percent Rule

In the summer of 2004, Google launched a small experiment that would reshape how we think about creativity in the workplace. Larry Page and Sergey Brin introduced the 20 percent rule, designed to create intentional space for exploration: engineers could spend one-fifth of their work time on projects completely of their own choosing.

The 20 percent rule is fundamentally about designing environments—both physical and systemic—that give creativity room to breathe. It's a recognition that innovation doesn't happen through constant grinding, but through deliberate, structured exploration.

At Google, this practice encouraged engineers to test ideas beyond their day-to-day responsibilities. While many projects gained traction through this spirit of exploration, not all of the company's iconic products were born directly from 20 percent time. For instance, Paul Buchheit created Gmail as part of his official role, though its culture of experimentation helped it grow into an email service now used by more than 1.8 billion people worldwide. Likewise, the concept that became AdSense was sparked through internal experimentation and later formalized into a system that would generate billions in revenue.

Google wasn't the first to recognize the power of margins; 3M had been practicing a similar approach since the 1940s, allowing employees to spend 15 percent of their time on passion projects. This policy led to innovations like Post-it Notes[20]—those teacher-treasured stickies came to us from an employee's curious exploration not some structured market research initiative.

Designing Creative Margins: Organizational Strategies

Creating margin isn't about working less. It's about working differently. Organizations that successfully implement margin time share several key characteristics:[21]

Structured Flexibility: Successful margin programs aren't completely unstructured. They provide clear guidelines:

- Specific time allocation (15–20 percent of work time)
- Expectations for documentation and potential implementation
- Mechanisms for sharing and evaluating creative explorations

Psychological Safety: Dr. Amy Edmondson's research on organizational psychology reveals that margin time requires more than just allocated hours. It needs an environment where the following occurs:

- Failure is seen as a learning opportunity
- Experimental thinking is encouraged
- People feel safe exploring unconventional ideas

Cross-Pollination Mechanisms: The most innovative margin programs create systems for sharing insights:

- Regular showcase events
- Collaborative platforms for sharing discoveries
- Opportunities for cross-departmental exploration

In schools, this might mean creating "innovation exchanges" where educators share experimental teaching approaches. Or it could mean establishing "classroom labs" where new instructional strategies can be tested in low-stakes environments before broader implementation.

Classroom Applications of Creative Margins

Genius Hour or 20 percent Time: Dedicate one class period per week (or 20 percent of a longer block) where students pursue passion projects related to the subject. For example:

- *Elementary*: Friday afternoon "Wonder Workshop" where students explore questions they've generated
- *Middle School*: "Innovation Lab" where students apply class concepts to solve real-world problems
- *High School*: "Deep Dive Sessions" where students explore specialized topics within the curriculum

Establish Structured Guidelines:

- *Create clear parameters*: projects must connect to learning standards, but students choose how
- *Develop checkpoints*: weekly progress journals, monthly "pitch meetings" to share developments
- *Design reflection tools*: simple templates where students document their process and learning

Building Psychological Safety:

- *Model productive failure*: share your own creative experiments that didn't work as planned

- *Create "idea prototyping" spaces*: whiteboards or digital spaces where rough ideas are welcomed
- *Use "yes, and" protocols*: teach students to build on each other's ideas rather than criticizing
- *Implement "soft deadlines"*: allow revisions and iterations without grade penalties

Enhance Cross-Pollination Opportunities:

- *"Gallery walks"*: where students visit and provide feedback on each other's in-progress work
- *Cross-grade partnerships*: where older students mentor younger ones on creative projects
- *"Expert panels"*: where students present solutions to authentic audiences (other classes, community members)
- *Digital showcase platforms*: where students can share their work and receive feedback

Personal Margin Design: Creating Your Creative Infrastructure

You don't need organizational permission to implement margin time in your own life. Many educators and professionals create their own infrastructure for creativity regardless of external structures or official policies. Productivity researcher Michael Hyatt frames this as moving beyond finding time to designing systems that prioritize creative exploration. It's the difference between hoping creativity might visit and creating conditions where it feels welcome to stay.

Let's get practical about implementation. Start by scheduling dedicated exploration time in your calendar—even 30 minutes weekly makes a difference. This isn't about hoping you'll "find time" (we never find what we're not actively looking for); it's about declaring that this time matters enough to protect. Many educators use the first portion of their planning period on a specific day as sacred "idea time," turning off notifications, closing their door, and focusing solely on exploring new teaching approaches.

Next, create physical and digital spaces specifically for idea capture. Think of these as idea traps—places where your fleeting insights can land rather than vanish into the ether. This might be a small notebook in your pocket, a dedicated app on your phone, or even a voice memo system for those ideas that strike while driving. The medium matters less than the habit of immediately capturing sparks before they fade.

Develop rituals that signal to your brain that it's time to shift into creative mode. Our brains love patterns and respond to consistent cues. Maybe it's a specific tea you brew before curriculum planning, a particular playlist that signals it's brainstorming time, or simply rearranging your physical space in a certain way. These are the neurological primers that help your brain transition into creative states more efficiently.

Finally, design low-stakes experimentation environments where you can play without pressure. Creativity withers under judgment. Create spaces—physical or temporal—where you can test ideas without immediately evaluating them. Many curriculum developers maintain what they might call a "curriculum sandbox"—a digital folder where they play with new instructional approaches before deciding which to develop further.

When we operate without margins, we're essentially running our creative engine at 100 percent capacity all the time—which inevitably leads to burnout and diminished innovation. It's like driving a car with the gas pedal pressed to the floor without ever allowing for maintenance. Eventually, something breaks down.

The Pareto Principle suggests that 80 percent of effects come from 20 percent of causes.[22] In creative margin time, this translates to a powerful insight: a small, intentionally designed portion of your time can produce breakthrough innovations.

Overcoming Challenges in Implementing Margins

Knowing that we need to add in creative margin and actually doing so in the real world are completely different. Let's address the very real challenges that make creative margins feel impossible in our already overcrowded lives.

Time constraints top the list for most educators. Between lesson planning, grading, meetings, and actual teaching, finding even 20 minutes for creative exploration can feel impossibly luxurious. Start by ruthlessly prioritizing. What tasks currently filling your schedule don't actually need your attention, could be streamlined, or might be delegated? Remember: saying yes to creative margin means saying no to something else. Make those choices consciously rather than letting circumstances choose for you.

Consider combining activities when possible. Your commute, exercise routine, or even household chores can become opportunities for creative input if not output. Listen to podcasts from different fields while driving. Use walking time to mentally explore teaching challenges from new angles. These aren't perfect solutions, but they create space for the cross-pollination of ideas even when dedicated margin time remains elusive.

Cultural expectations present another significant barrier, particularly in educational environments that value visible busyness over reflective practice. When colleagues or administrators question your "thinking time," be prepared to communicate its value in terms that resonate with organizational priorities. Share specific examples of how margin time can lead to instructional innovations or improved student outcomes. The language of results often persuades where philosophical arguments fall flat.

More importantly, lead by example. When you protect creative margins and produce innovative results, you create permission for others to do the same. Educational leaders who intentionally block time for "innovation development" can shift departmental culture when teachers see the quality of curriculum emerging from this protected time.

Perhaps the most insidious barrier is our own personal resistance—that inner voice questioning whether we "deserve" creative time when so many urgent tasks clamor for attention. Challenge this guilt directly. Creative margin isn't self-indulgence; it's strategic investment in your professional capacity and sustainability. Would you question the value of maintaining equipment in a factory? Your creative mind deserves at least the same maintenance consideration.

If guilt still lingers, start small. Even five minutes of deliberate creative attention creates value. Begin with these micro-margins and gradually expand as you experience their benefits firsthand. Like building any habit, consistent small steps often prove more sustainable than dramatic overhauls that quickly collapse under their own ambition.

As we prepare to explore how creativity becomes a competitive edge, remember that your most groundbreaking ideas are waiting in the margins. Implementing even ten minutes of margin time in your own day—perhaps during lunch or a planning period—can yield unexpected insights into classroom management or differentiation strategies. Margin isn't about doing less—it's about creating space for something more.

Applying Creative Thinking Practices: The Mosaic Method

Once you've made space for creativity through margins and built structures to support creative thinking, the next challenge becomes applying these practices—especially when connecting across different areas. While unstructured exploration has its place, many people benefit from frameworks that guide their thinking without constraining it.

Enter the Mosaic Method, a deceptively simple yet powerful framework for connecting ideas across seemingly unrelated domains. Developed by my team and me at the Institute for Arts Integration and STEAM, this four-step process

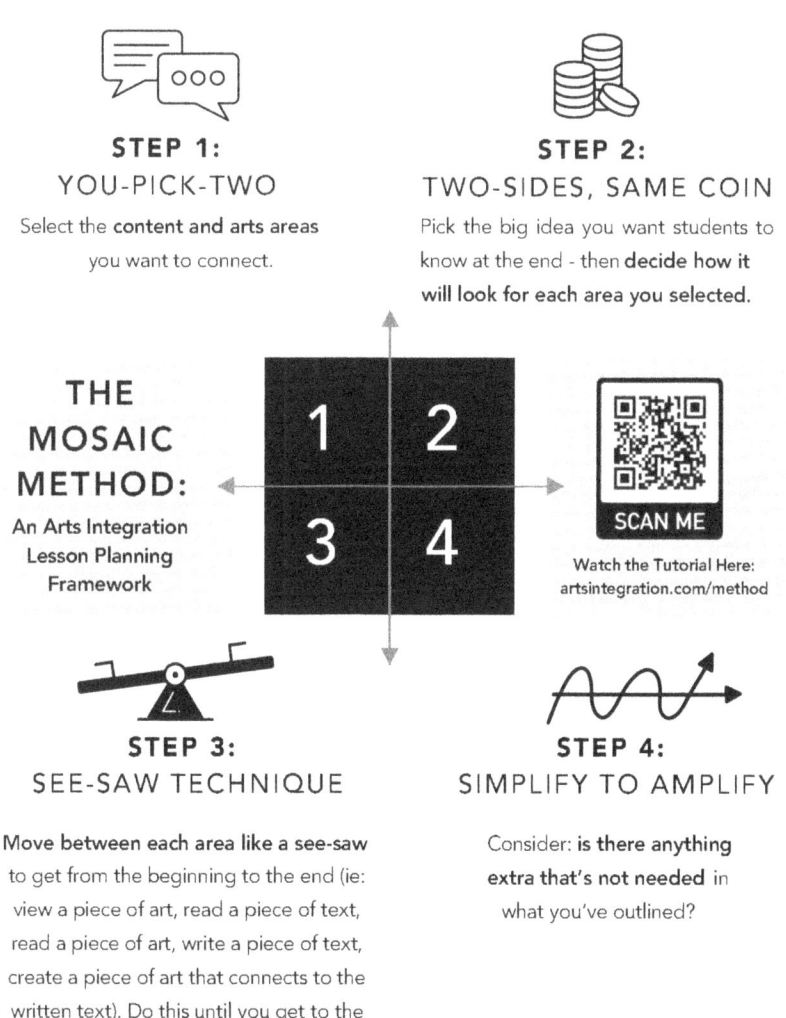

FIGURE 6.1

helps us rethink problem-solving and creative exploration. While originally designed for educators integrating arts into the curriculum, its principles apply to any creative endeavor.

Step 1: You-Pick-Two

The first step is about intentional connection. Just as a mosaic artist selects different tiles to create a broader image, you choose two areas that might not immediately seem related. This could be anything from "fractions and music" to "World War II and photography"—the key is finding unexpected bridges between domains.

Astronaut and scientist Dr. Mae Jemison describes arts and science as "two sides of the same coin"—a concept that perfectly captures this method's core philosophy. By deliberately choosing two disparate areas, you create fertile ground for innovative thinking.

Step 2: Two-Sides, Same Coin

Here's where the magic happens. You define the ultimate goal or "big idea" you want to explore. What's the core insight you're seeking? This becomes your metaphorical coin—with content and creative approach representing its two sides.

For instance, if exploring World War II through photography, your coin might be understanding how visual storytelling reveals historical narratives. The content side explores specific battle details, while the arts side examines photographic techniques.

Step 3: The See-Saw Technique

Imagine learning as a dynamic, back-and-forth movement. You don't simply teach content or artistic skill in isolation. Instead, you continuously shift between domains, allowing each to inform and illuminate the other.

A typical see-saw might look like this:

- View a historical photograph.
- Analyze its compositional elements.
- Read a text about the historical context.
- Create a new interpretation through artistic practice.
- Reflect on how the process changed understanding.

Step 4: Simplify to Amplify

Creativity isn't about complexity—it's about clarity. This final step involves ruthlessly eliminating unnecessary elements. As the method's creators note, educators often "throw the kitchen sink" at projects. The goal is creating the most direct path to meaningful insight.

Putting the Steps Together

Implementing the Mosaic Method as a part of your creative process is simple. Here's how:

- Select two seemingly unrelated domains (e.g., mathematics and dance).
- Identify a core concept that connects them (e.g., patterns).
- Create a learning journey that alternates between both domains (mathematical pattern analysis → choreographic pattern creation → mathematical evaluation).
- Strip away unnecessary complexity to focus on key connections.
- Reflect on new insights generated through this cross-domain approach.

Try this for yourself using the template found here in figure 6.2:

THE MOSAIC METHOD PLANNER

STEP 1:
YOU-PICK-TWO

Content:

Arts Area:

STEP 2:
TWO-SIDES, SAME COIN

This is your coin!

What **big idea** do you want students to know **by the end**?

How does this big idea appear in the content area?

How does this big idea appear in the arts area?

STEP 3:
SEE-SAW TECHNIQUE

List your steps (going back and forth between content and arts areas) until you get to your coin:

STEP 4:
SIMPLIFY TO AMPLIFY

Is there anything that is making this too complicated and can be cut out? If so, list it here and eliminate:

The Institute for Arts Integration and STEAV, 2024. Artsintegration.com

FIGURE 6.2

Beyond Arts Integration: The Mosaic Method as a Creative Thinking Tool

While originally designed for educational contexts, the Mosaic Method offers a universal approach to creative problem-solving:

- **Interdisciplinary Connection:** By forcing connections between seemingly unrelated domains, you train your brain to think more flexibly. This is crucial in an age of AI, where human creativity means making unexpected links.
- **Structured Exploration:** The method provides a framework that prevents creative paralysis. Instead of waiting for inspiration, you create a systematic approach to generating innovative ideas.
- **Cognitive Flexibility:** Moving between different domains builds neural pathways. Each "see-saw" movement challenges your brain to think differently, increasing cognitive adaptability.

Practical Applications

Here are some ideas for bringing the Mosaic Method into your teaching practice:

- **Science + Storytelling**: Students learn about the water cycle by creating stories from a water droplet's perspective, combining scientific facts with narrative elements. They create comic strips showing the droplet's journey through evaporation, condensation, and precipitation.
- **Math + Music**: Students explore fractions through rhythm, creating musical patterns that represent different fraction relationships (quarter notes, eighth notes, etc.). They compose short pieces that demonstrate understanding of both mathematical concepts and musical structure.

- **History + Visual Arts**: Students studying the Civil Rights Movement analyze protest photography techniques, then create their own visual representations of historical events using similar compositional principles.
- **Geography + Poetry**: Students study landforms and climate regions while learning about descriptive language and imagery. They create poems that accurately represent the scientific characteristics of different biomes while using literary devices.
- **Literature + Physical Education**: Students reading "The Odyssey" design a physical obstacle course that represents Odysseus's journey, with each station requiring both physical challenges and knowledge of the text.
- **Coding + Social Studies**: Students create simple programs that simulate historical trade routes, combining their understanding of economic systems with computational thinking.
- **Chemistry + Design**: Students studying molecular structures create 3D models that are both scientifically accurate and aesthetically considered, explaining both the chemical properties and their design choices.
- **Economics + Performing Arts**: Students create theatrical scenarios that demonstrate complex economic principles like supply and demand, market competition, or economic inequality.
- **Statistics + Journalism**: Students analyze data sets on community issues, then create journalistic pieces that accurately represent the statistical findings while telling compelling human stories.

This method isn't restricted to just the classroom, either. Here are some other examples of how the Mosaic Method can be used in your daily life as well:

Professional Development

- **Data Analysis + Storytelling**: Combine statistical insights with narrative techniques to make presentations more engaging. Instead of just sharing numbers, craft a story that gives context and meaning to the data.

- **Strategic Planning + Visual Thinking**: Map out business goals using visual frameworks borrowed from art composition. Create vision boards that combine analytical goals with creative visual representation.
- **Technical Documentation + User Experience**: When writing technical materials, apply principles from consumer psychology to make them more user-friendly and accessible.

Personal Growth:

- **Fitness + Productivity**: Design workout routines based on work productivity cycles. Match high-intensity interval training with project sprint methodologies, creating parallel physical and mental work patterns.
- **Cooking + Cultural Study**: Explore a different culture's cuisine while learning about its history and traditions. Create meals that represent historical periods or cultural movements.
- **Gardening + Mental Health**: Design garden spaces based on psychological principles of stress reduction and attention restoration. Create specific zones for different cognitive states (reflection, creativity, focus).

Home Life:

- **Home Organization + Psychology**: Arrange living spaces based on flow psychology, designing rooms that support specific mental states or family interactions.
- **Family Traditions + Learning**: Create family rituals that combine celebration with skill development. For example, holiday cooking that incorporates both cultural traditions and opportunities to learn new cooking techniques.
- **Budgeting + Game Design**: Transform financial planning into a game with levels, challenges, and rewards, applying game mechanics to practical financial goals.

Innovation doesn't happen in silos. It emerges in the spaces between—in the unexpected connections we're brave enough to explore.

Reflection Exercises to Expand and Level Up

Consistent, structured reflection documents creative experiences while actively creating new cognitive pathways. It's not the quantity of reflection that matters, but the quality—structured, intentional practices that move beyond simple documentation to genuine insight generation.[23]

Effective Reflection Techniques

Ready to add more active reflection to your creative mix? Here are some techniques to get you started.[24]

Journaling with Purpose

Journaling isn't about documenting every mundane detail. It's about creating a dialogue with yourself. Specific reflection prompts can transform a simple notebook into a powerful creative development tool:

- "What surprised me today?"
- "Where did I feel most/least creative?"
- "What obstacle did I transform into an opportunity?"

Mind Mapping

Visual representation can unlock insights that linear writing might miss. Create mind maps that

- trace the evolution of an idea,
- explore connections between seemingly unrelated concepts, and
- visualize your creative journey

Creative Interviews

Schedule monthly "creative check-ins" with yourself. Prepare questions as if you were interviewing a fascinating colleague about their creative process:

- What's working in my current approach?
- Where am I feeling stuck?
- What experiment do I want to try next?

Performance Review for Creativity

Treat your creative practice like a professional development opportunity. Create a quarterly self-assessment that includes the following:

- Creative goals achieved
- Skills developed
- Challenges encountered
- Unexpected learnings

Practical Implementation

In her work on innovation and entrepreneurship, Stanford professor Tina Seelig has documented a powerful approach to systematic reflection, which she calls "failure résumés."

Unlike traditional résumés that showcase successes, Seelig maintains detailed records of projects that didn't work, grants she didn't receive, and approaches that fell short of expectations. This documentation practice helped shape her influential creativity curriculum at Stanford, where students learn to view setbacks as data points rather than personal shortcomings.[25]

You can adapt this reflection practice to your own work. Music teachers might document approaches to teaching rhythm that didn't connect with students. Science teachers could track experiments that yielded unexpected results. English teachers might record discussion techniques that fell flat. By systematically documenting these experiences rather than trying to forget them, you build a personal knowledge base that yields insights for future work.

This approach transforms failure from a dead end into a strategic resource. Each "failed" idea becomes potential fuel for future innovation. Creating systems that capture these experiences objectively, without self-judgment, turns disappointments into valuable data rather than sources of frustration.

Creating a Reflection Environment

The environment for reflection is as crucial as the practice itself. For reflection to happen naturally, we need to design a space that invites introspection and creativity—a place where you can release, relax, and review your work with both compassion and curiosity.

For a while, my brother Andy had his home office in his basement. It constantly felt like he was headed "down to the hole" to work, with no windows and only harsh fluorescent lighting. Once he moved his desk upstairs to an open space flooded with natural light, he noticed an immediate improvement in both his mood and productivity.

Our physical surroundings have a direct influence on our cognitive processes. Exposure to natural light, views of greenery, or even indoor plants can reduce cognitive stress and enhance creative thinking. A reflection space might include a comfortable chair positioned near a window, soft natural lighting, and minimal technological distractions.

The rituals we create around our reflection space become as important as the space itself. Some creators light a specific candle, others brew a particular type of tea. These are neurological triggers that signal to our brains: "Now is the time for deep thinking."

Keep in mind, reflection happens after the creative work is complete. Trying to reflect on your creative work while you're creating will only hold you back. Allow yourself the freedom to create without worrying about whether it's any good. Then, review your work with the mindset that reflection isn't about judgment, but about understanding. It's the bridge between experience and innovation.

Throughout this chapter, we've explored the external scaffolding that allows innovative thinking to flourish. The journey begins with simple habits, sustained by thoughtful systems, and continually refreshed through reflective practice. These foundations are essential, but they're only part of the story. As you implement these approaches, you'll begin to notice patterns in how you specifically navigate the creative process.

Each of us has a unique creative fingerprint—a distinctive way of perceiving challenges, processing information, and generating solutions. In the next chapter, we'll explore how to identify your personal creative strengths, preferences, and patterns. You'll discover your individual creative code—the specific combination of thinking styles, environmental needs, and collaborative approaches that unlock your highest creative potential.

By understanding your unique creative makeup, you'll be able to customize the practices we've explored here, creating a creative ecosystem tailored precisely to your needs. This personal roadmap will help you navigate creative challenges with greater confidence and flexibility, while strengthening your capacity to bring innovative thinking to both your professional practice and personal growth.

Key Takeaways

1. Creativity is a habit that can be cultivated through intentional practices of mind-body connection, systematic exploration, and deliberate margin creation.

2. The most innovative thinking emerges not from constant focus, but from creating intentional spaces for exploration, rest, and unexpected connections.

3. By using frameworks like the Mosaic Method, we can systematically break down traditional thinking barriers and generate novel ideas across seemingly unrelated domains.

4. Reflection is not passive documentation, but an active process of decoding experiences, identifying patterns, and transforming insights into actionable creative potential.

5. In an age of artificial intelligence, our most distinctly human creative advantage lies in our ability to make unexpected connections, embrace uncertainty, and continuously reimagine possibilities.

PRACTICE STRATEGY: Playlist

Time to create a soundtrack that represents you and your unique life experiences.

1. Before you begin to create your playlist, think about your life's journey so far.
    a. Does there seem to be a common theme emerging?
    b. What are some major life events that you've experienced?
    c. Are there songs that could represent those events?

2. Begin to form a list of songs that could help you tell your unique story. Think about what it is about the song that appeals to you.
    a. Are there any specific lines in the song that you relate to?
    b. Do you just like the beat or the melody?
    c. Does it make you think of a certain person, place, or memory?

3. Create a playlist of ten to twelve songs that will best tell your story up to now. Include the name of the song and the recording artist, and a short explanation of why you chose it.

Notes

1. Academy of Achievement. (n.d.). "Maya Lin." *American Academy of Achievement.* https://achievement.org/achiever/maya-lin/

2. Wasser, F. (2015, November 10). "Creativity and the Mind-Body Connection." KNPR's State of Nevada. https://knpr.org/show/knprs-state-of-nevada/2015-11-11/creativity-and-the-mind-body-connection

3. Oppezzo, M., & Schwartz, D. L. (2014). "Give Your Ideas Some Legs: The Positive Effect of Walking on Creative Thinking." *Journal of Experimental Psychology: Learning, Memory, and Cognition*, 40(4), 1142–52. https://doi.org/10.1037/xlm0000027

4. Huang, L. (2021, August 11). "How 'Mind-Body Dissonance' Leads to Creative Thinking." INSEAD Knowledge. https://knowledge.insead.edu/leadership-organisations/how-mind-body-dissonance-leads-creative-thinking

5. Koch, S. C., Riege, R. F. F., Tisborn, K., Biondo, J., Martin, L., & Beelmann, A. (2019). "Effects of Dance Movement Therapy and Dance on Health-Related Psychological Outcomes. A Meta-Analysis Update." *Frontiers in Psychology*, 10, 1806. https://doi.org/10.3389/fpsyg.2019.01806

6. Aloizou, V., Linardatou, S., Boloudakis, M., & Retalis, S. (2024). "Integrating a Movement-Based Learning Platform as Core Curriculum Tool in Kindergarten Classrooms." *British Journal of Educational Technology*, 55(1), 78–97. https://doi.org/10.1111/bjet.13511

7. HeartMath Institute. (n.d.). "Heart-Brain Communication." https://www.heartmath.org/research/science-of-the-heart/heart-brain-communication/

8. Barnett KS, Vasiu F. (2024, October 2). "How the Arts Heal: A Review of the Neural Mechanisms Behind the Therapeutic Effects of Creative Arts on Mental and Physical Health." *Front Behav Neurosci*. 18:1422361. doi: 10.3389/fnbeh.2024.1422361. PMID: 39416439; PMCID: PMC11480958.

9. Clear, J. (n.d.). "The Habits Guide: How to Build Good Habits and Break Bad Ones." James Clear. https://jamesclear.com/habits

10. Booth, E. (n.d.). "The Habits of Mind of Creative Engagement." Eric Booth. https://ericbooth.net/the-habits-of-mind-of-creative-engagement/

11. Murakami, H. (2008). *What I Talk About When I Talk About Running: A Memoir.* Alfred A. Knopf.

12. Duncan, W. (n.d.). "Seven Behaviors That Will Unleash Your Creativity." Duncan Wardle. https://duncanwardle.com/seven-behaviors-that-will-unleash-your-creativity-2

13. Schrager, S., & Sadowski, E., (2016). "Getting More Done: Strategies to Increase Scholarly Productivity." *Journal of Graduate Medical Education*, 8(1), 10–13. https://meridian.allenpress.com/jgme/article/8/1/10/201041/Getting-More-Done-Strategies-to-Increase-Scholarly

14. McCoy, J. M., & Evans, G. W. (2002). "The Potential Role of the Physical Environment in Fostering Creativity." *Creativity Research Journal*, 14(3–4), 409–26. https://doi.org/10.1207/S15326934CRJ1434_11

15. Fransz, R. (2022). "How Systems Thinking Unlocked More Creativity Than I Could Ever Dream Of." UX Magazine. https://uxmag.com/articles/how-systems-thinking-unlocked-more-creativity-than-i-could-ever-dream-o

16. Dixit, J. (2009, May 21). "Paula Scher on Failure." *Psychology Today*. https://www.psychologytoday.com/us/blog/brainstorm/200905/paula-scher-failure

17. Ho, E., Jeon, M., Lee, M., Luo, J., Pfammatter, A., Shetty, V., & Spring, B. (2021). "Fostering Interdisciplinary Collaboration: A Longitudinal Social Network Analysis of the NIH mHealth Training Institutes." *Journal of Clinical and Translational Science*, 5(1), 1–36. https://10.1017/cts.2021.859

18. Project Zero. (n.d.). "PZ's Thinking Routines Toolbox." Harvard Graduate School of Education. https://pz.harvard.edu/thinking-routines

19. Pressfield, S. (2016). *The Artist's Journey*. Black Irish Entertainment LLC.

20. Goetz, K. (2011, February 1). "How 3M Gave Everyone Days Off and Created an Innovation Dynamo." Fast Company. https://www.fastcompany.com/1663137/how-3m-gave-everyone-days-off-and-created-an-innovation-dynamo

21. Chae, H., & Park, J. (2020). "The Effects of Routinization on Radical and Incremental Creativity." National Center for Biotechnology Information. https://www.ncbi.nlm.nih.gov/pmc/articles/PMC9967832/

22. Guy-Evans, O. (2022). "Pareto Principle (The 80-20 Rule): Examples and More." Simply Psychology. https://www.simplypsychology.org/pareto-principle.html

23. Blondin, H. (2020, October 27). "The Importance of Creative Reflection." Holly Blondin. https://hollyblondin.com/466/the-importance-of-creative-reflection

24. Brown, N. (n.d.). "Using Creative Methods to Reflect." Nicole Brown. https://www.nicole-brown.co.uk/creative-reflections/

25. Seelig, T. (2016, March 2). "The Secret Sauce of Silicon Valley." Medium. https://tseelig.medium.com/the-secret-sauce-of-silicon-valley-535a7dd11858

PART FOUR

THE OFFERING

7

The Creative Edge

> *Chapter Guiding Question: How can we thoughtfully and intentionally fuse all of these ideas about creativity together?*

By the late 1980s, Japan's Shinkansen trains zoomed across the countryside as some of the fastest in the world. Yet they had a serious flaw—whenever they exited a tunnel, they created a thunderous boom that echoed for a quarter mile. The trains' blunt-nosed design compressed air ahead of them like a piston as they sped through tunnels. When they finally emerged, the built-up air exploded outward with a disruptive crack that rattled nearby communities.

For Eiji Nakatsu, this wasn't just a technical headache. As a lead engineer at Japan Railways and an avid birdwatcher, he saw it as a creative puzzle begging for a solution outside conventional engineering wisdom.

Nakatsu didn't crack open research papers or engineering textbooks for inspiration. Instead, he turned to something seemingly unrelated: nature. Specifically, he looked at the kingfisher, a bird that dives from air into water with barely a splash. The kingfisher's uniquely shaped beak allows it to transition between elements with minimal resistance.

Could the same principle work for a train moving from a tunnel into open air?

Nakatsu and his team began testing designs that mimicked the kingfisher's beak. The result transformed train travel: the aerodynamically designed nose eliminated the tunnel boom while also reducing air resistance, allowing the train to run 10 percent faster while using 15 percent less energy.[1]

As artificial intelligence increasingly masters individual domains, this uniquely human ability to forge meaningful connections across disciplines becomes our greatest advantage. Whether in medicine, technology, business, or the classroom, breakthrough innovations increasingly spring from those who thoughtfully integrate diverse fields of knowledge and experience.[2]

This chapter explores how to cultivate this integrative creativity—a sustainable practice that gives us a genuine edge in an AI-driven world. We'll decode your own creative patterns, develop a competitive edge through creative thinking, and navigate common obstacles that block our progress. Most importantly, we'll explore how to thoughtfully weave together everything we've learned about creativity into a cohesive approach that works specifically for you.

Cracking Your Unique Creative Code

Your creative mind works like a combination lock. There's no universal code—each person's lock opens differently. Yet too often, we force ourselves into someone else's creative process, then wonder why we can't produce breakthrough ideas on demand.

One of the most damaging myths we tell ourselves is that some problems require creativity while others just need logical thinking. This artificial divide doesn't just limit our creative potential—it blinds us to opportunities for innovation. Creativity isn't a fixed skill you use in some situations and shelve in others. It shifts depending on the challenge, proving that every problem— no matter how logical it seems—has room for creative solutions.

Finding solutions through unexpected connections isn't just a happy accident. Research shows several key elements that innovative problem-solvers share:

1 Pattern Transfer

Pattern transfer involves looking for similar patterns in unrelated fields rather than trying to solve problems from scratch. Professionals who regularly explore fields outside their expertise solve problems more efficiently than those who stay within their domain.[3] For educators, this might mean studying business management strategies to develop more innovative classroom systems or examining design thinking to reimagine curriculum development.

2 Constraint Reframing

Constraint reframing means treating limitations as creative catalysts rather than obstacles. Teams that deliberately work within constraints often generate more innovative solutions than those without boundaries. We see this in schools with limited resources, where educators develop new approaches to teaching precisely because constraints force creative adaptation.

3 Solution Archaeology

Solution archaeology involves examining how similar problems have been solved in different contexts before seeking new solutions. Breakthrough innovations often come from adapting existing solutions from unexpected places. This explains why educational approaches borrowed from other cultures can revitalize American classrooms, or why healthcare protocols adapted from aviation safety transform patient outcomes.

These elements and applications extend far beyond traditional "creative" fields. When hospital teams apply choreography principles to emergency room flow patterns, they reduce wait times. When manufacturing plants use music theory to analyze assembly line rhythms, productivity increases. While these aren't traditional creative challenges, the solutions come from creative thinking.

Understanding your creative code means recognizing your natural problem-solving patterns and having the courage to follow them, even when they lead you down unexpected paths. As our world becomes increasingly automated, this ability to make unexpected connections and trust our unique problem-solving patterns becomes even more crucial.

Understanding Your Creative Patterns

One way to crack your creative code is to look for clues from your own past breakthroughs. This helps you unveil the creative patterns that impact your work over time. Author James Clear suggests that these patterns are highly individual—what works for one person may completely block another.[4] To find what works for you, look at the following:

Environment

Your physical surroundings actively participate in your creative process, not just serving as background noise. These factors subtly rewire our thinking and perceptions so seamlessly that we rarely even notice.

Some teachers discover their best curriculum ideas in silent classrooms after the last student leaves, when the energy of the day still lingers but the demands have subsided. Others find their creative spark ignites during the controlled chaos of faculty meetings where different perspectives collide, or while supervising recess as they observe students' natural learning patterns in unstructured play.

State of Mind

Your state of mind creates conditions where ideas either flow or stagnate. Your emotional and mental state acts as a "creative possibilities" filter.

Many educators find their creative edge sharpens under pressure—the looming deadline of an upcoming observation or lesson plan pushes their thinking beyond comfortable patterns. Others find pressure shuts down their creative faculties entirely. These folks produce their best work during the relaxed atmosphere of summer or quarterly planning blocks when expanded time horizons allow ideas to develop naturally.

What matters here is recognizing which mental and emotional conditions open your particular creative channels.

Social Context

Social context determines whether connections happen within your mind or between minds.[5] The presence or absence of others can alter how ideas form and develop.

Many teachers experience creative breakthroughs during collaborative planning sessions, where the friction between different perspectives generates possibilities they wouldn't have considered on their own. This could be something as simple as weekly forty-minute "Thursday Thinks" sessions where educators bring teaching challenges for group exploration.

Others need solitude to process and integrate ideas, finding that conversations provide raw material that must be refined in quiet reflection. A curriculum director I worked with schedules "meeting days" and "thinking days," protecting the latter from interruptions so she can make connections in the silence.

Regardless of your approach, take the time to intentionally recognize whether you thrive in collaboration or solitude. Understanding this can unlock a more direct path to creativity.

Activities

Activities serve as different doorways to the creative mind. What you're physically doing when insights strike reveals important clues about your creative process.

Some educators find breakthroughs happen while actively working on lesson plans, directly engaging with the challenge at hand. Others discover their best ideas arrive obliquely, while driving home as their minds decompress, or while making dinner as their attention shifts to tactile tasks.

Your body isn't separate from your creative process; it's an integral part of it. The activities that occupy your hands often free your mind to make unexpected connections.

Time

Time patterns reveal the natural rhythms of your creative energy. Your cognitive abilities fluctuate predictably throughout the day, influenced by circadian rhythms, energy levels, and attention cycles.[6]

You (like me) might be a quintessential morning planner, your mind sharpest when freshly rested, ideas flowing before the demands of the day create cognitive load. Or you might be like my husband Kevin, who finds his creativity peaks in the evening hours when the day's experiences have settled and can be recombined in new ways.

Similarly, work duration patterns matter—some teachers produce their best innovations in short, intense creative bursts of thirty minutes, while others need extended two-hour sessions to move past obvious ideas into truly original territory. These temporal patterns reveal the biological realities of how your particular brain processes information.

The Power of Cross-Pollination

Your creative code also includes how you prefer to combine different domains of knowledge. Our brains forge new connections most effectively when we actively engage with diverse fields of knowledge. As we've seen in previous chapters, getting outside our individual field can offer tremendous benefits to innovating inside of it.

The secret to this is finding your unique way of facilitating these connections. Some people read magazines, newsletters, and books with content spanning from the latest medical technology to education pedagogy to marketing strategies for online companies. Others like to stay within their own field but purposefully rotate through different projects within their week because they each spark unexpected insights. We aren't one-dimensional beings; we instinctively look for multiple ways of approaching and understanding the world. Knowing how your mind best makes these connections is crucial for developing your creative edge.

For educators, these cross-domain connections can update stale teaching approaches. I've seen teachers with experience in community theater apply improvisation techniques to their math instruction. They were delighted to see increased student participation and conceptual understanding. They stopped seeing math problems as facts to memorize and started seeing them as scenes students could explore.

This cross-pollination works across all subjects. Physics teachers who connect projectile motion to basketball help students understand abstract concepts through familiar activities. Music teachers who incorporate history help students place compositions in their cultural context. And art teachers who integrate science help students see beauty in the connected nature of all things.

Developing a Creative and Competitive Edge

In today's rapidly changing landscape, a competitive advantage doesn't come from doing things faster or cheaper; it comes from bringing uniquely human perspectives to problems. Creating a competitive advantage through creativity enables us to see opportunities others miss and develop solutions others can't replicate.[7]

Embracing creativity allows us to reframe problems in ways that reveal new approaches. For educators, this might mean reconsidering the fundamental purpose of assessment rather than simply digitizing existing tests. It involves connecting disparate ideas to form unique solutions, such as merging outdoor education principles with technology instruction. And it enables adapting to changing circumstances more fluidly than rigid systems, which is particularly valuable in educational environments where student needs continuously evolve.

Organizations and individuals who thrive in the AI era share a common trait: they excel at integrative thinking. This means combining

- technical knowledge (understanding your field's fundamentals);
- emotional intelligence (reading and responding to human needs);
- creative intelligence (making novel connections and seeing fresh patterns); and
- contextual intelligence (grasping the broader implications of your work).

The edge doesn't come from having each of these individually but from finding unique ways to weave them together. For example, if your school is struggling with student apathy and engagement, studies show that an effective solution is providing hands-on, relevant experiences that appeal to student interests.

To create this, you might try using "integration studios"—spaces where teachers from different disciplines collaborate on cross-curricular projects connecting technical skills with real-world applications. After working with thousands of teachers on these types of collaborative projects, here are just a few examples they've developed and have used successfully with their students:

- **The Innovators of History:** Students design an escape room based on a historical problem-solving scenario *(contextual intelligence)*. They incorporate engineering principles to build puzzles and challenges *(technical knowledge)*, collaborate to create an engaging and immersive experience *(emotional intelligence)*, and develop creative clues and storylines to enhance gameplay *(creative intelligence)*.

- **The Empathy-Driven Public Art Project**: Students research a social issue and create a public mural or digital artwork to raise awareness *(contextual intelligence)*. They apply various art techniques *(technical knowledge)*, design their work to evoke an emotional response *(emotional intelligence)*, and incorporate symbols and metaphors for deeper meaning *(creative intelligence)*.

- **The Future of Fashion: Wearable Technology:** Students design clothing that integrates smart textiles, such as temperature-sensitive fabric or LED patterns *(technical knowledge)*. They consider how fashion influences self-expression and identity *(emotional intelligence)*, develop unique and innovative garment designs *(creative intelligence)*, and examine how wearable technology is changing industries like healthcare and sports *(contextual intelligence)*.

This approach both improves academic performance and changes how students approach learning. Students stop asking, "Will this be on the test?" and start asking "How does this connect to the real world?"

The Differentiation Paradox

Even though we know the advantages of bringing creativity into our classrooms, there remains a persistent paradox: the more specialized and technical a field becomes, the more valuable creative differentiation becomes.

Take standardized testing, for example. Designed to measure knowledge and proficiency, these tests frequently suppress creativity by prioritizing rote memorization and uniformity. Research has shown that this emphasis can reduce intrinsic motivation and limit opportunities for creative exploration.[8]

In an environment where the correct answer is already predetermined, the act of questioning, experimenting, and synthesizing new ideas—the very foundation of creativity—is discouraged. This kind of focus on a binary system of right and wrong, yes or no answers isn't doing our students any favors for the future.

In his book *The Opposable Mind: How Successful Leaders Win Through Integrative Thinking*, Roger Martin explains that successful leaders don't see choices as either/or decisions. Instead, they hold two opposing ideas in their minds and work through the tension to produce a creative, better outcome.[9] We can develop this "opposable mind" by

- challenging assumptions,
- considering alternative perspectives,
- learning from diverse experiences, and
- being comfortable with complexity and ambiguity.

All of these experiences are the genetic markers of creativity. Yet, the structures of our educational system often work against this kind of thinking.

The tension between standardization and creativity mirrors the paradox that Martin describes. Creativity thrives in ambiguity, yet our systems are designed for clarity and order. If we are to prepare for a future where artificial intelligence automates routine tasks, we must prioritize the one skill AI cannot replicate: the ability to think in new and unexpected ways.

Build Your Moat

In the world of business strategy, a "moat" refers to a sustainable competitive advantage that protects a company from competitors. In the creative economy—where ideas, originality, and adaptability define success—the moat isn't built on patents, proprietary technology, or sheer market dominance. Instead, it's forged from the elements that make you distinctly *you*.

1 Unique Combinations

Start by looking at your diverse skill set and passions—especially the ones that seem unrelated. Often, the most valuable creative advantages come from unexpected intersections. Ask yourself the following:

- What are two or more disciplines I know well that others rarely combine?
- Where do my professional expertise and personal interests overlap?
- How can I merge these areas to create something distinct?

Here is an example: An educator with a background in both math and music might design classroom experiences that develop more intuitive ways to represent statistics through sound and rhythm.

2 Personal Perspective

Your unique experiences—where you grew up, the challenges you've overcome, your cultural influences—shape how you see the world. The more you lean into these, the more authentic and differentiated your creative work becomes.

Ask yourself the following:

- What life experiences have shaped my approach to problem-solving?
- What insights do I have that others in my field might overlook?
- How can I incorporate my personal story into my work in a meaningful way?

Here is an example: A teacher who grew up bilingual might integrate multilingual storytelling to build language connections for students.

3 Relationship Understanding

No matter how advanced AI becomes, human connection remains irreplaceable. The ability to understand emotions, motivations, and social dynamics gives creatives a strategic edge that no algorithm can replicate.

Ask yourself the following:

- What emotional insights do I bring that are valuable in my work?
- How can I use storytelling, empathy, or psychology to enhance what I create?
- In what ways can I design experiences that deeply connect with people?

Here is an example: An English teacher who also performs in community theater might use improvisational techniques to create more engaging expository writing.

4 Adaptive Learning

Creativity is not a static skill—it's a process of continuous growth. Your ability to evolve based on new knowledge and feedback determines how strong your moat remains over time.

Ask yourself the following:

- How often do I experiment with new techniques, ideas, or perspectives?
- What feedback loops can I create to refine my approach?
- How do I turn failures or setbacks into creative breakthroughs?

Here is an example: A science teacher notices her students keep struggling to understand ecological relationships. So she adapts her lesson to include having students create a sculptural relief using mixed media to represent the layers of a biome, incorporating principles of depth, texture, and composition from visual art. By constructing overlapping food webs with wire and organic materials, students not only visualize ecological relationships but also apply artistic techniques like balance and contrast to reinforce their understanding of interdependence in nature.

Unlocking Untapped Potential

At its core, building a creative advantage is about integration. For educators, this means stepping beyond rigid frameworks and finding ways to connect personal strengths, unexpected ideas, and adaptive strategies into teaching. It's becoming (or continuing to be) an educator who inspires curiosity, cultivates problem-solving, and fosters environments where students don't just consume knowledge, but actively construct it.

When teachers embrace creativity as a professional asset, they not only enhance student learning but also future-proof their own careers. The ability to adapt, synthesize diverse ideas, and engage learners in dynamic ways is what makes an educator indispensable in a rapidly changing world. Schools may shift priorities, technology may evolve, but the ability to think in ways that machines cannot is what will always set creative educators apart.

For students, the impact is even greater. By experiencing learning environments that emphasize creativity and integrative thinking, they move beyond passive memorization into a mindset of possibility. They develop the skills to see challenges from multiple angles, question assumptions, and imagine solutions beyond the obvious. These are the very abilities that will give them a true competitive edge—not just in academics, but in life.

As AI continues to automate tasks once thought to be uniquely human, the defining advantage of the future will not be information retention, but the ability to innovate, connect, and create.

Those who develop their creative edge will be the ones shaping the future, not just reacting to it.

Sidestepping the Excuses: Time, Overwhelm, and Comparison

Building a creative competitive edge sounds great in theory, but putting it into practice comes with some real challenges. The most common roadblocks—not enough time, feeling overwhelmed, and the endless trap of comparison—go beyond logistical challenges; they stem from resistance, a concept Steven Pressfield unpacks in *The War of Art*. Resistance shows up as procrastination, fear, and distraction, convincing us that we're too busy, too drained, or not talented enough to create something meaningful.[10]

But as we've seen in previous chapters, creativity thrives on commitment, not random inspiration. Pressfield makes a sharp distinction between amateurs and professionals: professionals show up, no matter how they feel. They push past doubt, refuse to let time constraints define them, and do the work anyway. If we want to build a true creative advantage, we need to do the same.

That starts with reframing our biggest creative barriers—not as obstacles, but as opportunities for innovation.

The Time Trap

"I don't have time to be creative" might be the most common creativity killer in existence. But lack of time isn't the real problem—it's our assumption about how much time creativity requires.

Researchers have discovered that it's not the actual amount of time available that impacts creative performance—it's how we *perceive* that time. When people view time limits as restrictive, their creativity suffers; when they see them as a challenge, their creative output actually improves.

In fact, having *some* constraints can enhance creativity rather than stifle it. Structured time frames often lead to more innovative ideas than unlimited time, as clear boundaries help focus cognitive resources and prevent procrastination. This flips the common belief that creativity thrives only in open-ended, unstructured settings.

Even more surprising? Studies suggest that just two to four hours of deep creative work per day can be optimal. It's not about how *much* time you have—it's about how you *use* it. Even short, focused sessions can lead to breakthrough ideas.

Here are some practical techniques for making the most of the time you have:

Timeboxing creates protected creative spaces within even the busiest schedule.[11] This technique involves setting a timer for a short, nonnegotiable period—often just ten minutes—dedicated exclusively to creative work. The defined boundary creates psychological safety that helps overcome the perfectionism that often blocks creative progress. When you know you only have ten minutes, you're less likely to overthink and more likely to simply begin.

When I was a music teacher, I used a time-boxing strategy I picked up in college called "First Five." Every day, I set aside the first five minutes of my planning period to brainstorm new curriculum concepts—no pressure, no judgment, just pure idea generation. I'd start with a simple *"What if ...?"* and let my creativity run. Over the course of a year, those tiny daily sessions added up, and by summer, I had enough fresh material to completely revamp my curriculum. The power of time-boxing is in its no-pressure consistency. Small, intentional bursts of creativity compound over time, leading to breakthroughs that wouldn't have happened otherwise.

Idea sprints capitalize on transition moments that would otherwise be lost. These are based on design sprints used by design teams to rapidly generate new solutions for solving problems or testing new products.[12] These brief bursts of focused creative thinking turn the "in-between" spaces of your day into productive idea generation sessions.

For this strategy to work, it's important to have a specific creative challenge ready. For example, you can keep a running list of upcoming science units on your phone and dedicate the four-minute passing periods between classes to generating one new activity idea for each topic. Or if you're an instructional coach, use the three minutes while your laptop boots up each morning to brainstorm new approaches to teacher feedback.

These sprints work because they're brief enough to fit into natural transitions yet focused enough to produce useful results. The constraint enhances creativity by forcing the mind to work efficiently without the opportunity for overthinking. Over time, these micro-sessions create a habit of creative thinking that becomes increasingly automatic.

Transformed waiting time converts previously frustrating delays into productive ideation opportunities.[13] The average educator spends hours each month just waiting—waiting for meetings to start, for copies to finish, for parents to arrive at conferences.

Rather than scrolling through social media or checking email during these moments, you can designate specific creative challenges for these unexpected time gifts. Try to sketch out a new idea or refine a process you've been thinking about. Or keep a running list of challenges or projects on your phone so you can chip away at them during unexpected delays.

Again, the effectiveness of this approach comes from preparation. It helps to have specific questions or work ready for these moments rather than trying to think them up on the spot. It also involves reframing waiting from an annoyance to an opportunity, a mental shift that reduces stress while increasing productivity.

For educators, these approaches create practical pathways to maintain a creative practice despite overwhelming schedules. Using the five minutes between classes to jot down one new teaching idea or converting part of lunch break into a quick brainstorming session with colleagues creates a regular practice of small tweaks that collectively make a big difference long term.

The Overwhelm Override

Creative block is the mental traffic jam that happens when too many thoughts compete for attention without a system to sort them. With an endless stream of inspiration from social media, AI tools, and everyday experiences, curation is mandatory. Instead of constantly chasing more ideas, the real challenge is managing the ones we already have.

Breaking projects into bite-sized steps, building routines that cut down on decision fatigue, and having a quick-response system for creative sparks can make all the difference. Even taking just two minutes to jot down a teaching idea when it hits can be the difference between it vanishing forever or turning into the next cutting-edge breakthrough.

Here are two strategies for combating overwhelm and turning it into manageable action:

1 Break projects into "micro-commitments."

Momentum starts with tasks so small they feel too easy to ignore. When a project feels overwhelming, our brains trigger resistance, making it harder to even begin. The trick is to break it down into *micro-commitments*—tiny, actionable steps that sidestep mental roadblocks.

Need to develop a new curriculum but don't know where to start? Instead of tackling it all at once, set a micro-commitment like *"write down ten big ideas"* or *"map big ideas to units."* Each completed step builds confidence and moves the project forward, making what once seemed impossible feel achievable.

Micro-commitments work because they create multiple *entry points* into the creative process. When teachers structure curriculum planning around tasks that take ten minutes or less, they make it easier to start—and, just as importantly, to keep going—even in the middle of a packed schedule.

2 Create a "decision-free zone."

Creativity flourishes when decision fatigue doesn't get in the way. The mental load of constant decision-making drains creative energy before the work even begins. A *decision-free zone* removes that friction by establishing preset routines and structures, allowing you to focus on the actual creative process rather than getting stuck deciding *how* to start.

For example, instead of approaching every lesson from scratch, create a go-to framework: a consistent sequence of steps you follow each time. Maybe that means always beginning with a brainstorming session, followed by a rough outline, then testing ideas with a small group before finalizing. By removing unnecessary decisions about *process*, you free up more mental space for *ideas*.

For educators, these strategies translate into practical applications that enhance creativity while acknowledging the realities of school environments. These approaches don't require additional time—they simply optimize the creative potential of the time already available.

The Comparison Trap

When we constantly measure ourselves against others' successes, we risk losing sight of our own creative instincts. The curated, polished work we see—especially on social media—can make it easy to feel like we're falling short. But comparison distorts reality, shifting our focus from meaningful progress to surface-level benchmarks that may have nothing to do with our actual goals.[14]

Breaking free from comparison requires adopting deliberate strategies that protect creative authenticity while still allowing for growth:

1 Define Success on Your Own Terms

Success isn't one-size-fits-all. Establishing personal metrics that align with your specific context, values, and goals is critical to determining what success looks like *for you*. Instead of measuring yourself against external expectations, shape your creative work around what will have the biggest impact on your students.

For example, rather than feeling pressure to replicate elaborate classroom setups or trendy teaching strategies, define success based on engagement, student growth, and the depth of learning happening in your space. When success is based on *impact* rather than *appearance*, creative energy is directed toward what truly matters.

2 Keep a "Wins Journal"

Our brains are wired to focus on what's lacking rather than what's working, which is why keeping a *wins journal* can be a game-changer. Documenting small victories—student breakthroughs, effective lessons, moments of connection—creates a tangible record of progress.

On tough days, reviewing these successes serves as a reminder of real impact, shifting the mindset from *"I'm not doing enough"* to *"Look at how far I've come."* This can be as simple as jotting down highlights in a planner, keeping a digital note of positive student feedback, or setting aside a few minutes each week to reflect on meaningful moments. The goal is to create an objective counterweight to the self-doubt that comparison often triggers.

3 Practice Strategic Ignorance

As my mentor Marie Forleo says, "create before you consume." Creativity needs space to breathe. Constant exposure to others' work—especially during the early stages of an idea—can lead to unintentional imitation or, worse, feeling stuck. *Strategic ignorance* means being intentional about when and how you engage with external influences.

For example, instead of constantly scrolling through education blogs or social media for new ideas, consider sketching out your own ideas first. Then, set specific times for professional inspiration, reviewing new strategies, or attending conferences periodically. This approach ensures you stay true to your creative genius while still staying informed of best practices and fresh approaches.

Reclaiming Your Creative Energy

Clearing creative roadblocks creates space for ideas to take shape, but developing creative skills takes practice. Small shifts, like time-boxing and micro-commitments, build momentum and make creativity a daily habit. The more consistently these strategies are used, the easier it becomes to generate, refine, and apply new ideas.

With the right mindset and tools, creativity becomes something you can access anytime, not just in rare moments of inspiration. The next step is learning how to strengthen creative thinking, apply it with purpose, and turn ideas into meaningful work.

The Creative Opportunity Cost

Every creative decision comes with an opportunity cost—not just in time or resources, but in the paths we don't take. Choosing to explore one idea means postponing another. Investing energy into refining a new approach means delaying implementation of something else. Unlike traditional decision-making, where trade-offs are often straightforward, creative opportunity costs are more complex, involving shifts in thinking, perspective, and long-term impact.

The Hidden Equation

Economists define opportunity cost as the value of what we give up to pursue something else.[15] But in creative work, the trade-offs go beyond efficiency. We aren't just exchanging time spent analyzing for time spent ideating—we're trading one way of thinking for another, one possible insight for an entirely different one.

Creative risks don't come with guarantees. Following a well-established method provides reliability, while experimenting with something new requires navigating uncertainty. The question isn't whether creative work has opportunity costs—it's whether those costs align with long-term goals rather than defaulting to short-term convenience.

Consider how creative choices play out in real-world educational settings:

- **Prioritizing Exploration Over Immediate Execution:** Investing time in exploring multiple approaches before settling on one takes longer but often leads to stronger, more effective outcomes. Educators who allow time for divergent thinking—brainstorming various ways to introduce a new concept, redesigning a lesson to include more student input—often create richer learning experiences than those who rush to implementation.

- **Investing in Long-Term Creative Growth Over Short-Term Productivity:** Professional learning time is often spent on immediate instructional needs, such as implementing new curriculum materials or meeting compliance requirements. But dedicating time to building teachers' creative capacity—through collaborative innovation, experimentation, or design thinking workshops—pays off in long-term adaptability and problem-solving skills.

- **Choosing Innovation Over Predictability:** A new teaching strategy, assessment method, or instructional model might be riskier than traditional approaches, but when aligned with long-term student engagement and deeper learning outcomes, the payoff often outweighs the uncertainty.

The Creativity Premium

Creative choices extend beyond individual projects; they shape entire industries, research fields, and cultural norms. Creativity often means trading certainty for possibility, established models for new approaches. In education, this plays out in the following ways:

- A teacher experiments with a project-based assessment instead of a traditional test, knowing that while it may take more effort to assess, it could lead to deeper student understanding.
- A district invests in student-led learning initiatives, recognizing that while outcomes may initially be less predictable than direct instruction, long-term student engagement and ownership of learning will likely increase.
- A school designs a flexible schedule to allow for interdisciplinary learning, knowing that while it requires logistical changes, it might unlock more meaningful connections between subjects.

Despite these trade-offs, creativity carries a unique premium: it creates possibilities that efficiency alone never will. While optimization improves what already exists, creative risks unlock what *could* exist. The biggest leaps don't come from working harder within the same system—they come from reimagining the system itself.

Making Strategic Creative Choices

Creativity isn't about making opportunity costs work for you. The challenge is being deliberate about where to invest time and energy so that creative risks align with long-term goals rather than defaulting to familiar efficiency.

As AI reshapes education, work, and creative fields, these trade-offs become even more critical. AI can generate content, analyze data, and automate processes, raising an essential question: *What's the opportunity cost of spending time on tasks AI can handle versus investing in the deeply human aspects of creativity?* The answer isn't to replace human creativity with AI but to redefine where human ingenuity holds the most value.

To navigate these choices effectively:

- **Choose creative risks that align with your long-term vision.** Creative investments should connect to a larger purpose. The question isn't just *"Is this a good idea?"* but *"Does this move me toward my broader goal?"* Whether it's rethinking grading practices, designing more inclusive learning experiences, or incorporating more creative autonomy for students, intentional investment leads to deeper impact.

- **Identify leverage points where small creative shifts can create big returns.** Not all innovation requires large-scale change. Sometimes, the most effective creative investments are small shifts that have exponential benefits—redesigning a classroom environment to promote collaboration, adjusting questioning strategies to encourage critical thinking, or integrating reflection practices to deepen learning.

- **Recognize when traditional efficiency might be limiting potential.** Streamlining processes can be valuable, but not when it comes at the cost of deeper learning or innovation. Sometimes, what appears inefficient in the short term—allowing students more choice, experimenting with flexible assessments, dedicating time to professional collaboration—actually leads to far greater long-term effectiveness.

The choices we make today will determine the role human creativity plays from now on. The creative risks we take—what we invest in, what we risk, and what we're willing to sacrifice for innovation—will shape not just our own work, but the future of humanity itself.

Your Throughline: Creative Skills, Mindsets, and Applications

Throughout this book, we've explored creativity from nearly every angle—from its neurological foundations to its practical applications, from the flow states that make it possible to the habits that make it sustainable. But understanding these elements individually isn't enough. The true power emerges when we intentionally weave them together into a cohesive whole.

As we've discovered, creativity acts as a dynamic ecosystem. Each component we've explored—creative skills, thinking patterns, expressive outlets, and practical applications—serves a crucial function in this ecosystem. Like an actual ecosystem, the health of the whole depends on the balance and integration of its parts.

The branches of creativity we examined in chapter 3 don't operate in isolation. Your technical skills enable more sophisticated creative thinking. Your creative thinking opens new channels for personal expression. Your personal expression informs how you apply creativity to solve real problems. And the results of that application circle back, deepening your technical skills and expanding your thinking capacity.

This integration happens at the neural level too. Remember how the *default mode network* (DMN) and *executive control network* (ECN) take turns in most cognitive activities? When engaging in creative experiences, these networks learn to work in concert rather than opposition. The same principle applies to your creative practice—elements that might seem contradictory (like structured technique and free exploration) actually enhance each other when properly integrated.

The most powerful creative breakthroughs come from finding the unique combination that works for you, rather than developing any single element to perfection. This is where your personal creativity code becomes essential.

The time patterns, environmental conditions, and social contexts that spark your creativity are the connective tissue that holds your creative ecosystem together.

Meanwhile, the mindsets that support this integration are sophisticated frameworks for processing experience. When faced with a teaching challenge, a creative educator doesn't just ask "How do I fix this?" but instead asks, "What might this problem be showing me that I couldn't see before?" This shift from problem-solving to opportunity-finding represents a core reorientation of how we engage with challenges.

This is why the practices we explored in chapter 6 matter so much. Daily creative habits build skills while simultaneously developing the neural pathways that make this integration possible. The morning pages exercise that seems disconnected from your teaching might be strengthening exactly the connective tissue your creative practice needs. The constraints exercise that feels limiting might be training the adaptive thinking required for your next breakthrough. If you're ready to take the leap and leverage creativity as your competitive edge, try using the essential question prompts from figure 7.1 as a starting point and see where they take you.

Each set of prompts aligns with a cyclical creative process that helps you focus on a problem (describe), get curious and consider how to address that problem (analyze), bring your unique perspective and experiences toward a potential solution (interpret), design a unique product or process that solves the problem (create), share your work with others (presentation), seek out feedback and determine what to use in order to make your creation better (evaluate), and finally review your end product or process to determine your next steps (reflect). These steps are part of the journey all creatives take to leave our legacy and process our unique human experience.

As artificial intelligence increasingly handles routine tasks, this integration becomes our unique advantage. AI can generate content, analyze data, and

30 ESSENTIAL QUESTIONS
through the CREATIVE PROCESS

 DESCRIBE
- How are the arts experienced?
- How do we gather evidence?
- What is the purpose of this work?
- What do you wonder about this piece?

 ANALYZE
- How are the arts understood?
- How do artists compose?
- How do arts elements effect the overall composition?
- What tools could you use to explore this work?

 INTERPRET
- How is this art form interpreted?
- How does interaction with this work provoke thinking?
- What connections do you see?
- How are connections represented?

 CREATE
- What influences choice-making?
- How can we compare and connect this with other work?
- Why is this work important?
- What limitations are present?
- What is creativity?
- How does an artist create meaning?

 PRESENTATION
- How do we use the arts to communicate?
- How can a viewer/listener comprehend what they are seeing/hearing?
- What makes this work effective?
- How can we use the arts to inspire action?

 EVALUATE
- Do audiences have responsibilities towards artists? If so, what are they?
- What can this work teach us about the world?
- What makes a thoughtful critique?
- Why does the artist choose to include this point of view?

 REFLECT
- How does this work deepen our understanding of ourselves?
- How does your observation influence your interpretation
- Why does this work make sense to you?
- How does this work make you feel or think differently?

FIGURE 7.1

even mimic creative styles, but it can't replicate the deeply personal synthesis that happens when a human brings their whole self—experiences, emotions, values, and vision—to a creative challenge.

In the end, creativity isn't something we do—it's who we are and the way we engage with the world. It's about bringing our full selves to our work, connecting disparate threads of knowledge, remaining open to unexpected possibilities, and having the courage to follow where they lead. The techniques and frameworks we've explored are simply tools to help you discover and refine your own creative voice.

Your creative edge is found in the unique way you integrate everything you've learned, filtered through your personal experience and directed toward the challenges that matter most to you.

Key Takeaways

1. Creativity thrives on meaningful connections, not isolated ideas. The ability to integrate knowledge across disciplines gives human creativity an edge in an AI-driven world.
2. Understanding your creative code unlocks your full potential. Identifying personal patterns—like when, where, and how you work best—allows you to refine your process and generate stronger ideas.
3. Cross-pollination fuels innovation. Engaging with diverse fields and applying insights from outside your domain leads to fresh perspectives and breakthrough solutions.
4. Creative work requires strategic investment. Every decision has an opportunity cost, and balancing short-term efficiency with long-term innovation is key to meaningful, sustainable progress.

5. The future belongs to those who think creatively. As automation takes over routine tasks, the ability to synthesize ideas, adapt quickly, and solve problems in novel ways will be the ultimate advantage.

PRACTICE STRATEGY: Build-a-Character

You're going to create a character for a story. This story is about a teacher's journey to a more creative classroom.

1. Pick your character. Is it a student? A teacher? An administrator? A parent?
2. Think about what that character's facial expression, body movement, gestures, voice and energy level might look and sound like. Write each of these down.
3. Next, write down answers to the following questions:
    a. What does this character want?
    b. What does this character need to achieve this?
    c. Where is this character stuck?
    d. What creative methods could this character use to become unstuck?
4. Optional (but highly suggested) step! Use your body to explore this character now and who they will become at the end of the story. Play around with their facial expression, body movement, gestures, voice and energy levels. Make them real.
    a. Note: this is going to feel weird. Do it anyway. Go to a quiet place where no one can bother you. If you have a mirror, that's even better. But the more you can embody these characters, the more you'll truly learn who they are and what they want/need.
5. Finally, write down who this character has become at the end of their journey.
    a. What do they look and sound like now?
    b. What kind of energy level do they now carry?
    c. What words or actions could best be used to describe them?

Notes

1. Baker, J. (2025, January 20). "From Bullet Trains to Green Buildings: Innovators Take Cue from Nature Through Biomimicry." Reuters. https://www.reuters.com/sustainability/land-use-biodiversity/bullet-trains-green-buildings-innovators-take-cue-nature-through-biomimicry-2025-01-13/

2. Swords, A. (2024). "The Opportunity Cost of AI." LinkedIn. https://www.linkedin.com/pulse/opportunity-cost-ai-alexander-swords-8nyic/

3. Young, S. (2008, January). "How to Find Creative Solutions to Non-Creative Problems." Scott H. Young. https://www.scotthyoung.com/blog/2008/01/08/how-to-find-creative-solutions-to-non-creative-problems/

4. Clear, J. (n.d.). "How to Find Your Hidden Creative Genius." James Clear. https://jamesclear.com/creative-genius

5. Zagonari, F., & Giacomoni, E. (2022). "Social Benefits and Individual Costs of Creativity in Art and Science: A Statistical Analysis Based on a Theoretical Framework." *PLoS One*, 17(4), e0265446. National Center for Biotechnology Information. https://www.ncbi.nlm.nih.gov/pmc/articles/PMC9045641/

6. Antes, A. L., & Mumford, M. D. (2009). "Effects of Time Frame on Creative Thought: Process Versus Problem-Solving Effects." *Creativity Research Journal*, 21(2–3), 166–82. http://dx.doi.org/10.1080/10400410902855267

7. Coetzee, F. (2023, December 28). "Creating Competitive Advantage Through Creativity, Creative Thinking, and Creative Problem Solving." Medium. https://nlpwithpurpose.medium.com/creating-competitive-advantage-through-creativity-creative-thinking-and-creative-problem-solving-01ac511e07ff

8. Holland, B. (2019, December 3). "The State of Creativity in America's Schools." Getting Smart. https://www.gettingsmart.com/2019/12/03/the-state-of-creativity-in-americas-schools/

9. Martin, R. (2009). *The Opposable Mind: How Successful Leaders Win Through Integrative Thinking*. Harvard Business Press.

10. Pressfield, S. (2002). *The War of Art: Break Through the Blocks and Win Your Inner Creative Battles*. Black Irish Entertainment LLC.

11. Kroolo. (2024, January 8). "What Is Timeboxing: Your Goal-Driven Time Management." https://kroolo.com/blog/timeboxing-a-practical-guide-to-goal-driven-time-management

12. Jake-Schoffman, D. E., & McVay, M. A. (2020). "Using the Design Sprint Process to Enhance and Accelerate Behavioral Medicine Progress: A Case Study and Guidance." *Translational Behavioral Medicine*, 11(2), 652–9. https://www.researchgate.net/

publication/346241321_Using_the_Design_Sprint_process_to_enhance_and_accelerate_behavioral_medicine_progress_a_case_study_and_guidance

13 Kong, R. (2023). "The Effect of Time Constraint Awareness on Creativity Test Performance." https://doi.org/10.21203/rs.3.rs-3214718/v2

14 Lehrer, J. (2012, March). "The Cost of Creativity." Wired. https://www.wired.com/2012/03/the-cost-of-creativity/

15 Minutes. (n.d.). "What Is Opportunity Cost?" https://minutes.co/what-is-opportunity-cost-its-the-variable-keeping-you-from-making-better-decisions-in-your-life-your-career-your-relationships-and-more/

8
Harnessing the Future

> *Chapter Guiding Question: How can we use our creativity as a guide for the twenty-first century?*

The Silk Pavilion at MIT's Media Lab often stops visitors in their tracks. There, in the center of the room, is a large three-meter-wide white igloo-shaped dome hanging gracefully from the ceiling—made by silkworms and robots working together.

The project began with a deceptively simple question: how might humans collaborate with other species to create new materials without depleting natural resources? Inspired by a silkworm's ability to spin a three-dimensional cocoon from a single thread, the project explored relationships between digital and biological construction. The team discovered that silkworms spin differently based on their environment, allowing designers to essentially "program" these tiny creatures through carefully calibrated conditions.

The process unfolded in two phases. First, a robot meticulously placed silk threads in patterns determined by the silkworms' natural behaviors. Then 6,500 live silkworms completed the structure, spinning dense patches in certain areas while leaving others more open—their work guided by environmental factors like heat and light. Each silkworm contributed a single silk thread about 1km long. Together, they created a dome-shaped masterpiece with a combined thread length rivaling the Silk Road itself.

Neri Oxman, the visionary behind this project, defies categorization in her work. With a background spanning medicine, architecture, and computer science, she brings a uniquely interdisciplinary perspective to her work. Leading MIT's Mediated Matter Group, she pioneers what she calls "material ecology"—an approach that treats design more like growing an organism than constructing an object. When her team later created Silk Pavilion II, they refined this concept further, employing seventeen thousand silkworms and demonstrating how biological manufacturing could scale for architectural applications.[1]

What makes Oxman's work so compelling goes far beyond this single project. She's designed buildings using structural principles from butterfly wings, created furniture that mimics human bone tissue, and developed wearable structures that interact with their surroundings. Her approach represents a fundamental shift in perspective. While traditional design typically starts with a form and then sources materials to build it, Oxman begins with the material properties themselves, allowing forms to emerge organically through environmental interaction.

In her lab, researchers blast through traditional boundaries between disciplines. Some program bacteria to produce pigments for sustainable textiles, while others develop fabrication systems inspired by how bees construct hives.

This merger of biology, technology, computation, and design offers a powerful metaphor for creativity in the twenty-first century. Rather than separating knowledge into discrete categories—art in one corner, science in another, technology in a third—these approaches allow disciplines to flow together, generating hybrid solutions to our most complex challenges.

Oxman's work demonstrates creativity's power to imagine previously invisible possibilities, going beyond mere problem-solving. She pushes us from crossing boundaries between disciplines to questioning whether those boundaries should exist at all.

Fresh perspectives like these—shifting from seeing buildings as objects we create to organisms we cultivate—represent exactly the kind of creative thinking we need to navigate our rapidly changing world. Throughout this book, we've explored how creativity emerges when we make unexpected connections and challenge our basic assumptions. Now, as artificial intelligence reshapes everything around us, this capacity for creative reimagining isn't just helpful—it's essential for our collective future.

What Science Tells Us Is Coming: Bridging the Gaps

We're standing at the brink of a significant shift in the way humans create. The World Economic Forum predicts that by 2030, creativity will be among the top three most valuable workplace skills, alongside critical thinking and complex problem-solving.[2] And it's not hard to see why.

The rise of artificial intelligence isn't just changing *what* we create—it's fundamentally transforming *how* we create. Technologies that can generate images, text, music, and code are rapidly reshaping creative fields that once seemed uniquely human. Meanwhile, climate change, global health challenges, and social inequities demand innovative solutions that go beyond conventional limits.

As the Cornell Tech research team puts it, "The future of creativity isn't about humans versus AI, but humans with AI."[3] This partnership between human imagination and computational power opens new realms of possibility, while simultaneously raising deep questions about creativity itself. What elements remain distinctly human in an age of generative AI? How do we prepare students and ourselves for creative futures we can barely imagine?

Science offers us some fascinating insights. Research suggests that as AI takes over more routine aspects of creative work, distinctly human creative capacities become increasingly valuable: our ability to frame meaningful problems, to combine insights across domains, and to infuse our work with emotional resonance and cultural understanding.[4]

But there's a catch. These higher-order creative capacities—the very skills that will distinguish human creativity in the AI age—are exactly the ones most education systems struggle to develop. While we've gotten better at teaching creative techniques, we're still figuring out how to nurture creative wisdom. This includes developing the judgment to know which problems are worth solving, which approaches might yield breakthrough solutions, and how to balance innovation with ethical responsibility.

This creates what researchers call the "creativity gap"—the growing distance between the creative skills and capacities we need for the future and those our current systems cultivate.[5] It's like we're preparing students to compete in a race while the finish line keeps moving.

Think about this: Bloomberg Media reports that sooner rather than later, diverse perspectives will shape creative fields more powerfully than technology itself. As AI systems get better at executing creative techniques, human creativity will increasingly be defined by the unique perspectives, experiences, and cultural insights we bring to our work. Yet most educational approaches to creativity still focus primarily on techniques rather than on developing authentic creative voices.

Similarly, other studies show that as technical barriers to creation fall, the most valuable creative skills shift from execution to conceptualization—from "how to create" to "what to create and why."[6] Yet most creativity education still emphasizes production skills over problem-finding and purpose-setting.

Bridging these gaps requires more than just tweaking existing approaches. It demands fundamentally reimagining how we develop creative capacity—starting with understanding how technology is reshaping creative work itself.

The Hype Cycle: Educational Technology's Rocky History

Let's state the obvious first: we've been here before. The history of education is marked by the echoes of "revolutionary technologies" that held the promise of transforming learning yet often fell short of their lofty claims.

I remember being a new teacher in the early 2000s when interactive whiteboards started replacing chalkboards in the classrooms of America. As a music teacher who had to draw multiple staves with the five-prong chalk holder so students could learn music notation, I craved these new whiteboards that could pull up predesigned staves in a second and write and erase notes with special interactive markers that didn't leave dust behind.

And I wasn't the only one—teachers all around me were begging for this new technology that could change everything from assessing students in real-time to providing personalized instruction to each student who approached the board. Administrators and tech companies heralded them as game-changers that would revolutionize teaching. School districts invested millions, teachers attended countless professional development sessions, and then most ended up as expensive projector screens, with their interactive capabilities largely unused or forgotten.

With disheartening regularity, this has been a recurring pattern. Each of these innovations—from educational filmstrips in the 1940s to overhead projectors and ditto machines in the 1960s, computer labs in the 1980s, DVDs and CDs in the 1990s, and iPads in the 2010s—arrived with the breathless expectation that they would revolutionize education. In the end, each adapted to a more subdued role than they had promised.

Why does this happen? The Gartner Hype Cycle[7] gives us some insight and explains why new educational technologies typically follow a predictable pattern:

- **The Technology Trigger**—A brand-new technology with enormous promise appears. Early adopters jump in, conference speakers become excited, and press releases pour forth.

- **The Peak of Inflated Expectations**—Excitement reaches fever pitch. This technology will revolutionize learning! Transform teaching! Solve educational inequity! Vendors make extravagant claims to have their products next in line for the upcoming budget cycle, and decision-makers, afraid of missing the next big thing, invest heavily.

- **The Trough of Disillusionment**—Reality sets in. There are constant technical difficulties. The implementation is more difficult than anticipated. There is insufficient training for teachers. The anticipated outcomes never come to pass. As the next flashy technology emerges, interest wanes.

- **The Slope of Enlightenment**—Persistent users start to see the real (as opposed to perceived) advantages of the technology. Implementations that are more realistic and measured start to provide long-lasting effects.

- **The Plateau of Productivity**—The technology finds its proper place in the educational ecosystem. It is typically less significant than first anticipated, but it is nevertheless useful in certain situations.

I've lived through this cycle multiple times as an educator. I watched colleagues burn countless hours mastering Bitmoji animations for their online and hybrid classes during the COVID-19 pandemic, only to have the technology become obsolete. I've seen schools invest heavily in fancy 3D printers with bells and whistles that no one could figure out, which then gathered dust after the initial excitement faded. I've seen virtual reality (VR) headsets purchased with great fanfare, then relegated to storage closets when maintaining them proved too time consuming.

This isn't to say educational technology hasn't made significant contributions. Generally speaking, however, those contributions have been more evolutionary than revolutionary. They've enhanced rather than transformed education. And their successful implementation has always depended more on thoughtful integration with teaching practice than on the inherent power of the technology itself.

So where does AI fit in this historical context? Is it simply the latest piece of instructional technology that will experience the same hype cycle? Or does it represent something fundamentally different?

The honest answer is both.

AI exhibits many characteristics of earlier educational technology fads. The grandiose claims, the hasty implementation without sufficient planning, and the emphasis on technology rather than pedagogy all seem oddly familiar. And like previous technologies, AI will almost certainly deliver less than its most enthusiastic proponents currently promise.

Yet there's an essential distinction with AI that suggests its impact may ultimately prove more significant than previous educational technologies. Unlike interactive whiteboards or iPads, AI isn't just a tool awaiting human direction. It's an adaptive system that can personalize responses, generate novel content, and even learn from interactions in ways that previous educational technologies simply couldn't.

The question isn't whether AI will transform education; it already has and will continue to do so. The question is whether that transformation will enhance teaching and learning in meaningful ways or disrupt them in ways that ultimately diminish educational experiences. The answer depends largely on how we choose to implement these technologies.

The Double-Edged Sword: AI as Disruptor in Education

Let me paint two very different scenarios of how AI might reshape education over the next decade.

First, picture a world in which artificial intelligence enhances the best elements of education. AI assistants are used by teachers to lessen administrative workload, customize lesson plans, and spot student misconceptions early. Students cultivate their understanding of AI in tandem with traditional literacies, engaging in collaboration with AI tools while enhancing uniquely human skills such as critical thinking, ethical reasoning, and creative problem-solving. The technology serves as a powerful complement to the human relationships at the heart of education.

Now, forget that first dream and imagine a world where AI becomes a disruptive force that erodes authentic learning. Schools increasingly turn to standardized AI systems that focus on quantifiable results, often at the expense of fostering deeper, more meaningful learning experiences. Students lose their capacity for original thought and internal knowledge, while getting better at producing AI-generated responses. Teachers find their professional judgment increasingly sidelined by algorithmic decision-making. Administrators looking to minimize costs substitute "AI facilitators" who only manage automated learning systems for certified teachers.

These aren't abstract thought experiments. Both futures are actively happening right now in schools across the country, and which one prevails will depend on the choices educators, policymakers, and community members make in the coming years. Here are some specific disruptions we need to navigate thoughtfully:

Disruption to Knowledge Acquisition

When I was in school, memorizing multiplication tables and state capitals wasn't just about having and retaining information. We were developing mental frameworks for understanding numerical relationships and geographic patterns. But what happens when AI can instantly deliver any fact, solve any equation, or produce any historical summary?

This instant access to information disrupts traditional knowledge acquisition in significant ways. The challenge isn't whether students should memorize less information (they probably should), but what cognitive foundations they must develop despite having AI assistance available. What mental models, conceptual frameworks, and core knowledge remain essential when facts are instantly accessible? How do we ensure students develop the background knowledge necessary to evaluate AI-generated information critically and use it creatively?

These aren't simple questions, and they vary by subject and developmental stage. A fifth grader still needs to internalize multiplication facts to develop number sense, even if calculators exist. But is it really necessary for high school students to memorize the periodic table when they will have AI support in their future careers? Perhaps it would be more beneficial for them to focus on grasping chemical principles and exploring their application in addressing unforeseen challenges, like those we encountered during the COVID-19 pandemic.

The challenge we face in this disruption isn't just about students learning less. It's in recognizing the underlying purposes of our curriculum and assessment are changing and being willing to redesign them if necessary. If we don't, we might fail to help students develop the key knowledge structures they need to think independently in an AI-assisted world.

Disruption to Assessment and Academic Integrity

Within weeks of ChatGPT's release on November 30, 2022, educators across the country faced a sobering reality: traditional assessments suddenly seemed pointless. Essays, problem sets, short answer questions—AI tools could generate plausible responses to all of them, often indistinguishable from student work. I saw this myself with teachers who were applying for our Arts Integration Certification program. By January of 2023, our organization had to include a notification that all applications would be run through an AI detector to determine originality. If more than 50 percent of the application was flagged as AI-generated, the applicant would be required to revise the application and resubmit. Applicants to our program range in age from thirty to sixty years. By the time we put this into place, we had already seen most of the applications being submitted shift from original work to mostly AI-generated for the essay questions and critical-thinking prompts.

This disruption cuts to the core of how we evaluate learning. When AI can write an essay analyzing "The Great Gatsby," complete an application, or solve a calculus problem step-by-step, what exactly are we assessing? The student's ability to generate an effective prompt? Their judgment in selecting and refining AI outputs? Or something else entirely?

I've spoken with many teachers wrestling with these questions. Some have reverted to locked-down, in-person assessments with no technology allowed. Others are redesigning assignments to focus on process documentation, in-class presentations, portfolios, or creative applications that showcase authentic student thinking. Many are simply hoping the problem will go away or that detection tools will be enough (they won't).

The more important challenge goes beyond catching cheaters. It's about reimagining assessment for a world where content generation is no longer a meaningful bottleneck. What matters isn't whether students use AI—it's whether they develop the conceptual understanding, critical thinking, and creative capabilities that AI can't provide.

Disruption to Teacher Roles and Professional Identity

The disruption to teaching itself may be the most significant and concerning. We're already seeing tremendous pressure to reduce education costs through technology, and AI offers a tempting avenue for those who view teaching primarily as information delivery rather than relationship-building.

Some edtech companies are subtly marketing AI tools as teacher replacements or arguing that schools can function with fewer certified educators by using AI to "scale" teaching. These approaches totally misunderstand what effective education involves. They reduce teaching to content delivery and basic feedback—precisely the elements AI can replicate—while ignoring the complex social, emotional, creative, and intellectual work that makes great teaching transformative.

The real danger isn't that robots will replace teachers. It's that we'll redefine teaching to focus on the aspects AI can't yet handle—emotional support, behavior management, and technology troubleshooting—while automating the intellectual heart of the profession: the thoughtful design of learning experiences, the nuanced assessment of student understanding, the adaptive response to student needs.

Teaching is more than explaining content and grading assignments. Teaching builds relationships that motivate learning, modeling thinking processes in real-time, and creating conditions where students develop not just knowledge but identity as learners.

The most thoughtful educational AI implementations recognize this reality. They focus on augmenting teacher capabilities rather than replacing them and handling routine tasks so teachers can focus on the high-value interactions that technology can't replicate.

The Equity Challenge

Perhaps the most troubling potential disruption involves educational equity. Without deliberate intervention, AI is likely to widen existing educational divides in several ways.

First, there's the basic access gap. Despite progress in closing the digital divide, significant disparities remain in access to devices, broadband internet, and technical support. Students in well-resourced schools will have access to the latest AI tools and guidance in using them effectively, while students in under-resourced schools may have limited or no access.

Then there's what researchers generally call the "usage gap"—differences in how technologies are implemented or utilized across schools. Affluent schools tend to use technology for creative production, critical thinking, and student-driven exploration. Less affluent schools more often use technology for basic skills practice, test prep, and highly structured activities. This pattern could repeat with AI, with disadvantaged students more likely to experience AI as a directive force rather than a creative tool.[8]

The result could be a new digital divide that's even more pervasive than previous versions—one where all students use AI, but some use it to amplify their thinking while others become dependent on it, their own cognitive development stunted in the process.

None of these disruptions are inevitable. But navigating them successfully requires moving beyond both techno-optimism ("AI will solve everything!") and techno-panic ("AI will destroy education!") to develop nuanced approaches that leverage AI's strengths while protecting what matters most in learning. This begins with confronting the ethical challenges AI presents head-on.

Ethical Crossroads: Navigating AI's Moral Maze

AI raises deep ethical questions for educators. These questions go far beyond "is using ChatGPT cheating?" to the heart of how these technologies are developed, deployed, and integrated into learning environments. Teachers find themselves on the front lines of these ethical dilemmas, often with minimal guidance or support.

The Theft of Creative Work

"Always heartbreaking to see arts institution encourage art theft over creativity imagination and skill! Instead of having AI do this trend, draw it! Paint it! Sculpt it! Create! AI is art theft."

These words from a celebrated cartoonist were in response to an AI trend my organization participated in on social media. We had created a "collector's item doll" using ChatGPT and shared it to our feed. This cartoonist's response, though, made us start to question not only the trend, but the deeper concerns around how these AI systems are generating this kind of content. His statements capture a sentiment shared by many artists, writers, and creators whose work has been scraped without permission to train generative AI systems.

Most large language models and generative AI systems were trained on vast data sets that include copyrighted creative works—books, articles, artwork, music, code—often without permission from or compensation to the original creators. When a student asks AI to "write in the style of Toni Morrison" or "create an image like Frida Kahlo," the system can do so because it has analyzed these artists' work without their consent.

For artists and writers, many of whom already struggle financially, this feels like both theft and existential threat. Their creative expressions, which are the product of years of development and personal experience, have been used to train systems that can now mimic their styles and potentially reduce demand for their original work.

On the flip side, we also received a response to the cartoonist's original objection from an educator who shared this:

> As long as no one is using AI and claiming that it is genuinely their 100 percent work of art and giving credit to AI, it is not theft. When people are studying art they often use the works of professional artists as a tool for learning and they utilize techniques or strategies that mimic the creations of others. I would not consider that theft, nor would most artists as long as credit is being given where it is due.

This isn't a simple debate and the questions that arise require us to think carefully about the values we model for students. When we use generative AI in classrooms, are we implicitly endorsing a model of creation that devalues individual creative labor? Are we teaching students that it's acceptable to use others' creative work without permission so long as the end result is convenient for us? As educators, we need to engage students in thoughtful conversations about these issues, rather than simply normalizing AI use without critical examination.

Bias and Representation in AI Systems

There's no getting around the difficult reality that AI systems often reproduce and amplify existing biases. Trained on data from a society with deep structural inequalities, these systems can perpetuate those same inequalities unless explicitly designed to counteract them.

The ethical implications for education are enormous. When AI systems contain biases related to race, gender, disability, language, or socioeconomic status, they risk reinforcing stereotypes, limiting opportunities, and undermining the fundamental educational goal of helping each student reach their full potential.

These biases are already appearing across educational AI applications:[9]

- Automated essay scoring systems that give lower scores to writing incorporating dialectal features typical of AAVE (African American Vernacular English), despite the content showcasing robust critical thinking
- Speech recognition systems that struggle to support students with diverse accents or speech disabilities
- "Personalized learning" algorithms that suggest less challenging content to students from underrepresented backgrounds[10]
- Facial analysis technologies designed to monitor student engagement often struggle to provide accurate results for students with darker skin tones
- Machine translation tools that perpetuate gender stereotypes in language translation

Teachers are facing the challenge of navigating these complex issues with little support or training. This means that a high school counselor utilizing an AI college recommendation system might not be aware that it is inadvertently guiding low-income students away from selective institutions. Similarly, an elementary teacher employing an AI reading program may not recognize that it is consistently undervaluing the potential of emergent bilingual students.

The ethical challenge extends beyond just recognizing these biases to deciding how to respond. Should teachers avoid AI tools entirely? Use them, but explicitly discuss their limitations with students? Try to correct for biases manually? These questions have no easy answers, but they demand thoughtful consideration rather than mass adoption with no game plan or professional development.

These ethical challenges aren't reasons to reject AI in education entirely. But they do demand thoughtful engagement rather than uncritical enthusiasm. We need to approach AI with both open minds and critical eyes, evaluating not just what these technologies can do but what values they embody and what consequences they might create.

By understanding these ethical dimensions, we can make more informed choices about how to integrate AI into education in ways that enhance rather than undermine our core educational values. This thoughtful integration becomes especially important when we consider how AI intersects with the creative capabilities we've explored throughout this book.

The Intersection of Creativity and Technology

The relationship between creativity and technology has always been complex, but today's technological revolution differs dramatically from those that came before. Previous shifts—from the printing press to photography to digital design tools—primarily changed how we executed creative ideas. Today's AI systems are increasingly involved in generating the ideas themselves.

When Adobe introduced Photoshop in 1990, it changed how designers worked but not what they conceived. The designer still had to envision the final image; Photoshop just made it easier to execute that vision. Today's AI tools like DALL-E and Midjourney can generate entirely new visual concepts from text prompts. They don't just execute ideas—they propose them.

This shift is what some researchers call "co-creative" technology—tools that participate in the creative process rather than simply facilitating it. It's the difference between a paintbrush that helps you realize your vision and a creative partner that contributes ideas of its own. One example of this is agentic AI. Agentic AI represents the next frontier beyond generative AI—systems designed to act autonomously to achieve goals with minimal human oversight. Unlike generative models that simply respond to prompts, agentic AI can plan, reason, and execute complex multistep tasks independently.[11]

This creates fascinating possibilities for creative collaboration. Imagine an AI agent that not only generates ideas but actively researches materials, experiments with different approaches, and implements solutions based on your creative vision. These systems could handle the more technical or repetitive aspects of creative work—researching historical painting techniques, organizing reference materials, or executing basic design elements—freeing human creators to focus on the truly innovative aspects of their work.

Here are some examples of various AI-human partnerships that are transforming creative work across many fields.

Architecture: Firms like Zaha Hadid Architects use AI systems that can generate thousands of design variations based on environmental, structural, and aesthetic parameters. Architects spend less time drafting and more time curating, refining, and imbuing these options with meaning and purpose.

Journalism: The Associated Press uses AI to generate routine financial earnings reports from around 4,400 companies each quarter. This frees up journalists to focus on investigative work and human-interest stories that algorithms can't capture. Instead of requiring writers to spend their time on reporting simple figures, it's redirecting their creative energy toward higher-value work, like the analysis of what those numbers mean.

Education: Teachers are using AI tools to generate multiple versions of practice problems and assessment tools, allowing them to provide more personalized learning experiences while focusing their creative energy on designing meaningful learning journeys and building connections with students.

This transformation isn't just changing what creative professionals do—it's redefining what makes human creativity valuable. Let's examine how these changes affect each branch of creativity we've explored throughout this book.

Connected to AI

As artificial intelligence continues to evolve, understanding and utilizing the Four Branches of Creativity becomes essential for distinguishing human creative capability from machine output. Each branch interacts with AI differently, offering insights into both the possibilities and limitations of machine creativity. Knowing these differences—and how to leverage them—helps us determine what and how to teach each creative branch.

Creative Skills and AI

In the realm of creative skills, AI has made remarkable progress. It can generate images, compose music, write code, and even mimic artistic styles with increasing sophistication. These capabilities might seem to challenge the value of human technical skills. In reality, AI reveals the importance of humans connecting technical proficiency with other creative branches. While AI can execute with nearly perfect technique, it lacks the internal compass that guides human creators in choosing which skills to apply and why.

Creative Thinking and AI

This branch reveals one of the starkest contrasts between human and artificial intelligence. While AI can process vast amounts of information and identify patterns humans might miss, it operates within the boundaries of its training data. In this respect, AI can be incredibly knowledgeable within its domain but unable to make those wild, unexpected connections that characterize human insight.

Human creative thinking remains distinctive in our ability to

- make intuitive leaps across seemingly unrelated content,
- question fundamental assumptions,
- generate truly novel approaches rather than variations on existing patterns, and
- understand context and nuance in ways that machines simply can't.

These are exactly the capabilities we can teach and cultivate in our classrooms and daily lives to enhance our ability to thrive in the uncertain future ahead.

Creative Expression and AI

If there's one area where human creativity truly shines, it's here. Creative expression involves translating personal experience, emotion, and meaning into creative output. While AI can process patterns and generate variations based on existing data, it cannot experience the emotional resonance, cultural context, or lived experiences that fuel genuine human innovation.

The same qualities that make human creativity vulnerable—our doubts, our personal histories, our emotional responses to the world—are what make it irreplaceable. AI might evolve to become a powerful collaborator in the creative process, handling aspects that benefit from computational efficiency and pattern recognition, but the spark of truly original creative insight remains distinctly human. It's the difference between a photograph of a sunset and actually watching the sky transform while feeling the evening breeze—both can be beautiful, but only one carries genuine meaning.

Creative Application and AI

In this branch, we see the most promising potential for human-AI collaboration. AI isn't replacing human creative application—it's amplifying it. What could be better than having a tireless assistant who can

- handle routine tasks while you focus on strategy,
- generate multiple variations of your ideas for testing,
- help implement solutions at scale, and
- provide data-driven insights to inform your creative decisions.

But here's the critical component: AI needs human guidance to ensure these applications are meaningful, ethical, and truly beneficial. We're the ones who understand context, consider implications, and make value-based decisions about how to apply creative solutions.

The New Creative Landscape

The future of creativity is about understanding how to combine the computational power of a supercomputer with the spark of human imagination. And while AI can handle the heavy lifting of processing and pattern-finding, humans bring the crucial elements that give those patterns meaning. In this wild new world, we humans have what I like to call our "3 I's"—three distinct elements that AI just can't match:

1. **Integration**—our ability to blend ideas across domains, connect emotions with logic, and see patterns that transcend data.
2. **Intention**—our capacity to create with purpose, guided by values and an understanding of human needs.
3. **Innovation**—our power to identify which problems are worth solving and design possibilities that go beyond existing patterns.

This collaboration between the "3 I's" is transforming creative work in exciting ways:

Augmented Ideation

AI tools can now generate hundreds of variations while we humans curate, refine, and infuse them with meaning. It's not about replacing our creative process but expanding it. Think about it like this: in traditional brainstorming, we might generate a dozen ideas in an hour. With AI assistance, we can explore hundreds of conceptual directions in minutes, freeing us to focus on the truly human part of creation—deciding which ideas matter and why.

I'm seeing this play out in classrooms where teachers who once struggled to help students generate story ideas now use AI as a springboard. The students don't just take what the AI suggests; they transform it, challenging assumptions and adding emotional depth that only human experience can provide.

This partnership works because humans and AI bring complementary strengths to the ideation process. AI excels at retrieving information, making connections across vast data sets, and generating variations on themes. Humans excel at emotional resonance, cultural context, and ethical judgment. When these strengths combine, we get ideation that's both broader and deeper than either could achieve alone.

The key is understanding that AI isn't your creative replacement—it's your inexhaustible brainstorming partner with infinite stamina. You remain the curator, the meaning-maker, the one who knows which ideas deserve to live and which ones don't serve your deeper purpose. Your human wisdom—shaped by lived experience, cultural understanding, and emotional intelligence—becomes more valuable, not less, in deciding what's truly worth pursuing.

Enhanced Implementation

The technical barriers that once limited creative expression are falling as AI handles more of the execution details, freeing us to focus on vision, strategy, and purpose. This shift fundamentally changes where we direct our creative energy.

Think about documentary filmmakers who previously spent weeks manually transcribing interviews. Now they can use AI to handle that tedious work, allowing them to invest more time in crafting powerful narratives and visual storytelling. Or consider educators developing customized learning materials who no longer need to start from scratch—they can rapidly prototype materials and then focus their expertise on pedagogical refinement and emotional connection.

This isn't cutting corners—it's simply redirecting human creativity to where it adds the most value. With AI handling routine implementation challenges, we can push further into unexplored creative territory. I've watched musicians who never learned traditional notation use AI to translate their hummed melodies into sheet music, opening collaboration with classically trained performers.

I've also seen non-programmers prototype functional apps by describing their vision to AI assistants. These tools don't replace the need for human creativity—they amplify it by removing technical obstacles that previously limited who could create and what they could create.

The most exciting aspect is how this shift democratizes creative production. Implementation barriers have historically limited who could bring their ideas to life. As AI lowers these barriers, we're seeing a flourishing of voices and perspectives that might otherwise have remained silent. The creative landscape becomes richer, more diverse, and more representative of the full spectrum of human experience.

Collaborative Intelligence

Right now, we're witnessing the evolution of an entirely new set of creative capabilities that simply didn't exist before AI entered our daily lives. It's like watching a new artistic medium emerge in real-time.

We're becoming fluent in "AI whispering"—the subtle art of crafting prompts that coax these systems toward unexplored territories. Instead of typing technically perfect instructions, we're developing a creative dialogue with these systems. I've watched educators who initially struggled with prompt writing transform into skilled collaborators who know exactly how to guide AI through questions and iterative feedback. They're not just using AI—they're dancing with it.

There's also this emerging skill called "synthetic discernment"—that gut-level ability to look at AI-generated content and instantly recognize not just what works or doesn't, but what holds the seed of something truly meaningful. It reminds me of how experienced editors can spot potential in a rough draft that others might dismiss. We're developing this sixth sense for creative possibility in machine outputs, seeing beyond the obvious to the transformative.

Then there's what philosopher Andy Clark describes as "cognitive assemblage"—our growing capacity to weave together human insight, AI capabilities, and real-world needs into something greater than the sum of its parts. This isn't about human *or* machine creativity; it's about creating a third space where they enhance each other in ways neither could achieve alone.

Perhaps most crucially, we're learning to navigate this territory with ethical awareness. Every new AI capability comes with profound questions about authenticity, attribution, and impact. I'm seeing thoughtful creators move beyond simply asking, "Can we?" to the more essential questions: "Should we?" and "How might this reshape human creativity in the long run?" We're not just technical pioneers but ethical ones.

These skills move far beyond technical know-how into new forms of creative literacy that are fundamentally reshaping the relationship between human imagination and machine capability. And this is precisely why our four-branch creativity framework matters more now than ever. Understanding how to develop and blend all aspects of our creativity has become our secret weapon in this increasingly automated world. Rather than competing with AI, we can use it thoughtfully to amplify what makes human creativity special in the first place.

The Rise of the Creative Machine: Computational Creativity in the Age of AI

When my daughter was seven, she once asked me if computers could think. Before I could answer, she followed up: "Could they ever think up something brand new, something nobody told them about first?"

Her instinctive question cuts to the heart of what makes computational creativity such a fascinating frontier. AI systems like DALL-E and Midjourney now generate images that range from breathtaking to bizarre, all without ever having held a paintbrush. Music composition algorithms produce symphonies without understanding the emotional resonance of a minor chord.

Computational creativity is a rapidly growing field that explores the potential for machines to exhibit creative behavior. It encompasses a wide range of techniques and approaches, from generative art and music to creative problem-solving and scientific discovery.[12]

One example of this kind of work is from Dominic Harris, a London-based digital artist whose immersive installations blur the boundaries between technology and art. Harris develops custom algorithms that respond to human movement, turning gallery visitors into active participants. His piece "Bloomed," for example, uses motion sensors to trigger flowers that bloom in response to visitor movements.[13]

Then there's Lee Cronin, a chemist at the University of Glasgow. Cronin and his team have developed an AI system that can generate new chemical compounds with desired properties. By analyzing vast databases of known compounds and using machine learning to identify patterns and relationships, the system can propose entirely new molecules that have never been synthesized before[14].

The algorithmic artist doesn't struggle with self-doubt or draw inspiration from a childhood memory. It doesn't know the thrill of a breakthrough after weeks of frustration. Yet its outputs can move us deeply, raising profound questions about what creativity truly is.

After all, if AI can now write essays, compose music, and generate art that most of us can't distinguish from human-created work—what exactly are we assessing when we evaluate creativity?

The new reality of AI's rapidly expanding set of technological breakthroughs makes assessing the value of creative work more important than ever. While billionaires like Bill Gates may espouse that teachers and healthcare professionals will be replaced in the future,[15] I wholeheartedly disagree. We'll still need nurses and doctors and principals and teachers, though the job may look different than it does today. In fact, it may be better because AI can handle the mundane tasks that slow our work and allow us to transform our focus into personalized instruction and care which led many of us to these professions in the first place. This will be dependent upon our answer to the question: "how much are we willing to let go?". Here are three shifts that can help educators navigate this new landscape:

1. ***Product AND Process***

In chapter 4, we explored the importance of assessing creative processes, not just products. While AI can generate impressive outputs, it doesn't engage in human-like creative processes. It doesn't experience curiosity, conceptual struggle, or emotional connection—all elements central to human creativity.

Forward-thinking educators are making creative processes more visible and valued:

- Elementary teachers encourage the use of creativity journals where students document their inspirations, attempts, revisions, and reflections.
- Middle school arts teachers assess students' project development through process portfolios showing work at different stages.
- High school STEM teachers (science, technology, engineering, and math) evaluate students' problem-solving pathways, not just their solutions.

By adjusting our focus to how students create—their question-asking, ideation, selection, development, and revision—teachers can evaluate distinctly human aspects of creativity that AI doesn't replicate.

2. ***From Solo Creation to Creative Collaboration***

The second shift recognizes creativity as inherently social rather than purely individual. While some computational creativity systems try to generate new works independently, others are designed to work with human creators. These systems act as creative partners, suggesting ideas, providing inspiration, or helping to refine and develop human-generated concepts.

While AI can generate content as this thought partner, it doesn't genuinely collaborate, negotiate different perspectives, or respond with emotional intelligence to human needs.

Educators are increasingly assessing collaborative creativity through approaches like these:

- Elementary design challenges where teams tackle problems together, with assessment focusing on idea-building and perspective-taking
- Middle school projects where students receive feedback from multiple sources and teachers assess how they integrated these differing ideas into their work
- High school in-class discussions focusing on current events and working together to explore problems and solutions

By evaluating how students create with others—sharing perspectives, building on ideas, resolving differences, and responding to feedback—teachers can assess creative capabilities that remain distinctly human even as AI advances.

3. *From Assigned Topics to Student-Directed Inquiry*

Student agency is critical when defining creative problems and purposes. While AI can generate content on assigned topics, it doesn't identify meaningful problems or pursue personally significant inquiries on its own.

Educators are changing their assignments to include the following:

- Elementary project-based learning units where students pursue self-chosen investigations, with assessment focusing on question quality and investigative persistence
- Middle school passion projects where students identify problems they care about, with evaluation focusing on problem definition and purposeful exploration

- High school impact initiatives where students develop solutions to self-identified community issues, with assessment examining problem framing and adaptive problem-solving

By noticing how students identify and define creative challenges—their ability to notice problems, ask meaningful questions, and pursue personally significant inquiries—teachers evaluate creative capabilities that AI cannot replicate.

These shifts don't mean abandoning the assessment of creative products. Student-created work remains important evidence of learning and accomplishment. But in an AI world, product assessment alone is insufficient. The most valuable creative assessment examines how students create, who they create with, and why they create—dimensions that remain distinctly human.

This evolution in creativity assessment certainly helps teachers differentiate human creativity from AI generation. But it also helps students develop the creative capabilities most likely to remain valuable in an AI-infused world: the ability to direct creative processes purposefully, collaborate creatively with others, and identify meaningful problems worth solving.

The rise of the creative machine isn't the threat to human creativity that so many fear, but an invitation to redefine and reinvigorate it. It's a call to explore new forms of creative partnership and to push the boundaries of what we think is possible. And it's a reminder that, even in an age of artificial intelligence, the most powerful creative force in the universe remains the human imagination.[16]

Tapping into Your Creative Genius

How do we harness the power of that imagination? After two decades of working with educators, students, and professionals across many different fields, there's one thing I know at my core to be true: each of us has a unique creative access point—a specific artistic area or creative approach that naturally resonates within us. For some, it's visual expression through drawing or photography. For others, it's the rhythm and movement of dance or music. Still others connect deeply with storytelling, design thinking, or building three-dimensional structures.

This is more than a preference; it's a gateway to your creative genius. It's your distinctive way of knowing and operating in the world that allows you to fulfill our fundamental human need to create. When you recognize and embrace your creative access point, you unlock a powerful catalyst that can transform how you approach challenges across all domains of your life.

As the founder of design firm IDEO and Stanford's d.school, David Kelley has observed thousands of people reconnecting with their creative confidence. His research shows that most adults don't lack creative ability—they lack creative confidence. Somewhere along the way, many of us absorbed the message that we weren't "the creative type," and that belief became a self-fulfilling prophecy[17].

Breaking through this barrier requires what Kelley calls "guided mastery"—an approach that helps you build confidence through small creative successes. Instead of big dramatic transformations, we focus on taking small, manageable steps that gradually expand your creative comfort zone.[18] We can adapt Kelley's approach as a means of finding, exploring, and leveraging our creative access points for the future that awaits.

Finding Your Creative Access Point

The first step in tapping into your creative genius is identifying your personal creative access point. Try these approaches:

1. **Reflect on flow experiences:** Think about times when you've been so absorbed in a creative activity that you lost track of time. What were you doing? This state of flow often signals a natural creative access point.

2. **Recall childhood joys**: Before you learned to self-censor, what creative activities brought you genuine pleasure? These early inclinations often point to our authentic creative channels.

3. **Notice where you naturally observe detail**: Do you find yourself analyzing the structure of music you hear? Noticing color combinations in your environment? Appreciating the storytelling in films? These attention patterns often reveal our creative strengths.

4. **Experiment across domains**: Try short creative exercises in different forms—writing, drawing, movement, music, construction—and note which feel most energizing and natural.

Once you've identified your creative access point, you can use it as a foundation for developing broader creative capabilities and applying them to challenges in your work and life.

Building Your Creative Practice

You can start building your own creative practice with "creativity microdoses"—brief, low-stakes creative challenges that are incorporated into your daily routine:

- Instead of taking your usual route to work, find a new path and notice three things you've never seen before.
- Take a common object on your desk and come up with five unconventional uses for it.
- Write a six-word memoir about your day before going to bed.
- Sketch a simple object from three different angles.
- Create a playlist that tells the story of your week.

These small exercises might seem trivial, but they're rewiring your brain, creating new neural pathways that support creative thinking. And as we learned in chapter 5, these small practices help prepare your mind to enter flow states more easily.

Since even brief creative engagements increase our capacity for divergent thinking (generating multiple solutions to a problem), these creativity microdoses help our adaptability and resiliency in the face of complex challenges.

As you build confidence, gradually increase the scope of your creative challenges:

- When facing a problem, commit to generating at least ten different solutions before selecting one to pursue.
- Set aside thirty minutes each week for "curiosity time"—exploring a topic that intrigues you but has nothing to do with your work.
- Find a "creativity accountability partner" with whom you can share your attempts, struggles, and breakthroughs.
- Create something every day for a week, no matter how small or simple.
- Practice "creative cross-training" by engaging with a creative form that's outside your comfort zone.

Applying the Four Branches to Your Creative Development

Let's look at how all of this connects to the Four Branches of Creativity we explored in chapter 3. Each offers a different pathway to tap into your creative potential.

Once we discover our creative access point, we use that area to develop specific **creative skills**. This means developing technical abilities in areas that interest you, whether that's learning basic coding, taking a drawing class, or exploring new teaching techniques.

As we build those skills over time, we become more confident in our abilities. This allows us to begin exploring other creative activities, which require us to use **creative thinking**. This is where the creative microdosing comes in, providing opportunities for us to make unexpected connections.

As you find your creative groove, you might find ways to bring more of yourself through **creative expression** into your work, whether that's through journaling, artistic practice, or simply bringing your unique perspective to collaborative projects.

Finally, through **creative application**, you could look for opportunities to implement creative approaches to real challenges in your classroom, workplace, or community through approaches like arts integration, STEAM, or project-based learning.

Why Integrated Approaches Work

The reason approaches like these work lies in how they leverage our natural creative access points while building bridges to other domains. These integrated approaches weave creativity into the fabric of learning and problem-solving, rather than treating it as a separate skill.

This integration creates five powerful benefits that apply equally to classroom learning and professional development:

1. **Deep Engagement and Ownership**: When we engage through our natural creative access points, we become active participants rather than passive recipients. Students in arts-integrated classrooms show higher motivation and investment in their learning because they connect to the material through their creative strengths. This same principle applies in professional settings—when we approach problems through our creative access points, we take greater ownership of the challenge and invest more deeply in finding solutions.

2. **Enhanced Critical Thinking**: Creative integration builds natural bridges between different types of thinking. A student exploring mathematical concepts through dance develops both spatial reasoning and abstract thinking simultaneously. A professional using visual mapping to understand complex data activates both analytical and aesthetic thinking. These complementary thinking modes enhance our ability to see problems from multiple angles and develop innovative solutions.

3. **Empowerment and Agency**: Both teachers and students report greater confidence and professional satisfaction in integrated creative environments. Teachers become facilitators of discovery rather than transmitters of information. Students become co-creators of their learning experience. Similarly, professionals who incorporate creative approaches into their work report greater autonomy and job satisfaction.

4. **Equitable Access to Success**: Everyone has creative capacities, but they manifest differently across individuals. Integrated creative approaches provide multiple entry points to learning and problem-solving, ensuring that diverse thinkers can contribute and succeed. In a world increasingly dominated by standardized systems, this equity of access becomes more crucial than ever.

5. **Connective Learning for Complex Challenges**: The most significant problems we face don't respect disciplinary boundaries. Climate change isn't just a scientific challenge—it's also social, economic, and ethical. Educational equity isn't just about pedagogy—it involves psychology, sociology, and policy. Integrated creative approaches prepare us to navigate these complex, interconnected challenges by developing our capacity for connective thinking.

And don't forget the importance of reflection and consistent action. These two areas are the difference between people who merely dabble in creativity and those who develop significant creative achievements.

When you approach challenges with curiosity rather than certainty, when you demonstrate resilience after creative setbacks, and when you show enthusiasm for learning across disciplines, you're creating a contagious culture of creativity that spreads to those around you.

By recognizing your unique creative access point and building deliberate practices around it, you're both developing discrete creative skills and cultivating your distinctive creative genius, your natural way of making meaningful contributions to our shared world.

Where Will You Go Next?

As you forge your creative path forward, reflect on which aspects of creativity have resonated most deeply with you throughout this journey. Perhaps you felt a spark of recognition when we explored flow states in chapter 5—those moments when time seems suspended and creative work becomes effortless. Or maybe the structured creative habits we examined in chapter 6 offered a framework that aligns with how you naturally operate.

Consider these questions: What problems light you up with curiosity? What challenges make you want to roll up your sleeves and dive in? These questions are the compasses pointing toward your unique contribution to the future.

Your unique response to these different facets of creativity isn't random—it's revealing something essential about how your creative mind works best.

The most meaningful creative practice emerges when we align our approaches with our natural cognitive rhythms rather than forcing ourselves into someone else's creative template. This doesn't mean avoiding challenges or staying in your comfort zone—quite the opposite. It means recognizing your starting point and building outward from there with both purpose and flexibility.

Remember the neuroplasticity principles we explored? Your brain physically rewires itself in response to how you engage with the world. Each creative challenge you embrace—whether it's developing a new teaching approach, redesigning your home environment, or solving a community problem—is building neural architecture that enhances your capacity for every future task. You're solving today's problems while developing tomorrow's capabilities.

This is why cultivating your creative practice isn't a luxury—it's a necessity for navigating an increasingly complex future. The challenges ahead will require all Four Branches of Creativity working in concert, bringing together different ways of thinking, different fields of knowledge, and different approaches to problem-solving. We need people who are developing unique ways of seeing things as they are and things as we want them to be—both the connections and the possibilities.

As we close this book, know that this isn't an ending but a beginning. The creative journey you're embarking on isn't a sprint to some distant finish line—it's an ongoing exploration of what's possible. Every creative act, no matter how small, is a miracle that contributes to the larger tapestry of human innovation and progress.

Your creativity matters. Not despite the rise of artificial intelligence and automation, but because of it. In a world where routine tasks are increasingly handled by machines, our uniquely human capacity for creativity in all its forms becomes more valuable than ever.

The future is waiting for your contribution. Whether you're a scientist combining different forms of knowledge, an artist pushing the boundaries of expression with new technologies, or someone who brings creative thinking to everyday challenges, your perspective and your creative voice are essential parts of humanity's next chapter.

So step forward boldly. Use the tools and insights you've gained from this journey. Trust in your creative capacity. Because the future isn't something that happens to us—it's something we create together, one innovative solution at a time.

Key Takeaways

1. Human-AI creative partnerships are redefining creative work. Rather than competing with AI, our creative future lies in developing new capabilities that leverage both machine efficiency and human insight.

2. The "3 I's"—*integration, intention, and innovation*—represent distinctly human creative advantages that will remain valuable regardless of how advanced AI becomes.

3. Computational creativity is reshaping how we assess creative work, requiring a shift from evaluating just products to examining processes, collaborative abilities, and problem-finding skills.

4. As technical barriers to creation fall, creative value shifts from execution to conceptualization—from "how to create" to "what to create and why"—requiring a rethinking of creative education.

5. Navigating the twenty-first century demands "integrative creativity"— the ability to blend diverse disciplines, perspectives, and approaches to address increasingly complex challenges in a rapidly changing world.

PRACTICE STRATEGY: Stepping In, Stepping Out

Two things can be true at the same time. There are always multiple perspectives and angles that impact our understanding of ideas and topics like creativity and artificial intelligence. For this final strategy, we're going to explore these two areas from different points of view.

1. Find a photograph that captures something (anything!) about creativity and artificial intelligence.
2. View that photograph from the perspective of a consumer. Then, answer these questions:

a. What do you see in this image?

   b. What questions do you have about this image?

   c. What feelings bubble to the surface as you look at this image?

3. Next, look at the photograph again, but this time from the perspective of an artist. Answer these same questions as an artist might:

   a. What do you see in this image?

   b. What questions do you have about this image?

   c. What feelings bubble to the surface as you look at this image?

4. Look at what you wrote from each perspective. What's the same? What's different?

5. Finally, using what you've identified in step 4, edit the photograph (either digitally or by printing it out and physically transforming it) to highlight YOUR perspective about creativity and artificial intelligence.

Notes

1 Wyss Institute for Biologically Inspired Engineering. (2013, May 28). "Spinning Up a Silk Pavilion." Wyss Institute at Harvard University. https://wyss.harvard.edu/news/spinning-up-a-silk-pavilion/

2 Bloomberg Media. (2024, January 5). "Representation Will Define the Future of Creativity More Than Technology." https://www.bloombergmedia.com/blog/representation-will-define-the-future-of-creativity-more-than-technology/

3 Cornell Tech. (2023, February 20). "AI vs. Artist: The Future of Creativity." https://tech.cornell.edu/news/ai-vs-artist-the-future-of-creativity/

4 Business Wire. (2024, April 15). "Futuri Shares Groundbreaking AI in Media Study at National Association of Broadcasters (NAB) Show 2024; Reveals a New Era of Human-AI Collaboration in Content Creation." Business Wire. https://www.businesswire.com/news/home/20240415609276/en/Futuri-Shares-Groundbreaking-AI-in-Media-Study-at-National-Association-of-Broadcasters-NAB-Show-2024-Reveals-A-New-Era-of-Human-AI-Collaboration-in-Content-Creation

5 Guilford, J. P. (1950). "Creativity." *American Psychologist*, 5(9), 444–54. https://doi.org/10.1037/h0063487

6   Siguaw, J. A., Simpson, P. M., & Enz, C. A. (2006, October 20). "Conceptualizing Innovation Orientation: A Framework for Study and Integration of Innovation Research'." *Journal of Product Innovation Management*, 23(6), 556–74. https://doi.org/10.1111/j.1540-5885.2006.00224.x

7   Gartner. "Gartner Hype Cycle." Accessed April 14, 2025. https://www.gartner.com/en/research/methodologies/gartner-hype-cycle

8   Mollenkamp, D. (2024, August 29). "Will AI Shrink Disparities in Schools, or Widen Them?" EdSurge. https://www.edsurge.com/news/2024-08-19-will-ai-shrink-disparities-in-schools-or-widen-them

9   Baker, Ryan S., & Hawn, A. (2021). "Algorithmic Bias in Education." *International Journal of Artificial Intelligence in Education*, 31, 600–40.

10 Reich, J., & Mimi, I. (2017). "From Good Intentions to Real Outcomes: Equity by Design in Learning Technologies." Digital Media and Learning Research Hub.

11 Purdy, M. (2024, December 12). "What Is Agentic AI, and How Will It Change Work?" *Harvard Business Review*. https://hbr.org/2024/12/what-is-agentic-ai-and-how-will-it-change-work

12 TechTarget. (n.d.). "Computational Creativity (Artificial Creativity)." https://www.techtarget.com/whatis/definition/computational-creativity

13 Merritt, R. (2023, May 25). "Butterfly Effects: Digital Artist Uses AI to Engage Exhibit Goers." NVIDIA Blog. https://blogs.nvidia.com/blog/ai-artist-dominic-harris/

14 Urquhart, J. (2018, July 19). "AI Robot Tests, Predicts and Even Discovers Reactions That Are New to Chemistry." Chemistry World. https://www.chemistryworld.com/news/ai-robot-tests-predicts-and-even-discovers-reactions-that-are-new-to-chemistry/3009276.article

15 Richards, B. (2025, February). "Bill Gates Says AI Will Replace Doctors, Teachers and More in Next 10 Years, Making Humans Unnecessary 'for Most Things.'" *People*. https://people.com/bill-gates-ai-will-replace-doctors-teachers-in-next-10-years-11705615

16 May, T. (2024, July 15). "Where the Creative Industry Is Heading and How to Survive the Next 15 Years." Creative Boom. https://www.creativeboom.com/tips/where-the-creative-industry-is-heading-and-how-to-survive-the-next-15-years/

17 Kelley, D., & Kelley, T. (2013). *Creative Confidence: Unleashing the Creative Potential Within Us All*. Currency.

18 Kelley, T., & Kelley, D. (2012, December). "Reclaim Your Creative Confidence." *Harvard Business Review*. https://hbr.org/2012/12/reclaim-your-creative-confidence

APPENDIX A: ARTS INTEGRATION, STEAM, AND PROJECT-BASED LEARNING

As you're reading through this book, you may be wondering about specific teaching approaches I refer to when discussing how to bring creativity into the classroom. The three I discuss most often are arts integration, STEAM (science, technology, engineering, the arts, and mathematics) and PBL (project-based learning). In this appendix, I'll be breaking down each approach so you can have a better understanding of what they are, when to use them, and how to implement them effectively within a school setting.

Arts Integration: Connecting Curriculum through Creative Expression

In 2009, second-grade teacher Candace Hutchinson faced a classroom where nearly half her students were struggling with fractions. Traditional methods weren't working, and test scores were declining. In desperation, she turned to her school's music teacher (me) for help.

Together, we created a lesson that connected music note values (quarter notes, half notes, whole notes) with mathematical fractions. Students physically moved to different beat patterns, created musical pieces based on fraction values, and composed their own "fraction songs." The result? Within three weeks, 92 percent of students showed mastery of the concepts on assessment, compared to just 46 percent before the intervention.

This is arts integration at its finest—not using arts as a decorative add-on, but as a genuine pathway to deeper understanding.

What Is Arts Integration?

At its core, arts integration is an approach to teaching and learning where content standards are taught and assessed equitably in and through the arts. It's not a curriculum but a methodology that brings together different subject areas through meaningful connections.

For something to truly be arts integration, it must fulfill three key criteria:

- connect a content standard (such as math, science, language arts, or social studies) with an arts standard (visual arts, music, dance, theater, or media arts) in a way that makes natural sense;
- teach both standards equitably throughout the lesson (not using one to merely enhance the other); and
- assess learning in both content areas.

This approach is fundamentally different from simply using art activities to make lessons more fun or engaging. It's not enough to just *use* another content or arts area. You must have a lesson connected back to naturally aligned standards in both the content and the arts area. When implemented correctly, arts integration becomes a powerful teaching approach that helps students understand, apply, and demonstrate their knowledge in unique ways.

The Arts Integration Continuum

Most educators don't immediately master arts integration. Instead, they progress through a continuum of implementation levels:

On one side of the continuum is *arts enhancement*. This is where we're using the arts in service of another content area—the arts are making the content "sticky." On the other side of the scale is *arts integration*. This is where both the content and the arts are being taught and assessed equitably.

ARTS INTEGRATION CONTINUUM CARD

Arts integration is a process, which means that it naturally unfolds over time and will look different in each classroom. Use this continuum card to discover where you are in your own integration journey and what your next steps could be moving forward.

BASIC LEVEL .... **HIGHEST LEVEL**

ENHANCEMENT	THEME-BASED	INQUIRY-DRIVEN	CO-TAUGHT	INTEGRATION
Uses one area to support or service another in a lesson.	Lesson is based upon a theme common in two areas.	Lesson in both areas centers around an essential question.	Lesson is co-taught by content teachers in two or more areas.	Lesson is co-planned by two content teachers and is grounded in equitably teaching and assessing standards in both areas.
Little to no discussion between content and fine arts area teachers about the lesson.	Some discussion surrounding the theme alignment between content and arts area teachers about the lesson.	Discussion and planning surrounding the essential questions between the content and arts area teachers about the lesson. Possible lesson collaboration.	Planning occurs between content and fine arts area teachers about the lesson. Portions of the lesson may be taught in each content area separately.	Planning occurs between content and fine arts area teachers about the lesson. The lesson may be co-taught or individually taught within a single classroom

The Institute for Arts Integration and STEAM   ArtsIntegration.com

FIGURE APPENDIX A.1

Think of it like the difference between a cupcake with icing on top and a blueberry muffin: The cupcake with icing looks and tastes great. But, you could remove the icing from the top and the cake would stay intact. This is like an arts enhancement lesson. If you can remove the arts part of the lesson and the lesson would still stay intact, you're using the arts in service of the content.

On the other hand, a blueberry muffin also looks and tastes good. But if you tried to remove the blueberries from the muffin, your muffin would crumble. This is like an arts integration lesson. You can't remove either the content or the arts part of the lesson without the lesson crumbling.

Both arts enhancement and arts integration are great! Just like cupcakes and muffins are both excellent pastries. We just need to know what we're using, why we're using it, and choose the approach with intention.

In between these two ends of the scale, there are three other sections: theme-based instruction, inquiry-based learning, and co-taught instruction. Each of these is a shade of arts integration. Each has a specific practice and purpose:

- **Enhancement**—Using one subject area to support or service another (like singing the "50 Nifty United States" song to memorize state names). This is where many people start out and that's okay. It's just not arts integration.

- **Theme-Based Instruction**—Creating lessons around a common theme in two areas. There may be some discussion surrounding the theme alignment between the content and fine arts teachers about the lesson. This is really a stepping stone toward looking at a common thread.

- **Inquiry-Driven Instruction**—Addressing a concept between content and arts areas centered around an essential question. There is discussion and planning surrounding the essential questions between the content and fine arts teachers about the lesson and maybe even some lesson collaboration. This can take on a lot of different looks based on the scheduling and flexibility available in a school.

- **Co-Taught Lessons**—Lessons taught collaboratively by teachers from different content areas. The planning occurs between the content and fine arts teachers about the lesson. Again, this can take on a lot of different possibilities. It may look like a project where one part is taught in the English language arts (ELA) classroom and the arts component is taught in the arts classroom. Or, it could be that the ELA and arts teacher teach the lesson together in the same room.
- **Arts Integration**—Lessons co-planned by teachers and grounded in equitably teaching and assessing standards in both areas. The planning occurs between the content and fine arts teachers about the lesson. The lesson can either be co-taught or individually taught within a single classroom. This happens after each standard being addressed has already been explicitly taught on its own, and an arts integration lesson is being used to apply their learning in an expanded context to provide a meaningful learning experience.

What's most important to remember about the continuum is this: not everything is meant to be fully arts integrated, nor can we always keep everything arts enhanced. There are steps in between that we can explore and bit by bit expand and deepen our teaching practice.

Understanding this continuum helps teachers recognize their current practice and identify steps toward more authentic integration.

Roles and Responsibilities

Sometimes, teachers question what their individual roles are in the arts integration approach. What are they responsible for? It's important to be clear on who does what and why before jumping in. This way, everyone has a clear picture of where they fit into this approach.

The role of the arts teachers is to teach their arts content first. They need to teach the skills and processes of their art form if our students have any chance of using them as an application of learning. This is a huge advocacy tool for arts teachers. Arts integration requires *more* dedicated arts instruction—not less. Many arts teachers worry that they will be replaced by classroom teachers teaching arts content. But that's not how this works. Arts teachers are the only ones who have the experience and training to provide the best possible skills and processes in their respective art forms. They need to focus on teaching those things during dedicated arts times.

They are also a collaborator in the approach. They can co-teach arts-integrated lessons and should be a partner in collaborative planning efforts. They can also model arts techniques for teachers and students. And finally, they are arts advocates. They are the folks who design and put on gallery shows and arts nights, and they can share arts strategies and techniques at professional development (PD) events. These teachers can help document and share the arts with all stakeholders in the community.

The role of the classroom teacher is to teach their content directly first and then work in collaboration with the arts teacher to create and implement an arts-integrated lesson that helps students apply their learning. Classroom teachers also need to teach the skills and processes of the content areas first. Which is why arts integration is an approach—it's meant to provide relevance, context and creation into the learning process. Classroom teachers are also collaborators. They can also co-teach lessons, work in collaborative planning with arts teachers and they can model content strategies and skills. Finally, they can also support arts advocacy by participating and even contributing to gallery shows, coming to arts nights—maybe even offering to help coordinate them—and in sharing arts integration strategies and lessons during PD events.

Each teacher is a valuable partner in this approach, and each teacher has something extraordinary to offer the other. It is a true collaborative effort.

When and How to Use Arts Integration Effectively

Arts integration works best as an intentional approach used strategically rather than constantly. The most effective implementations emerge when students need to apply knowledge in new contexts or when concepts benefit from multiple modes of representation. This approach particularly shines when learners struggle with traditional methods, when complex ideas need concrete expression, or when engagement has waned with conventional teaching approaches.

The most effective arts integration begins with standards alignment—identifying genuine connections between content and arts objectives rather than forcing artificial links. Successful implementation builds on explicit instruction first, then uses integration as a way for students to apply what they've learned in both domains. This means teaching fraction concepts directly before having students compose music using those same mathematical relationships. The power lies in collaboration across disciplines, where content expertise meets artistic knowledge to create something more meaningful than either could accomplish alone. Throughout the process, both the journey and destination matter; students gain as much from experimenting with artistic processes as they do from completing polished final products.

Assessment remains crucial but takes a different form in integrated learning. Rather than separate tests for each subject, effective arts integration employs authentic assessments that measure understanding in both domains simultaneously—perhaps a scientific explanation illustrated through visual arts or a mathematical concept demonstrated through dance.

Remember: the goal of arts integration isn't to force arts into every lesson; rather, it's to activate multiple pathways to understanding and application of content. We want to use this approach when it genuinely deepens learning and creates transformative educational experiences.

STEAM Education: Where Arts Meet STEM

STEAM education takes the traditional STEM approach (science, technology, engineering, and mathematics) and infuses it with the arts to create a more holistic, creative learning experience. Unlike the separate subject areas approach we often see in schools, STEAM embraces the natural connections between disciplines to create powerful learning experiences that prepare students for a complex, innovation-driven world.

What Is STEAM Education?

STEAM education is an approach to learning that uses science, technology, engineering, the arts, and mathematics as access points for guiding student inquiry, dialogue, and critical thinking. This is defined by several key elements that must be present to qualify as a STEAM lesson or experience.

First, STEAM is an integrated approach to learning, similar to arts integration, that requires an intentional connection between standards, assessments and lesson design/implementation. It's not just adding art projects to science lessons—it's deliberately weaving together learning objectives across disciplines.

At its core, true STEAM experiences involve two or more standards from science, technology, engineering, math, and the arts to be taught *and* assessed in and through each other. This means both the STEM content and the arts content need equal attention in both instruction and assessment.

The STEAM approach differs from arts integration in that it centers around inquiry, collaboration, and an emphasis on process-based and project-based learning. Students don't just memorize facts—they explore, question, and create throughout the whole learning experience.

Perhaps most importantly, STEAM education requires utilizing and leveraging the integrity of the arts themselves. The arts aren't just decorative additions but essential components with their own rigorous standards and processes.

Beyond Integration: The STEAM Process and Implementation

The most powerful STEAM learning typically lives in the interdisciplinary and transdisciplinary spaces, where students see knowledge not as isolated subjects but as interconnected tools for understanding and transforming the world.

Interdisciplinary learning explicitly connects subjects in meaningful ways. Students might learn the science of light and color while simultaneously exploring how artists use these principles, seeing direct connections between the disciplines.

Transdisciplinary learning occurs when subjects blur completely around authentic challenges or problems. Students might tackle designing an energy-efficient, aesthetically pleasing public space—seamlessly blending principles of engineering, environmental science, design, and mathematics in service of a real-world application.

Bringing STEAM to life in the classroom follows a process that mirrors how professionals solve complex challenges in the real world, using both interdisciplinary and transdisciplinary methods along the way:

1. **Focus through Inquiry**—Begin with an essential question or problem to solve that naturally connects STEM and arts content. This question becomes the driving force behind the learning experience.

2. **Uncover Standards**—Identify the specific standards from both STEM and arts disciplines that align with your inquiry. This ensures the learning remains rigorous and purposeful.

3. **Brainstorm**—Encourage students to generate multiple possibilities and approaches. This mirrors the divergent thinking processes used by both scientists and artists in their work.

4. **Build Knowledge**—Engage students in researching both the STEM and arts components of the challenge. This research phase builds the foundational understanding needed to create innovative solutions.

5. **Create**—Students design and develop their solutions, applying knowledge from across disciplines. This hands-on phase engages students in the messy, iterative process of bringing ideas to life.

6. **Present and Refine**—Students share their creations and reflect on both process and product. Peers and possibly industry professionals (if available) provide feedback that can be used to refine the process and product in any reiteration phases needed. This final step reinforces learning and develops communication skills essential for future success.

This process transforms classrooms into studios and laboratories where students don't just learn about concepts—they apply them to meaningful challenges, developing both knowledge and the skills to use that knowledge effectively.

How STEAM Differs from Arts Integration

While both STEAM and arts integration involve connecting disciplines, there are important distinctions:

Arts integration focuses specifically on connecting an arts standard with a content standard (like math or science) in an equitable way. For example, teaching fractions through music notation would be arts integration if both math and music standards are being taught and assessed equally.

STEAM, meanwhile, is broader in scope—it creates learning environments where science, technology, engineering, arts, and math interact in authentic ways. Rather than pairing two subjects, STEAM creates a multidisciplinary learning ecosystem where multiple subject areas flow together around genuine problems or questions.

The difference is subtle but important: arts integration typically creates powerful connections between two disciplines, while STEAM creates a space where multiple disciplines converge around authentic challenges.

Why STEAM Matters Now More Than Ever

We live in a world where innovation happens at the intersection of disciplines. The most groundbreaking solutions rarely come from isolated expertise in a single subject—they emerge when different ways of thinking collide and collaborate.

STEAM education prepares students for this reality by teaching them to think across boundaries, to see connections where others see divisions, and to approach problems with both analytical rigor and creative imagination. We are at a point where it is not only possible, but imperative that we facilitate learning environments that are fluid, dynamic, and relevant. Our complex world demands education that mirrors its interconnected nature, and STEAM provides a framework for that kind of learning.

The shift to STEAM isn't about abandoning the rigor of STEM education—it's about enhancing it with the creative approaches, design thinking, and innovative spirit that the arts bring to the table. In doing so, we prepare students not just to navigate the future, but to create it.

Project-Based Learning: Creating Authentic Learning Experiences

When we talk about powerful teaching approaches, project-based learning (PBL) consistently rises to the top of the list. Unlike the traditional "learn it now, maybe apply it later" model we're all familiar with, PBL flips the script by starting with real challenges that naturally pull students into learning. I've seen this approach transform classrooms from places of passive consumption to dynamic spaces of creation and discovery.

What Is Project-Based Learning?

At its heart, project-based learning is about students tackling meaningful problems over time. It's process-driven rather than focused on memorizing facts. The learning happens as students engage with compelling questions that don't have Google-able answers.

PBL is about addressing real challenges that matter beyond classroom walls, rather than simply assigning work for the sake of grades. When students see their work has genuine purpose, motivation takes care of itself. And the magic happens when students share their finished products with real audiences—suddenly the stakes are higher, and so is the quality of their work.

But there's a big difference between simply doing projects and true project-based learning. Traditional projects can be solitary affairs focused on creating a product. Every student typically makes the same thing, following the same steps. PBL, on the other hand, requires collaboration, focuses on the journey as much as the destination, and gives students significant voice in shaping their path and outcomes.

The Connection to Arts Integration and STEAM

You might have noticed how naturally PBL overlaps with arts integration and STEAM approaches. They're kindred spirits in many ways. All three center on inquiry and creative process. The same collaborative exploration that makes STEAM education so powerful also drives effective PBL experiences.

These approaches also all break down traditional subject boundaries. Just as STEAM weaves together science, technology, engineering, arts, and math, PBL regularly crosses disciplinary lines to solve messy, real-world problems.

This makes it incredibly natural to incorporate arts standards alongside other content areas.

Among all three, there is a shared commitment to authentic application. Students aren't just learning about concepts—they're using them to create something meaningful. Consider a driving question like "How can we design public art that tells the story of our community's history?" This naturally braids together visual arts, social studies, and even engineering principles in a context that matters.

Implementing PBL in the Classroom

So how do you actually do this? The PBL implementation process follows a reliable sequence while preserving plenty of room for student voice:

1. Teacher provides an "entry event."
2. Students take on the project, possibly assigning roles.
3. Students gather background knowledge needed for their projects.
4. Teacher and students work collaboratively to develop criteria for evaluating projects.
5. Students design, create and prepare projects for presentation.
6. Students present the project.
7. Students reflect on the process and evaluate projects.

If you're looking to transform existing projects into true PBL experiences, start by framing them with compelling questions that allow for real student choice. Work backward from the final product to ensure clarity while still enabling creative exploration. And please, start small! Begin with one class or unit to refine your approach before expanding. Build bridges from what you already do well by adding more inquiry and student voice to familiar projects.

The Value of Connecting PBL and the Arts

The arts are already project-based by nature—artists create works that express ideas and solve problems. When we embrace the structure and intentionality of PBL in arts education, we add rigor by infusing more inquiry and student voice into the creative process.

This approach helps prepare students for a future none of us can predict. With job markets evolving and new careers emerging constantly, our task is to cultivate adaptable, creative problem-solvers ready for whatever comes next—including careers in the arts.

By combining the creative processes inherent in the arts with structured inquiry, we create learning experiences that go far beyond test preparation. Arts educators can make this shift without sacrificing the integrity of their discipline—in fact, PBL often enhances arts instruction by providing meaningful contexts for applying artistic skills to authentic challenges.

PBL creates more powerful learning through approaches that naturally complement each other, connecting classroom learning to the real world in ways that stick with students long after the final bell rings.

The Benefits of Using Arts Integration, STEAM, and Project-Based Learning

For schools that commit to embracing arts integration, STEAM, and/or PBL with integrity, the results are astounding. Schools that intentionally use these approaches find student achievement rises by 10 percent or more across the board.[1]

No longer can we say that creativity, innovation, and meaningful learning cannot exist in schools today. Instead, schools must be brave enough to look beyond traditional approaches (which yield very little result) for hands-on, minds-on approaches like arts integration, STEAM, and PBL that have a proven track record of working. Here's why:

1. **Student Buy-In**—Students become active participants in their learning when the arts are intentionally integrated. This, in turn, provides an opportunity for students to own the learning and have a vested interest in their own success.

2. **Builds Critical Thinking Skills**—Students engage in critical thinking and construct personal meaning through their learning in arts-integrated lessons. They develop the skills to work through problem-solving and to innovate new solutions. This builds grit and perseverance capacities in all learners.

3. **Empowerment for Teachers and Students**—Instructors become facilitators of creative learning and are empowered in their own professional growth. Teachers feel fulfilled and able to provide a hands-on learning environment for their students.

4. **Affords Equity**—These approaches yield an equitable learning environment for all learners through their own access points.

5. **Provides Connective Learning**—They also furnish a research-based pathway to teaching twenty-first-century learning skills and natural avenues for differentiation.

Perhaps the most compelling reason to embrace these approaches is that the arts provide universal access points to learning. Think about it: everyone connects with at least one art form in some way. Whether that's singing in the shower or doodling while listening to a lecture, everyone has an arts access point. It's our job as teachers to find that access point and use that as an avenue for students to explore ideas, share their perceptions, solve problems, and make sense of the world around them. Arts integration, STEAM, and PBL are approaches that not only embrace our humanity but allow us to experience humanity together.

Note

1. Judith Phillips, John Harper, Kayla Lee and Elise Boone. Arts Integration and the Mississippi Arts Commission's Whole Schools Initiative, John C. Stennis Institute of Government and Mississippi Arts Commission, 2020, accessed March 29, 2025. https://mswholeschools.org/wp-content/uploads/2020/12/Stennis_Full-Report.pdf

APPENDIX B: HOW I WROTE THIS BOOK

If you like to read the back of the book first to find out how the story ends before investing time into the plot, then you're my kindred spirit. I do this all the time, especially with fiction, and I make no apologies. So if you're reading this before you've read the rest of the book, I see you and I'm here for it. And if you've reached this part after reading everything else, I applaud your patience. It's a gift I often ask for and rarely receive.

The biggest question I think anyone reading this book will have is whether I used artificial intelligence to write it. It was the question I thought about most before even starting. Here I was, preparing to argue that creativity remains humanity's greatest advantage in an increasingly AI-driven world—while simultaneously wondering how I might use AI to support my own creative process. Was this a contradiction? Or an opportunity to practice exactly what I was preaching?

Complicated answer: yes—I used artificial intelligence as a support tool for writing this book. Simultaneously, no—I did not use AI-generated text in the manuscript and all work here is original to myself. Any edits suggested by AI have been reworked in my own writing.

But it's way more nuanced than either of these answers suggest, which is where I think many of get so much wrong right now. We miss the details that make the difference. So let me be clear about how I used AI and what that means, because I think it matters.

The Human-AI Creative Partnership

All of the written text in this book is original to me. This book's core ideas, experiences, anecdotes, and insights are mine. They come from twenty years in education, countless classroom observations, workshops with thousands of teachers, and my own journey as a creative practitioner. The research synthesis draws from my extensive reading and understanding of the field. The stories and examples are real—things I've witnessed, experienced, or verified through reliable and cited sources.

What AI provided was something different but equally valuable: a thought partner, research assistant, editor, and writing coach all rolled into one. I followed the guidance from The Author's Guild on how to use AI ethically in the writing process.[1] I understand that the systems and algorithms that artificial intelligence uses are often trained on uncompensated work from other authors and artists, which is one of the ethical dilemmas we are working through at this moment. As an author and artist myself, I do not want to take advantage of someone else's work in order to create my own. Therefore, I provided my AI tools with only samples of my own writing, to ensure it was using and referencing only my previous work, voice, and cadences as it supported me throughout the writing process. Even though the Author's Guild recognizes that the limited ways I used AI in this process as outlined below fall within ethical practices, I believe it's important to disclose how I used AI to ensure transparency and to reflect that it was used for specific purposes and as a collaborative tool, not as an author itself.

Here's what that looked like in practice:

- **Organizing research**: I had folders full of articles, studies, and notes. AI helped me categorize them, identify patterns, and suggest connections between seemingly disparate pieces of information.

- **Structuring ideas**: I'd write through a set of topics and ideas within a chapter, and AI would suggest areas that needed expansion or clarification. This was especially helpful because I wrote chapters whenever I had time in my week, which meant there were occasions when I forgot what I had written before. There were also times when I thought I had explained a section clearly, and AI pointed out there were gaps that needed to be filled for the reader to best understand the overarching theme.

- **Brainstorming Partner:** When I experienced writer's block or struggled to articulate a complex concept, AI served as a brainstorming partner. I'd describe what I was trying to express, and AI would offer various phrasings to help me find my voice. These phrasings were never the perfect result, but they were often enough to spark a better combination or get me started on the right path.
- **Editing assistance:** AI helped identify repetitive phrases, awkward transitions, and opportunities to make my writing more engaging without changing the core content or mimicking someone else's style.
- **Citation formatting:** Properly formatting references is tedious but essential work. AI helped ensure my citations were consistent and correctly formatted.

What AI didn't do was generate the book itself. It didn't create the core ideas, develop the central arguments, or fabricate examples. The voice you've read throughout these pages is authentically mine, shaped by my experiences, values, and perspective on creativity and education.

The Irony Isn't Lost on Me

There's a certain poetry in using AI to help write a book about human creativity. Throughout this process, I've experienced firsthand the dynamic I describe in these pages: AI is exceptional at certain tasks (organizing information, suggesting patterns, identifying inconsistencies) but remains fundamentally limited in others (generating authentic personal experiences, making meaning from information, or developing truly original ideas).

Working with AI reinforced my central thesis: when we use technology as a tool rather than try to replicate human creativity, we free ourselves to focus on what we do best—making unexpected connections, finding personal meaning, and sharing authentic human experiences.

The Creative Process Remains Human

What I hope this open and honest account of my writing process demonstrates is that creativity isn't threatened by AI—it's amplified by it when we approach the partnership thoughtfully. The book you've just read isn't less creative because AI helped in its development; it's simply a different kind of creative work, one that leverages new tools while remaining grounded in human experience and insight.

In the classroom, in professional settings, and in our personal creative pursuits, this is the model I believe we should embrace: using AI for what it does well, while recognizing and cultivating the uniquely human creative capacities that set us apart.

Every word in this book passed through my human filter of experience, knowledge, and values. Every idea was evaluated against my understanding of what matters in education and creativity. The AI didn't write this book—I wrote this book and used AI to ensure it was the best quality possible, with the human element always in the driver's seat.

And that, ultimately, is what I believe the future of creativity looks like: not humans versus machines, but humans and machines, each contributing what they do best to create something neither could accomplish alone.

Now *that's* creative.

Note

1 Authors Guild. "AI Best Practices for Authors." Last modified April 9, 2024. https://authorsguild.org/resource/ai-best-practices-for-authors/.

BIBLIOGRAPHY

Academy of Achievement. "Maya Lin." American Academy of Achievement. Accessed April 3, 2025. https://achievement.org/achiever/maya-lin/.

Aguilera, Ana Maria. "Theories of Creativity Explained." Ana Maria Aguilera, 2022. https://anamariaaguilera.com/creativity-theories/.

Alabbasi, Ahmed M. A., Sue Hyeon Paek, Daehyun Kim, and Bonnie Cramond. "What Do Educators Need to Know About the Torrance Tests of Creative Thinking: A Comprehensive Review." *Frontiers in Psychology* 13 (2022): 1000385. https://doi.org/10.3389/fpsyg.2022.1000385.

Allegretto, Sylvia, Emma García, and Elaine Weiss. "Public Education Funding in the US Needs an Overhaul." Economic Policy Institute, 2022. https://www.epi.org/publication/public-education-funding-in-the-us-needs-an-overhaul/.

Almulla, Mohammed A. "Constructivism Learning Theory: A Paradigm for Students' Critical Thinking, Creativity, and Problem Solving to Affect Academic Performance in Higher Education." *Cogent Education* 10, no. 1 (2023). https://doi.org/10.1080/2331186X.2023.2172929.

Aloizou, V., S. Linardatou, M. Boloudakis, and S. Retalis. "Integrating a Movement-Based Learning Platform as Core Curriculum Tool in Kindergarten Classrooms." *British Journal of Educational Technology* 55, no. 1 (2024): 78–97. https://doi.org/10.1111/bjet.13511.

Amabile, Teresa M. *Creativity in Context: Update to The Social Psychology of Creativity*. Boulder, CO: Westview Press, 1996.

Amabile, Teresa M., and Michael G. Pratt. "The Dynamic Componential Model of Creativity and Innovation in Organizations: Making Progress, Making Meaning." *Research in Organizational Behavior* 36(5) (2016): 157–83. https://doi.org/10.1016/j.riob.2016.10.001.

American Psychological Association. "The Science of Creativity." *GradPSYCH* 7, no. 1 (2009): 14. https://www.apa.org/gradpsych/2009/01/creativity.

Antes, A. L., and M. D. Mumford "Effects of Time Frame on Creative Thought: Process versus Problem-Solving Effects." *Creativity Research Journal* 21, no. 2–3 (2009): 166–82. http://dx.doi.org/10.1080/10400410902855267.

Authors Guild. "AI Best Practices for Authors." Last modified April 9, 2024. https://authorsguild.org/resource/ai-best-practices-for-authors/.

Baker, J. "From Bullet Trains to Green Buildings: Innovators Take Cue from Nature Through Biomimicry." Reuters, January 20, 2025. https://www.reuters.com/sustainability/land-use-biodiversity/bullet-trains-green-buildings-innovators-take-cue-nature-through-biomimicry-2025-01-13/.

Baker, Ryan S., and Aaron Hawn. "Algorithmic Bias in Education." *International Journal of Artificial Intelligence in Education* 31 (2021): 600–40.

Barnett KS, Vasiu F. "How the Arts Heal: A Review of the Neural Mechanisms Behind the Therapeutic Effects of Creative Arts on Mental and Physical Health." *Front Behav Neurosci*. 2024 Oct 2;18:1422361. doi: 10.3389/fnbeh.2024.1422361. PMID: 39416439; PMCID: PMC11480958.

Bentley, Peter. "Can Robots Be Creative?" BBC Science Focus, 2021. https://www.sciencefocus.com/future-technology/can-robots-be-creative.

Bielec, Sylwia. "A Growth Mindset in the Arts." Learn Quebec, January 2022. https://blogs.learnquebec.ca/2022/01/a-growth-mindset-in-the-arts/.

Blondin, Holly. "The Importance of Creative Reflection." Holly Blondin. Accessed April 3, 2020. https://hollyblondin.com/466/the-importance-of-creative-reflection.

Bloomberg Media. "Representation Will Define the Future of Creativity More Than Technology." Bloomberg Media, 2024. https://www.bloombergmedia.com/blog/representation-will-define-the-future-of-creativity-more-than-technology/.

Boaler, Jo. *Mathematical Mindsets: Unleashing Students' Potential Through Creative Math, Inspiring Messages, and Innovative Teaching*. San Francisco: Jossey-Bass, 2016.

Booth, Eric. "The Habits of Mind of Creative Engagement." Eric Booth. Accessed April 3, 2025. https://www.ericbooth.net/essays-feed/the-habits-of-mind-of-creative-engagement.

Brown, Nicole. "Using Creative Methods to Reflect." Nicole Brown. Accessed April 3, 2025. https://www.nicole-brown.co.uk/creative-reflections/.

Business Wire. "Futuri Shares Groundbreaking AI in Media Study at National Association of Broadcasters (NAB) Show 2024; Reveals A New Era of Human-AI Collaboration in Content Creation." Business Wire, April 15, 2024. https://www.businesswire.com/news/home/20240415609276/en/Futuri-Shares-Groundbreaking-AI-in-Media-Study-at-National-Association-of-Broadcasters-NAB-Show-2024-Reveals-A-New-Era-of-Human-AI-Collaboration-in-Content-Creation.

Catterall, James S. *Doing Well and Doing Good by Doing Art: The Effects of Education in the Visual and Performing Arts on the Achievements and Values of Young Adults*. Los Angeles: Imagination Group/I-Group Books, 2009.

Ceria, Marina, host. "João Carlos Martins: The Maestro Finds New Hope." Episode 16. In *The Loss Encounters*. Podcast audio, June 20, 2024. https://www.thelossencounters.com/episodes/2024-06-20-joao-carlos-martins.

Chacur, K., Serrat, R., Villar, F. et al. "You Must Learn to Age": Reflections on and Adaptations to Age-Related Changes Among Older Artists and Craftspeople. Population Ageing 18, 391–414 (2025). https://doi.org/10.1007/s12062-024-09466-5

Chae, Heesun, and Jisung Park. "The Effects of Routinization on Radical and Incremental Creativity." National Center for Biotechnology Information, 2020. https://www.ncbi.nlm.nih.gov/pmc/articles/PMC9967832/.

Clear, James. "Habits." James Clear. Accessed April 3, 2025. https://jamesclear.com/habits.

Clear, James. "How to Find Your Hidden Creative Genius." James Clear. Accessed April 3, 2025. https://jamesclear.com/creative-genius.

Coetzee, F. "Creating Competitive Advantage Through Creativity, Creative Thinking and Creative Problem Solving." Medium, 2023. https://nlpwithpurpose.medium.com/creating-competitive-advantage-through-creativity-creative-thinking-and-creative-problem-solving-01ac511e07ff.

Cornell Tech. "AI vs Artist: The Future of Creativity." Cornell Tech, 2023. https://tech.cornell.edu/news/ai-vs-artist-the-future-of-creativity/.

Creative Live. "Science of Creativity." Creative Live. Accessed April 3, 2025. https://web.archive.org/web/20250424105132/https://www.creativelive.com/blog/science-of-creativity/.

Csikszentmihalyi, Mihaly. *Flow: The Psychology of Optimal Experience*. New York: Harper & Row, 1990.

De Bono, Edward. *Lateral Thinking: A Textbook of Creativity*. London: Penguin, 2016.

Deci, Edward L., and Richard M. Ryan. *Intrinsic Motivation and Self-Determination in Human Behavior*. New York: Springer Science & Business Media, 1985.

Dixit, Jay. "Paula Scher on Failure." *Psychology Today*, May 13, 2009. https://www.psychologytoday.com/us/blog/brainstorm/200905/paula-scher-failure.

Drexel University School of Education. "How to Inspire Creativity in the Classroom." Drexel University. Accessed April 3, 2025. https://drexel.edu/soe/resources/teacher-resources/inspire-creativity-in-the-classroom/.

Duncan, Wardle. "Seven Behaviors That Will Unleash Your Creativity." Duncan Wardle. Accessed April 3, 2025. https://duncanwardle.com/seven-behaviors-that-will-unleash-your-creativity-2/.

Dweck, Carol S. *Mindset: The New Psychology of Success*. New York: Random House, 2006.

Edmondson, Amy C. "Psychological Safety and Learning Behavior in Work Teams." *Administrative Science Quarterly* 44, no. 2 (1999): 350–83.

Ellingrund, Kweilin. "Generative AI and the Future of Work in America." McKinsey Global Institute, July 26, 2023. https://www.mckinsey.com/mgi/our-research/generative-ai-and-the-future-of-work-in-america.

Feist, Gregory J. "The Function of Personality in Creativity: Updates on the Creative Personality." In *The Cambridge Handbook of Creativity*, edited by James C. Kaufman and Robert J. Sternberg, 113–30. Cambridge: Cambridge University Press, 2019.

Florida, Richard. *The Rise of the Creative Class*. New York: Basic Books, 2002.

FlowLab. "Neuroplasticity and Flow." FlowLab. Accessed April 3, 2025. https://flowlab.com/en/mental-fitness-blog/neuroplasticity-and-flow-training/.

Franklin, S. W. "The Surprising Origins of Our Obsession with Creativity." Behavioral Scientist, 2023. https://behavioralscientist.org/the-surprising-origins-of-our-obsession-with-creativity/.

Fransz, Robin. "How Systems Thinking Unlocked More Creativity Than I Could Ever Dream Of." UX Magazine, 2022. https://uxmag.com/articles/how-systems-thinking-unlocked-more-creativity-than-i-could-ever-dream-o.

Gaines, J. "Fostering Creativity: 12 Strategies to Boost Creative Skills." PositivePsychology.com, 2020. Accessed April 3, 2025. https://positivepsychology.com/creativity/.

Gartner. "Gartner Hype Cycle." Accessed April 14, 2025. https://www.gartner.com/en/research/methodologies/gartner-hype-cycle.

Georgia Department of Education. "Assessment and Evaluation: What's the Difference." Georgia Department of Education. Accessed April 3, 2025. 20Assessment_and_Evaluation_Whats_the_Difference.

Giles, Rebecca M. "10 Ways to Promote Artistic Expression." Exchange Press. Accessed April 3, 2024. https://hub.exchangepress.com/articles-on-demand/27403/.

Gnezda, Nicole M. "Cognition and Emotions in the Creative Process." *Art Education* 64, no. 1 (2011): 47–52. https://doi.org/10.1080/00043125.2011.11519111.

Goetz, Kaomi. "How 3M Gave Everyone Days Off and Created an Innovation Dynamo." *Fast Company*, February 1, 2011. https://www.fastcompany.com/1663137/how-3m-gave-everyone-days-off-and-created-an-innovation-dynamo.

Guilford, J. P. "Creativity." *American Psychologist* 5, no. 9 (1950): 444–54. https://doi.org/10.1037/h0063487.

Guilford, J. P. *The Nature of Human Intelligence*. New York: McGraw-Hill, 1967.

Guy-Evans, Olivia. "Pareto Principle (The 80-20 Rule): Examples and More." Simply Psychology, 2022. https://www.simplypsychology.org/pareto-principle.html.

Hancock, Jonathan. "What Are Your Values?" Mind Tools. Accessed April 3, 2025. https://www.mindtools.com/a5eygum/what-are-your-values.

HeartMath Institute. "Heart-Brain Communication." HeartMath Institute. Accessed April 3, 2025. https://www.heartmath.org/research/science-of-the-heart/heart-brain-communication/.

Hinton, Jeffrey. "How Did We Get Here: A Brief History of American Standardized Testing." Jeffrey Hinton, December 8, 2020. https://web.archive.org/web/20240303060527/https://www.jeffreyahinton.com/post/how-did-we-get-here-a-brief-history-of-american-standardized-testing.

Ho, Eric, Jeon, Minjeong Jeon, Minho Lee, Jinwen Luo, Angela Pfammatter, Vivek Shetty, and Bonnie Spring. "Fostering Interdisciplinary Collaboration: A Longitudinal Social Network Analysis of the NIH mHealth Training Institutes." *Journal of Clinical and Translational Science* 5(1) (2021): 1–36. https://10.1017/cts.2021.859.

Holland, Beth. "The State of Creativity in America's Schools." Getting Smart, December 3, 2019. https://www.gettingsmart.com/2019/12/03/the-state-of-creativity-in-americas-schools/.

Holmes, Sarah E. "No Child Left Behind: A Failing Attempt at Reform." *Inquiries Journal/Student Pulse* 2(12) (2010). http://www.inquiriesjournal.com/a?id=337

Huang, Li. "How 'Mind-Body Dissonance' Leads to Creative Thinking." INSEAD Knowledge, August 11, 2021. https://knowledge.insead.edu/leadership-organisations/how-mind-body-dissonance-leads-creative-thinking.

Jake-Schoffman, Danielle E., and Megan A. McVay. "Using the Design Sprint Process to Enhance and Accelerate Behavioral Medicine Progress: A Case Study and Guidance." *Translational Behavioral Medicine* 11, no. 7 (2020): 652–59. https://www.researchgate.net/publication/346241321_Using_the_Design_Sprint_process_to_enhance_and_accelerate_behavioral_medicine_progress_a_case_study_and_guidance.

Jung, Rex E., and Richard J. Haier. "Creativity and Intelligence: Brain Networks That Link and Differentiate the Expression of Genius." In *Neuroscience of Creativity*, edited by Oshin Vartanian, Adam S. Bristol, and James C. Kaufman, 233–54. Cambridge: MIT Press, 2013.

Karwowski, Maciej. "Creative Mindsets: Measurement, Correlates, Consequences." *Psychology of Aesthetics, Creativity, and the Arts* 8, no. 1 (2014): 62–70. https://doi.org/10.1037/a0034898.

Karwowski, M., R. Royston, and R. Reiter-Palmon, R. "Exploring Creative Mindsets. Variable and Person-Centered Approaches." *The Psychology of Aesthetics, Creativity, and the Arts* 13, no. 1 (February 2019): 36–48. https://doi.org/10.1037/aca0000170.

Kaufman, James C., and Ronald A. Beghetto. "Beyond Big and Little: The Four-C Model of Creativity." *Review of General Psychology* 13, no. 1 (2009): 1–12. https://www.normanjackson.co.uk/uploads/1/0/8/4/10842717/four_c_model_of_creativity.pdf.

Keller, Evelyn Fox. *A Feeling for the Organism: The Life and Work of Barbara McClintock.* New York: Henry Holt, 1984.

Kelley, David, and Tom Kelley. *Creative Confidence: Unleashing the Creative Potential Within Us All.* New York: Currency, 2013.

Kelley, Tom, and David Kelley. "Reclaim Your Creative Confidence." *Harvard Business Review*, December 2012. https://hbr.org/2012/12/reclaim-your-creative-confidence.

Koch, S. C., R. F. F. Riege, K. Tisborn, J. Biondo, L. Martin, and A. Beelmann. "Effects of Dance Movement Therapy and Dance on Health-Related Psychological Outcomes. A Meta-Analysis Update." *Frontiers in Psychology* 10 (2019): 1806. https://doi.org/10.3389/fpsyg.2019.01806.

Kong, Rowena. "The Effect of Time Constraint Awareness on Creativity Test Performance." Research Square, 2023. https://doi.org/10.21203/rs.3.rs-3214718/v2.

Kotler, Steven. "3 Science-Based Strategies to Increase Your Creativity." Ideas.TED.com, 2021. https://ideas.ted.com/3-science-based-strategies-to-increase-your-creativity/.

Kroolo. "What Is Timeboxing: Your Goal-Driven Time Management." Kroolo, 2024. https://kroolo.com/blog/timeboxing-a-practical-guide-to-goal-driven-time-management.

Kupers, Elisa, and Marijn van Dijk. "Creativity in Interaction: The Dynamics of Teacher-Student Interactions during a Musical Composition Task." *Thinking Skills and Creativity* 36 (2020). https://doi.org/10.1016/j.tsc.2020.100648.

Lee, Jae Hwa, and Soyeon Lee. "Relationships between Physical Environments and Creativity: A Scoping Review." *Thinking Skills and Creativity* 48 (2023). https://www.sciencedirect.com/science/article/pii/S1871187123000469.

Lehrer, J. "The Cost of Creativity." *Wired*, March 2012. https://www.wired.com/2012/03/the-cost-of-creativity/.

Magsamen, Susan, and Ivy Ross. *Your Brain on Art: How the Arts Transform Us.* New York: Random House, 2023.

Martin, Roger L. *The Opposable Mind: How Successful Leaders Win through Integrative Thinking.* Boston: Harvard Business Press, 2009.

May, Tom. "Where the Creative Industry Is Heading and How to Survive the Next 15 Years." Creative Boom, 2024. https://www.creativeboom.com/tips/where-the-creative-industry-is-heading-and-how-to-survive-the-next-15-years/.

McCoy, J. M., and G. W. Evans. "The Potential Role of the Physical Environment in Fostering Creativity." *Creativity Research Journal* 14, no. 3–4 (2002): 409–26. https://doi.org/10.1207/S15326934CRJ1434_11.

McCraty, Rollin, and Maria A. Zayas. "Cardiac Coherence, Self-Regulation, Autonomic Stability, and Psychosocial Well-Being." *Frontiers in Psychology*, 5 (September 29, 2014): 1090. doi:10.3389/fpsyg.2014.01090. PMID: 25345802; PMCID: PMC4179616.

Merritt, Rick. "Butterfly Effects: Digital Artist Uses AI to Engage Exhibit Goers." NVIDIA Blog, May 25, 2023. https://blogs.nvidia.com/blog/ai-artist-dominic-harris/.

Minutes. "What Is Opportunity Cost?" Minutes. Accessed April 3, 2025. https://minutes.co/what-is-opportunity-cost-its-the-variable-keeping-you-from-making-better-decisions-in-your-life-your-career-your-relationships-and-more/.

Mississippi Arts Commission, Stennis Institute of Government and Community Development Full Report. Mississippi Arts Commission, 2020. Accessed March 29, 2025. https://mswholeschools.org/wp-content/uploads/2020/12/Stennis_Full-Report.pdf.

Mollenkamp, Daniel. "Will AI Shrink Disparities in Schools, or Widen Them?" *EdSurge*, August 19, 2024. https://www.edsurge.com/news/2024-08-19-will-ai-shrink-disparities-in-schools-or-widen-them.

Murakami, Haruki. *What I Talk About When I Talk About Running: A Memoir*. New York: Alfred A. Knopf, 2008.

NeuCollins, Tempest. "Encouraging a Growth Mindset Through Art." 2019. National Education Association. Accessed April 3, 2025. https://www.nea.org/professional-excellence/student-engagement/tools-tips/encouraging-growth-mindset-through-art.

Newsham, G. "Twin Towers Tightrope Walker Philippe Petit Recalls Daring Feat 50 Years Later: 'Artistic Crime of the Century.'" *New York Post*, July 27, 2024. https://nypost.com/2024/07/27/us-news/twin-towers-tightrope-walker-philippe-petit-recalls-daring-feat-50-years-later-artistic-crime-of-the-century/.

Oppezzo, Marily, and Daniel L. Schwartz. "Give Your Ideas Some Legs: The Positive Effect of Walking on Creative Thinking." *Journal of Experimental Psychology: Learning, Memory, and Cognition* 40, no. 4 (2014): 1142–52. https://doi.org/10.1037/a0036577.

Paris Review. "Maya Angelou, The Art of Fiction No. 119." Interviewed by George Plimpton. *The Paris Review* 116 (Fall 1990). https://www.theparisreview.org/interviews/2279/the-art-of-fiction-no-119-maya-angelou.

Park, Namgyoo K., Monica Youngshin Chun, and Jinju Lee. "Revisiting Individual Creativity Assessment: Triangulation in Subjective and Objective Assessment Methods." *Creativity Research Journal* 28, no. 1 (2016): 1–10. https://doi.org/10.1080/10400419.2016.1125259.

Peterson, T. W. "The Positive Psychology of Persistence and Flexibility." Dr. Paul Wong, 2020. http://www.drpaulwong.com/the-positive-psychology-of-persistence-and-flexibility/.

Pink, Daniel H. *A Whole New Mind: Why Right-Brainers Will Rule the Future*. New York: Riverhead Books, 2006.

Pressfield, Steven. *The Artist's Journey*. Black Irish Entertainment LLC, 2016.

Pressfield, Steven. *The War of Art: Break through the Blocks and Win Your Inner Creative Battles*. Black Irish Entertainment LLC, 2002.

Project Zero. "Thinking Routines." Harvard Graduate School of Education. Accessed April 3, 2025. https://pz.harvard.edu/thinking-routines.

Purdy, Mark. "What Is Agentic AI, and How Will It Change Work?" *Harvard Business Review*, December 12, 2024. https://hbr.org/2024/12/what-is-agentic-ai-and-how-will-it-change-work.

Reich, Justin, and Mizuko Ito. "From Good Intentions to Real Outcomes: Equity by Design in Learning Technologies." Digital Media and Learning Research Hub, 2017. https://clalliance.org/wp-content/uploads/2017/11/GIROreport_1031.pdf.

Richards, Bailey. "Bill Gates Says AI Will Replace Doctors, Teachers and More in Next 10 Years, Making Humans Unnecessary 'for Most Things.'" People, March 29, 2025. https://people.com/bill-gates-ai-will-replace-doctors-teachers-in-next-10-years-11705615.

Riley, Susan. "Creativity Is Not a Soft Skill. It Is a Must-Have Mindset for the 21st Century." The 74 Million, September 21, 2020. https://www.the74million.org/article/riley-creativity-is-not-a-soft-skill-it-is-a-must-have-mindset-for-the-21st-century-how-teachers-can-nurture-it-in-their-students/.

Ripley, Amanda. *The Smartest Kids in the World: And How They Got That Way.* New York: Simon & Schuster, 2013. "Amanda Ripley Compares US Education System to Best Education System in the World" (February 13, 2014). Aspen Institute. https://www.aspeninstitute.org/blog-posts/amanda-ripley-smartest-kids-in-the-world-aspen-institute/.

Roberts, Jennifer L. "The Power of Patience." *Harvard Magazine*, October 2013. https://www.harvardmagazine.com/2013/10/the-power-of-patience.

Robinson, Ken. "Do Schools Kill Creativity?" Filmed February 2006. TED video, 19:24. https://www.ted.com/talks/sir_ken_robinson_do_schools_kill_creativity.

Runco, Mark A., and Robert S. Albert. "Creativity Research: A Historical View." In *The Cambridge Handbook of Creativity*, edited by James C. Kaufman and Robert J. Sternberg, 3–19. Cambridge: Cambridge University Press, 2010. https://doi.org/10.1017/CBO9780511763205.003.

Said-Metwaly, Sameh, Wim Van den Noortgate, and Eva Kyndt. "Approaches to Measuring Creativity: A Systematic Literature Review." *Creativity: Theories-Research-Applications* 4, no. 2 (2017): 238–75. https://intapi.sciendo.com/pdf/10.1515/ctra-2017-0013.

Samara, Thedia. "The Psychology of Creativity: Exploring the Mindset Connection." Medium, 2023. https://medium.com/@drthediasamara/the-psychology-of-creativity-exploring-the-mindset-connection-46e0f1bbc443.

Sawyer, R. Keith. *Explaining Creativity: The Science of Human Innovation.* New York: Oxford University Press, 2012.

Schrager, Sarina, and Elizabeth Sadowski. "Getting More Done: Strategies to Increase Scholarly Productivity." *Journal of Graduate Medical* 8, no. 1 (2016): 10–13. https://meridian.allenpress.com/jgme/article/8/1/10/201041/Getting-More-Done-Strategies-to-Increase-Scholarly.

Seelig, Tina. "The Secret Sauce of Silicon Valley." Medium, March 2, 2016. https://tseelig.medium.com/the-secret-sauce-of-silicon-valley-535a7dd11858.

Shryack, Sari. "The History of Creativity." Sari Studio, 2019. https://www.sari.studio/blog-1/the-history-of-creativity.

Siguaw, Judy A., Penny M. Simpson, and Cathy A. Enz. "Conceptualizing Innovation Orientation: A Framework for Study and Integration of Innovation Research." *Journal of Product Innovation Management* 23, no. 6 (2006): 556–74. https://doi.org/10.1111/j.1540-5885.2006.00224.x.

Swords, Alexander. "The Opportunity Cost of AI." LinkedIn, 2024. https://www.linkedin.com/pulse/opportunity-cost-ai-alexander-swords-8nyic/.

TeachThought Staff. "The 3 Modes of Thought: Divergent, Convergent Thinking." TeachThought, 2025. https://www.teachthought.com/critical-thinking/3-modes-of-thought-divergent-convergent-thinking/.

Technology Networks. "Study Pinpoints Origins of Creativity in the Brain." Technology Networks Neuroscience News and Research, July 2024.

TechTarget. "Computational Creativity (Artificial Creativity)." TechTarget, April 5, 2019. Accessed April 3, 2025. https://www.techtarget.com/whatis/definition/computational-creativity.

Time. "Science: Portrait of an Ace." *Time*, May 31, 1954. https://time.com/archive/6884620/science-portrait-of-an-ace/.

Tishman, Shari. *Slow Looking: The Art and Practice of Learning Through Observation*. 1st ed. New York: Routledge, 2017. https://doi.org/10.4324/9781315283814.

Topolinski, Sascha, and Rolf Reber. "Gaining Insight into the 'Aha' Experience." *Current Directions in Psychological Science* 19, no. 6 (2010): 402–5. https://doi.org/10.1177/0963721410388803.

Urquhart, James. "AI Robot Tests, Predicts and Even Discovers Reactions That Are New to Chemistry." *Chemistry World*, July 19, 2018. https://www.chemistryworld.com/news/ai-robot-tests-predicts-and-even-discovers-reactions-that-are-new-to-chemistry/3009276.article.

Velázquez, José A., Nancy L. Segal, and Blanche N. Horwitz. "Genetic and Environmental Influences on Applied Creativity: A Reared-Apart Twin Study." *Personality and Individual Differences* 75 (2015): 141–6. https://doi.org/10.1016/j.paid.2014.11.014.

Veloglovsky, Miriam. "Navigating the Dichotomy of a Creative Process vs. Creative Product." Miriam Beloglovsky. Accessed April 3, 2025. https://miriambeloglovsky.com/navigating-the-dichotomy-of-a-creative-process-vs-final-product.

Villines, Zawn (2022, April). "What Is a Flow State and How to Achieve It." Medical News Today, 2023. https://www.medicalnewstoday.com/articles/flow-state#flow-vs-hyperfocus.

Virtual Lab School. "Cultivating Creativity and Innovation: Environments and Materials." Virtual Lab School. Accessed April 3, 2025. https://www.virtuallabschool.org/fcc/creative-expression/lesson-3.

Wagner, Tony. *Creating Innovators: The Making of Young People Who Will Change the World*. New York: Scribner, 2012.

Walden University. "What's the Difference Between Hard and Soft Skills." Walden University. Accessed April 3, 2025. https://lifelonglearning.waldenu.edu/resource/what-is-the-difference-between-hard-skills-and-soft-skills.html.

Wasser, Fred. "Creativity and the Mind-Body Connection." KNPR's State of Nevada, November 11, 2015. https://knpr.org/show/knprs-state-of-nevada/2015-11-11/creativity-and-the-mind-body-connection.

Wieschermann, Dominik. "Four Principles of Navigating the Subjectivity of Creative Work." LinkedIn, 2024. https://www.linkedin.com/pulse/four-principles-navigating-subjectivity-creative-work-wieschermann-ed6xe/.

Wilson, Robert Evans Jr.. "Surprise! Creativity Is a Skill Not a Gift." *Psychology Today*, June 30, 2013. https://www.psychologytoday.com/us/blog/the-main-ingredient/201306/surprise-creativity-is-skill-not-gift.

World Economic Forum. "These Are the Jobs That AI Can't Replace." World Economic Forum, May 2023. https://www.weforum.org/stories/2023/05/jobs-ai-cant-replace/.

Wu, Yihan, and Wilma Koutstaal. "Creative Flexibility and Persistence." *Consciousness and Cognition* 105 (2022): 103410. https://www.sciencedirect.com/science/article/abs/pii/S1053810022001490.

Wyss Institute for Biologically Inspired Engineering. "Spinning Up a Silk Pavilion." Wyss Institute at Harvard University, May 28, 2013. https://wyss.harvard.edu/news/spinning-up-a-silk-pavilion/.

Yang, Heng-Chen, and Hsin-Yih Cheng. "Creativity of Student Information System Projects: From the Perspective of Network Embeddedness." *Computers & Education* 54, no. 1 (2010): 209–21. https://doi.org/10.1016/j.compedu.2009.08.004.

Young, Scott H. "How to Find Creative Solutions to Non-Creative Problems." Scott H. Young, January 2008. https://www.scotthyoung.com/blog/2008/01/08/how-to-find-creative-solutions-to-non-creative-problems/.

Zagonari, Fabio, and Elena Giacomoni. "Social Benefits and Individual Costs of Creativity in Art and Science: A Statistical Analysis Based on a Theoretical Framework. *PLoS One*, 17(4): e0265446." National Center for Biotechnology Information, 2023. https://www.ncbi.nlm.nih.gov/pmc/articles/PMC9045641/.

Zelizer, Julian E. "How Education Policy Went Astray." *The Atlantic*, April 2015. https://www.theatlantic.com/education/archive/2015/04/how-education-policy-went-astray/390210/.

INDEX

3 I's of creativity 235
20 percent rule
   comparison with 3M's margin time 149
   Google's innovation policy 148

adaptive learning 182
Amodei, Dario 212
artificial intelligence (AI)
   advent of 5
   bias in systems 215
   challenges and opportunities 14
   comparison with human creativity 33
   democratization of creative production 222
   disruptor in education 7
   distinctive features compared to past educational technologies 217
   effects on creativity and education 193
   ethical challenges and societal concerns 13, 213, 223
   functions as research assistant and editor 255
   historical background and societal impact 12
   impact on creative flow 131
   impact on creative implementation 221
   impact on creative work and education 214
   impact on creativity and education 263
   impact on education 11, 218
   impact on education and creativity 211
   impact on human creativity 43
   limitations in creativity 26
   limitations in creativity and emotional intelligence 13
   role in creative ideation 221
   use as support tool in writing 254
arts enhancement
   definition of 241
   definition within continuum 239
arts integration
   arts teachers, roles of 243
   benefits for student achievement 251
   classroom teachers, roles of 243
   continuum 239
   co-teaching in 240
   criteria 239
   definition and classroom application 238
   definition and continuum 241
   effective use and assessment 244
   impact on learning and creativity 138
   professional development and educational impact 268
   student engagement and empowerment 252
   universal access points for learning 252
assessment
   impact on flow 129
   role in creative development 85
   see also creativity assessment
assessment and academic integrity 220
assessment of creativity 225
attention 126
augmented ideation 220

bias in AI systems 215
Big-C creativity 41
biomimicry 181
Boaler, Jo 123
brain-derived neurotrophic factor (BDNF) 127
brain hemispheres 123
branches of creativity 217
   see also Four Branches of Creativity
business strategy 190

INDEX

challenge-skill balance 122
cognitive flexibility exercises 129
cognitive reserve 127
collaborative intelligence 222
comparison trap 188
computational creativity
    definition and scope 224
    impact on creative assessment 235
connection points
    cross-disciplinary collaboration benefits 145
    examples of cross-pollination 146
    Oblique Strategies 146
connective learning 232
constraint reframing 183
constraints 64
convergent thinking 35
co-teaching in arts integration 240
creative access point
    definition and identification 228
    recognition and practice building 233
creative activities 185
creative advantage 183
creative application
    amplification by AI 219
    assessment via Requirements Model 96
    definition and real-world examples 67
    educational methods and assessment 68
    implementation in real challenges 231
creative choices in education 191
creative collaboration
    educational assessment methods 226
    human-AI partnerships 216
    social context and group dynamics 38
creative confidence
    concept and reclaiming strategies 262
    development through experience 72
    guided mastery approach 228
creative development
    importance of integration 45
    key takeaways summary 45
creative differentiation 189

creative ecosystem 194
creative edge
    components of 181
    developing unique integrative thinking 187
    integration of knowledge and personal experience 197
creative education 235
creative energy 190
creative environments
    design principles 71
    embracing individual differences 40
    importance of supportive spaces 67
    role in creativity 71
creative exercises 64
creative expression
    assessment via Systems Model 96
    forms and emotional processing 66
    human uniqueness versus AI 219
    integration into work and collaboration 231
    personal and communal significance 65
creative habit
    cultivation strategies 171
    examples of established routines 141
    home life integration 171
    intentionality and consistency 141
    personal growth applications 171
creative habits
    building rituals gradually 142
    foundation for flow 128
    importance of daily practice 140
    personalization and consistency 142
    structured frameworks 233
creative literacy 223
creative margin
    challenges in implementation 153
    definition and implementation strategies 151
    idea capture techniques 152
    low-stakes experimentation environments 152
    overcoming personal resistance 154

INDEX

practical tips for scheduling and space design 152
rituals for creative mindset 152
creative margins, classroom applications 150
creative microdosing 231
creative mindset
    components of mental agility 71
    curiosity, resilience, and enthusiasm 233
    definition of 71
    role in creative process 71
    transferability across domains 71
    types of mindsets 71
creative mindsets
    measurement and impact 261
    shift from problem-solving to opportunity-finding 195
creative opportunity cost 190
creative overconfidence 72
creative patterns 184
creative practice
    development of 61
    integration of elements 71
    necessity for future challenges 234
    ongoing development 71
    practice strategy 'Yes, And ...' 133
creative process
    design thinking methodology 86
    essential question prompts and cyclical steps 196
    importance in creativity 86
    importance in education 225
    individual uniqueness and myths 182
    personal creative code 175
    personal growth through creativity 86
    unique creative fingerprint 175
creative product 86
creative reflection
    effective techniques 172
    environment design 172
    failure résumés 173
creative risks 191
creative self-efficacy 62

creative skills
    assessment via Taxonomy of Creative Design 96
    definition and examples 63
    development through deliberate practice 61
    role in education and assessment 64
creative spectrum
    4-C Model explanation 41
    definition and overview 41
creative teaching 73
creative theft 213
creative thinking
    assessment challenges and educational integration 65
    assessment via Guilford Model 95
    distinctiveness from AI 218
    mental processes and innovation 64
    role in skill development 231
creative thinking styles 34
creative workplaces 68
creativity
    amplification through AI collaboration 256
    assessment of. see creativity assessment
    barriers in schools 17
    challenges in assessment 81
    challenges in education 21
    challenges of measurement in education 19
    complex nature and nurturing 106
    creative process stages 13
    cultivation as habit 7
    definition and components 25
    definition and cultivation 31
    definition and development as practice 61
    definition of 5
    development and nurture 29
    equity gap in schools, 21
    Four Branches model 63
    future implications across fields 43
    habit formation in education 140
    historical perspectives on value 81

human capacities enhanced by
    flow 131
human creative advantage 176
human element in creative process 257
impact of values on innovation 81
importance as uniquely human
    trait 20
importance for future careers 21
importance for future jobs 12
importance in AI and future
    challenges 213
importance in AI era 41, 190
importance in education 5
integration in curriculum 14
integration with foundational and tech
    education 16
interplay of branches and ecosystem
    metaphor 69
interplay of different types 41
intersection with technology 8
key takeaways 175
measurement and assessment
    considerations 69
measurement challenges 21
measurement of 81
mental health benefits 33
modern measurement challenges 81
neuroscience of 7, 31
overview 61
relationship to hard and soft skills 29
relationship with values in education
    and business 81
research and theories overview 261
role as human superpower 44
role in education 9, 12
role in education and workforce 15
role in interdisciplinary innovation 213
social phenomenon 27
using creativity to bridge educational
    divides 18
creativity and AI 183
creativity and intelligence 261
creativity and persistence 266
creativity assessment
    authentic contexts 105
    balancing structure and freedom 105
    balancing transparency and
        flexibility 104
    case study of Central Park East
        Secondary School 102
    challenges of objectivity 101
    developmental focus 104
    effective educator practices 101
    key takeaways 106
    models and measurement 89
    multiple evaluators and measures 104
    overview 91
    practical strategies for schools 103
    practice strategy: theme and
        variations 107
    predictive validity 79
    Torrance Tests of Creative Thinking 79
    triangulation of subjective and
        objective methods 263
creativity assessment models
    integration in business and
        healthcare 94
    overview of four key models 90
    see also Four Models
creativity development in education 127
creativity gap 214
creativity in education
    state and nurturing in schools 261
    Torrance's early observations 79
creativity in professions 29
creativity microdoses 229
creativity myths 32
creativity premium 192
creativity types 103
critical thinking
    development through arts-integrated
        lessons 252
    enhancement through creative
        integration 232
Cronin, Lee 224
cross-pollination
    combining diverse knowledge
        domains 186
    role in fueling innovation 197
Csikszentmihalyi, Mihaly 26

daily rituals
    characteristics of effective rituals 143
    examples in education 143
    impact on cognitive flexibility and focus 142
dance movement therapy 262
decision-free zone 188
deep engagement and ownership 231
Default Mode Network 32
defining success 189
design sprint process 261
developmental variations in flow 129
digital environments 70
divergent thinking 34

education
    balancing tech skills and foundational skills 16
    focus and purpose since twentieth century 5
    historical development 19
    purpose since twentieth century 20
    socioeconomic disparities in access 11
educational environment 130
educational equity 212
educational system 190
educational technology 215
education policy 21
education system 20
Elementary and Secondary Education Act 11
empowerment and agency 232
environmental design
    applications in classroom settings 144
    intentional design over aesthetics 144
    role in creative productivity 143
equitable access to success 232
equity gap
    impact on creativity in education 17
    in creativity education 5
equity in education
    afforded by arts integration and PBL 252
    creative learning opportunities 21
ethics in AI 213

ethics of artificial intelligence 223
evaluation 85
Executive Control Network 32

failure résumés 173
feedback loops
    components of effective loops 145
    importance for innovation 144
five pillars of creative practice 142
flexibility 129
flow
    benefits of 121
    conditions for access 121
    definition of 121
    neural mechanisms of 121
    role in creativity and education 131
    strategies for cultivation 132
flow cycles 126
flow mindset 72
flow proneness 124
flow state
    brain wave activity during 123
    chemical processes involved 123
    definition and achievement 265
    definition and benefits 7
    definition of 121
    neural mechanisms during 123
flow states 233
flow triggers
    identification of 125
    incorporation into routines 125
4-C Model
    Big-C creativity 41
    explanation 41
    Little-c creativity 41
    Mini-c creativity 41
    Pro-c creativity 41
Four Branches of Creativity
    alignment with assessment models 95
    application to personal development 230
    integration for problem-solving 234
    model 63
Four Models
    Guilford Model 90, 93, 95

Requirements Model 91, 92, 96
Systems Model 92, 93, 96
Taxonomy of Creative Design 90, 93, 96
future of work 14

Gartner Hype Cycle 216
Google's innovation policy 148
    see also 20 percent rule
group flow 128
groupthink 39
growth mindset 71
guided mastery approach 228
Guilford Model
    application in assessment 90
    application in educational settings 93
    focus on cognitive creative skills 90

Harris, Dominic 224
heart-brain connection 138
Highlights for Children 18
home creative spaces 70
human-AI creative partnership 254
human-AI creative partnerships 235
human creativity
    '3 I's' framework 220
    unique synthesis beyond AI capabilities 197
human imagination 227

idea sprints 185
innovation 172
innovation orientation 264
innovative classrooms 69
integrated approaches 231
integrated creativity assessment 98
integration studios 188
integrative creativity
    importance in AI-driven world 182
    necessity for 21st century challenges 235
integrative thinking 188
interdisciplinary collaboration 261

Johnson, Lonnie 28
journaling 172

Kent, Corita 61
knowledge acquisition 219
lateral thinking 36

Lin, Maya 135
Little-c creativity 41

Martins, João Carlos 125
material ecology 212
McClintock, Barbara 130
mentorship programs 18
micro-commitments 187
mind-body connection
    role in creative thinking 136
    role in creativity 261
mind mapping 172
mindset shifts 73
Mini-c creativity 41
mistake mapping
    definition and practice 141
    transforming failure into learning 142
molecular biology 121
Mosaic Method
    arts integration lesson planning framework 155
    creative thinking tool beyond arts integration 159
    practical applications in education 159
    professional development applications 160
    See-Saw Technique (step 3) 156
    Simplify to Amplify (step 4) 157
    Two-Sides, Same Coin (step 2) 156
    You-Pick-Two (step 1) 156
movement 136
Myers, Garry Cleveland 17

Nakatsu, Eiji 181
neural networks in creativity 194
neuroplasticity

effects of creative practice 126
  foundation for creative flow 124
  importance of practice and use 127
  principles in creativity
    development 234
  role in creative thinking 33
novelty 91

Oblique Strategies 146
opportunity cost
  concept and relation to AI 263
  role in creative decision making 191
  see also creative opportunity cost
opposable mind, 190
optimal anxiety 123
overwhelm 187
Oxman, Neri 212

Pareto Principle 153
pattern transfer 183
performance review 173
persistence 129
persistence and flexibility 128
personal perspective 181
physical environment 262
practice strategy
  Build-a-Character exercise 198
  Headlines 21
  iNotice 3, 75
  Magazine Cover 45
  playlist creation 176
  Stepping In, Stepping Out 235
  Theme and Variations 107
  Yes, And … 133
Pro-c creativity 41
process and product 87
progress loops 63
project-based learning (PBL)
  connection with arts education 251
  definition and characteristics 249
  implementation process 250
  relation to arts integration and
    STEAM 249
psychological safety

  impact on creativity in workplaces 68
  role in creative margins 149

recovery periods
  strategic rest as cognitive tool 147
  techniques for cognitive recovery 147
reflection and consistent action 232
relationship understanding 182
Requirements Model
  concept and application 91
  strengths and limitations 92
resolution 91
Rodin, Auguste 126

Salience Network 32
Shinkansen trains 181
Silk Pavilion 211
social context 185
solution archaeology 183
standardized testing
  historical origins and impact on
    education 11
  history in America 261
  impact on creativity and motivation
    189
  perceived impact on creativity 17
  relationship with poverty 17
status hierarchies 39
STEAM
  role in arts integration 9
  role in enhancing creativity and
    learning 251
STEAM education
  comparison with arts integration 247
  core elements 245
  definition 245
  importance in contemporary
    education 248
  process and implementation steps 246
strategic creative choices 192
strategic ignorance 189
structured reflection 65
student-directed inquiry 226
subjectivity in creativity assessment 100

synthesis 91
Systems Model
    definition and social dimension 92
    strengths and limitations 93

Taxonomy of Creative Design
    application in educational and business settings 93
    framework for assessing creative products 90
teacher roles 211
3M's margin time 149
    see also 20 percent rule
time and creativity 186
timeboxing 184
time management 184

Torrance, E. Paul
    early observations on creativity in education 79
    see also Torrance Tests of Creative Thinking
Torrance Tests of Creative Thinking 79
transformed waiting time 186
transient hypofrontality 124

unique combinations 181

van Gogh, Vincent 100

wins journal 189
World Economic Forum 12
Wright brothers 28

ABOUT THE AUTHOR

Susan M. Riley is an internationally recognized educator, author, and founder of the Institute for Arts Integration and STEAM—the world's largest online professional development provider for teachers and leaders using arts-integrated approaches. She has spoken at the United States Department of Education, National Public Radio, and Americans for the Arts, and her articles have been featured in numerous publications worldwide. She lives in Westminster, Maryland, with her husband Kevin and daughter Emma.